Death in the

Dining Room

AMERICAN CIVILIZATION

A series edited by Allen F. Davis

Death
in the
Dining
Room

and Other Tales of

Victorian Culture

by Kenneth L. Ames

 TEMPLE UNIVERSITY PRESS   PHILADELPHIA

Temple University Press,

Philadelphia 19122

Copyright © 1992 by Temple University.

All rights reserved

Published 1992

Printed in the United States of America

The paper used in this publication is

acid free for greater permanence.

Published with the assistance of

the Getty Grant Program

Library of Congress Cataloging-in-Publication Data

Ames, Kenneth L.

Death in the dining room and other tales of Victorian culture /

Kenneth L. Ames.

p. cm. — (American civilization)

Includes bibliographical references (p.) and index.

ISBN 0-87722-891-4 (cl)

1. Material culture—United States. 2. United States—Social life and

customs—19th century. 3. United States—Popular culture—History—19th

century. I. Title. II. Series.

E168.A517 1992 91-33635

973.5—dc20 CIP

973.891

mH.

FOR HEATHER AND HOLLY

Contents

Acknowledgments

Where do ideas and understandings come from? In my case, I recognize that many of them were generated or refined through the numberless interactions with others that have enriched and informed my life. I welcome this opportunity to thank some of the people who have in one way or another helped me think about culture and material culture. First, I am grateful to my parents, who took me at a very young age to the Wadsworth Atheneum in Hartford, where my eyes and my mind were opened to the importance of things. And I am grateful to the Wadsworth Atheneum for being there today, in some ways changed but in more important ways still the same, and still a place where people can have powerful formative experiences. I am indebted to Dale K. Haworth, distinguished professor of art history at Carleton College, for luring me to the academic discipline of art history years ago and for staying in touch with me ever since. And I appreciate the genial encouragement of the graduate art history faculty at the University of Pennsylvania back in the distant days when I was a graduate student. All faculty were supportive, but I owe particular debts to Frederick Hartt, who showed me the value of visual analysis, to Robert C. Smith, who demonstrated repeatedly the power of words to explicate the affective impact of things, and to George B. Tatum, who taught me that the histories of arts and ideas are inseparable. At Franklin and Marshall College, sculptor and architect Edmund Whiting helped me understand visual thinking, while team-teaching experiences with Ira Grushow and Harry Butler helped me form a broader notion of culture.

First at Franklin and Marshall and subsequently at the Winterthur Museum and the University of Delaware, I taught—and was taught by—many thoughtful and creative students. Much of the material in this book was worked out in graduate classes for the Winterthur Program in Early American Culture. Winterthur's position as a research center drew to it many scholars from whom I learned a great deal. I also owe much to my former colleagues at Winterthur and Delaware and to my current colleagues at the New York State Museum. And there are all those helpful, encouraging, and sometimes inspirational people I have met at conferences or through professional organizations who have been part of an ongoing informal support group and mutual aid society. I thank all of them but particularly Bill Alderson, Eleanor Alexander, Mary Alexander, Jay Anderson, Bill Ayres, David Barquist, Dennis Barrie, Larry Berkove, Michele Bogart, Leslie Bowman, Donna Braden, Cynthia Brandimarte, Bradley Brooks, Karin Calvert, Charles and Mary Grace Carpenter, Tom Carter, Ed Chappell, John Cherol, Bob Christensen, Cliff Clark, Liz Cohen, Gail Colglazier, Ann Condon, Ned Cooke, Joe Corn, Wanda Corn, Bill Cotton, Wayne Craven, Betsy Cromley, David Dangremond, Avi Decter, Bert and Ellen Denker, Ulysses Dietz, Diane Douglas, David Driscoll, Michael Ettema, Doris Fanelli, Bill Faude, Sue Finkel, Oscar Fitzgerald, Mac Fleming, Benno Forman, Sherry Fowble, John Freeman, Maxine Friedman, Susan Garfinkel, Wendell Garrett, Gayle Gibson, Beverly Gordon, Alan Gowans, Kasey Grier, Steve Hall, Mary Ellen Hayward, Mary Lynn Stevens Heininger, Mary Ellen Hern, Dean Herrin, Don Hibbard, Bill Homer, Adrienne Hood, Bill Hosley, David Kahn, Wendy Kaplan, Ann Kohls, Gary Kulik, Amanda Lange, Neil Larson, Jackson Lears, Grant McCracken, John Maass, Bill Mahar, Victor Margolin, Karal Ann Marling, Katherine Menz, Christopher Monkhouse, Peter Mooz, Marianna Munyer, Kirk Nelson, Jessica Nicoll, Stacia G. Norman, Amy Osaki, Nancy Packer, Elizabeth C. Panhorst, Clark Pearce, Bob Peck, Carol Petravage, Dianne Pilgrim, Jerry Pocius, Sumpter Priddy, Jules Prown, Ian Quimby, Elizabeth Redmond, Ellen Rosenthal, Rodris Roth, Bob St. George, Susan Schoelwer, David Schuyler, Joan Severa, Dini Silber, Jim Sims, Deborah Smith, Ellen Snyder-Grenier, John Stephens, Ian Stewart, Damie Stillman, Peter Strickland, Marx Swanholm, George Talbot, Page Talbott, Lonn Taylor, Eleanor S. Thompson, Gretchen Townsend, Charles Venable, Deborah Waters, Charles Watkins, Ruth Weidner, Stephanie Wolf, Anne Woodhouse, and Michael Zane.

I am also deeply indebted to many at museums and libraries around the country who went out of their way to answer questions, locate data, or obtain photographs for me. I particularly want to thank Anne W. Ackerson, Pamela Boynton, Dick Brauer, Sarah Burns, Fran Carroll, Michael Flanagan, Karen Fordyce, Barbara Hall, John Hamilton, Peter Hill, Kath Howe, Joanne Kosuda-Warner, Andy Kraushaar, Paula Pergament, Terry Prior, Maureen Quimby, Lore Squier, Milo Stewart, and Susan

Whetstone. At the New York State Museum and New York State Library I received valuable assistance from Ron Burch, Patricia Cacciotti, Jim Corsaro, Joyce Patterson, John Scherer, Craig Williams, Melinda Yates, John Yost, and others. I thank these people and all the institutions that provided me with images and allowed me to reproduce them here. Special words of gratitude are also due to Gail J. Ames, who allowed me to publish images of many objects in her collection and, more important, provided me with many years of support, encouragement, and friendship.

This book was finished at the New York State Museum, but it is in many ways a product of my tenure at Winterthur. I am grateful to that institution for its continuing support of scholarly activity over the years. I particularly want to acknowledge my debt to former Directors Charles van Ravenswaay and Jim Smith for aiding and abetting my work, occasionally at some cost to themselves. I also owe much to my friend and former colleague Scott Swank, who vigorously defended academic freedom and unrestricted inquiry while he was deputy director at Winterthur. Scott encouraged me to call them as I saw them—and I did.

Many staff members at Winterthur have been immensely helpful. The folks in the library have been exemplary. Winterthur's library is world class, and so is the service. Much of the credit for that goes to Neville Thompson, whose knowledge of the bibliography of American material culture is legendary. Neville helped me locate countless facts and images. I greatly appreciate her generous assistance. I also thank my friend Katharine Martinez, head of Winterthur's library, for making the resources of the library accessible to me and for her enthusiastic encouragement of my work.

Many of the fine images in this book were provided by Winterthur's capable photographers. My thanks to them and to Alberta Brandt for her deft supervision of photograph production and sales. I also profited over the years from the work of the dedicated clerical staff at Winterthur and am happy to acknowledge the help of Patricia Bullen, Linda Carson, Pat Elliott, Ann Marie Keefer, Pauline Larkin, Jane Mellinger, Trish Mercer, Sandra Mitchell, and many others.

One of the great pleasures of my line of work has been linking up with kindred souls who see the world, or at least parts of it, much the way I do. I have been fortunate to enjoy the friendship, good humor, and support of several people with such parallel vision. I am pleased here to acknowledge my considerable debt to Simon Bronner, Harvey Green, Michael Hall, Michael Owen Jones, Gene Metcalf, Tom Schlereth, Marsha Semmel, Dell Upton, John Vlach, and Susan Williams. Each one of them has good-naturedly given me encouragement, inducement, provocation, or correction as appropriate. Each has shared understandings and insights generously. I have learned much from them and value their continuing friendship. I also take pleasure in my long association with Jim Loewen. Jim helped me think about social and cultural issues years ago when we were freshman roommates at Carleton College. I am still learning from him.

This book would not have happened at all if it had not been for the kind invitation from Allen Davis to consider publishing with Temple. I thank him for the invitation and thank Janet Francendese and Mary Capouya for enthusiastically shepherding this project through the system and Irene Glynn for the copyediting. And I want to thank designer Richard Hendel and everyone at Temple University Press for making this such an attractive and accessible book.

Finally, I thank Nancy Garrison, who, for better or worse, really does see the world as I do. She provided judicious doses of support and criticism as needed and in various ways helped make this a better book. The title and many of the better passages are hers.

Introduction

This book explores American Victorian culture through its "tangible proofs."[1] It examines the unspoken assumptions and persuasions of everyday life through the things that framed and gave meaning to that life. It peers into the internal world of culture through the external world of material culture.

Two comprehensions shape and pervade the text. The first is that ordinary goods perform a variety of tasks, play a variety of roles, in everyday life. One of my major purposes here has been to articulate and explore the varied tasks and roles performed by a few classes of objects in Victorian America. The second comprehension is that culture is a complex package of beliefs and behaviors and that this package is riddled with ambiguities and contradictions. My second major purpose has been to show how some of the ambiguities and contradictions of Victorian culture were expressed in these same goods. My overriding historical goal has been to contribute to a richer and more subtle understanding of American Victorian culture.[2]

Using the word "understanding" when dealing with culture might be promising a little more than I can deliver. Culture is not necessarily understandable. It surely is not rational. Nor is it coherent. My argument here is that culture is both insistent and muddled. Culture pervades life in the form of things, behaviors, ideas, laws, morals, and opinions. At its most effective, it is stealthy, lurking where we do not expect it. But culture is not monolithic, consistent, or integrated. It is often deeply contradictory and self-subverting. The subtext of this book is that culture and individual lives are characterized by profound ambiguity and ambivalence. Both were central factors of Victorian life.

The truth of this becomes clear in the explorations in this book. Meanings turn out to be numerous, conflicting, and changing. People in Victorian America were deeply conflicted over most of the central issues that occupy human societies—issues of power and power relations, the distribution of wealth and resources, gender roles and expectations, definition and enforcement of appropriate beliefs and behaviors, and resolution of tensions between continuity and change. Many people in Victorian America were unsure of how they felt about their own culture. Throughout the text,

I have tried to indicate something of the Victorians' ambivalence. And I have tried to reveal my own. For if the Victorians were ambivalent about their culture, it seems fair to say that late moderns are just as ambivalent about that culture. This book is meant as an essay in cultural interpretation. In this context, ambivalence upon ambivalence seems fitting. There are, after all, few certainties about issues that truly matter. And there are also very real limits to knowledge about the past. I have tried in the pages that follow to indicate some of the conditions that affect and constrain historical inquiry and our ability to recreate historical realities.

My ambivalence extends to matters of evaluation. I think the written texts make clear my own very mixed feelings about Victorian culture and its products. This may startle some readers. But the time has long passed when authors writing about material culture can be expected to celebrate uncritically the goods they analyze. Many of the objects in this book are remarkable products of humankind. I hope that people experience a sense of discovery as they leaf through these pages. Indeed, to make that experience likely, I have tried to gather images that are not familiar, not hackneyed. Visual excitement is important. But I hope readers will be willing to move from the objects to the culture behind those objects. They will find that the beliefs and behaviors those objects sustain are just as fascinating as the goods—and sometimes very troubling. Positive elements are often offset or undercut by negative elements, the empowerment of some compromised by the victimization of others. In looking at a few slices of Victorian culture through five different material culture lenses, I have tried to illuminate a range of readings and to suggest losses as well as gains, costs as well as benefits, as people in the last century tried to superimpose order on a shifting and uncertain world.

This is, then, a study in contextualization. Such studies revolve around the central issue of meaning. Again and again, I have tried to figure out what something meant. No responsible evaluation of an object can ignore the question of meaning. Like poisoned apples, pretty goods can serve sinister ends.

Material culture assumes a prominent place in this book. Sometimes it is the subject of inquiry. Sometimes it becomes a way of inquiry. My argument is not that material culture is superior to other ways of knowing, but that it is different. The view of the world revealed through material culture is not the same as that attained through words. For that matter, the world of things and the world of words are not the same. Things and words draw on different systems of perception and cognition. Objects have both philogenetic and ontogenetic primacy. The earliest humans probably used tools before they developed coherent speech. Infants engage material culture before they can talk. When they become adults, they often use material culture to express that which they cannot, will not, or dare not speak. Things occupy a distinctive place on the field of human culture, providing data, advancing agendas, and supporting and embodying assumptions often not expressed elsewhere.

A word about method. My approach throughout has been Aristotelian. Every chapter either begins with an object or a group of objects or, in the course of discussion, provides extensive analysis of one or more objects. Beginning with objects, giving primacy to objects, promotes lines of inquiry that may be quite different from those generated by word-oriented scholarship. While I have not crafted this book as a discourse on method, I believe that my method can be easily reconstructed from the texts. A key tenet of my approach is that goods and words are both culturally constructed artifacts. As such, they may or may not be equal, but they are separate. Some who write about material culture privilege words over things. They write about goods from words. They try to puzzle out the meaning of things from what others have written or said about things. I think this is a mistake. I have tried to err in the opposite direction, privileging things over words. I have written about goods from goods. The gain from this approach is access to cultural values not expressed verbally. The loss is one of refinement, nuance, and specificity. Understandings from things are often grosser, more general, than understandings from words. Thus my discussions are appropriately and consciously broad and general.

This book makes no attempt to provide an inclusive survey of Victorian material culture or even Victorian domestic material culture. The Victorians were an intensely materialistic people. It would take many volumes to do justice to the extraordinary proliferation of goods characteristic of their world. Instead, I have focused on five categories of goods, each providing access to some different aspect of everyday life and commonplace culture. These goods range in date from the 1850s to the early years of the twentieth century. They also range widely in price, from highly fashionable, expensive, one-of-a-kind goods produced for the very wealthy to mass-produced items that cost the nineteenth-century equivalent of two or three of today's dollars. Most of my examples are drawn from the East Coast and the Midwest, although all the phenomena discussed had international manifestations. This is not, then, a narrowly American story. The culture described here was lived in America but extended beyond this country. Although it may have taken on a distinctive flavor here, much of it was either formulated elsewhere or created in response to external cultural forces.

The first chapter examines the furnishings Victorians placed in their front halls. These objects support a discussion of the Victorians' specialized use of space, their pervasive self-consciousness, and their ritualization and ceremonialization of commonplace events of daily life. The second chapter turns to dining rooms and more particularly to the immense sideboards that were installed in the homes of the wealthy around the middle of the century. These objects provide opportunities for further consideration of ritual and ceremony in affluent Victorian homes. They also provide occasions to analyze Victorians' understanding of the relationship between nature and humankind and to observe cultural and gender conflict.

Inexpensive embroidered mottoes are the subject of the third chapter. These seemingly limited artifacts turn out to provide eloquent testimony to the contradictory union of visions of progress grounded in technological development and understandings of appropriate beliefs and sentiments grounded in religion and tradition. The fourth chapter continues to explore themes of religion and tradition within the domestic realm, looking at parlor organs and their use in a variety of social strategies in which women play prominent parts. Finally, the fifth chapter studies seating furniture and posture as material culture, showing how interrelated issues of class, gender, and power were played out in goods and body language.

This book is meant to be suggestive and, at some level, experimental. For one thing, my approach is impressionistic. This is not a work of the new particularism. I have tried to paint with a broad brush, to capture sweeping and pervasive cultural forces. These forces surely had differing impacts on millions of individuals, and there are just as surely millions of individual stories to be told. I have tried to touch on a few elements that might be constant in many if not all of those stories. But personal stories will in large part be retrieved from words. My emphasis has been on culture knowable through things.

In like manner, I have not discussed or even touched on most of the familiar great events of the nineteenth century. Readers will find no meaningful mention of the Civil War, for example, and almost nothing about national politics. These omissions are intentional. While culture responds to—and is constructed to accommodate—wars, disasters, crimes, and various misfortunes, individually such events often have little impact on its general configurations. The violent and often tragic events that fill newspapers are real enough but are frequently overwhelmed and washed away by the great sweep of culture. The juggernaut of culture rolls over nearly everything in its path.

One of my purposes in writing this book has been to suggest ways to think about culture, ways to locate culture in things. My historical argument is that goods were critical to the workings of Victorian culture and that any attempt to understand that culture must take those goods into account. But in the end, I am more interested in provoking thought and inquiry about things and culture than in providing answers to questions about Victorian America. I hope that in some small ways this book will help people develop an anthropological curiosity about the world around them.

Congruent with the spirit of experimentation, this book has three texts. The primary text is the images. I am grateful to the staff at Temple University Press for their enthusiastic acceptance of the idea that images are crucial to this book and need to be presented with clarity and force. In fact, of course, the real primary texts are the objects recorded in the images. In a museum setting, it would have been theoretically possible to assemble the objects into an order that, even without words, would have made some sense. A book format, however, requires images, and for the purposes of comprehension, these images are conventionally accompanied by captions. Read sequentially and in conjunction with examination of the images, this second text of captions sketches an outline of the major arguments of each chapter. Many of these captions are also mini essays, each exploring an idea or concept provoked by the image. The captions can thus be read in order or at random. Yet a third text, the linear discussion that constitutes the major verbal component of the book, provides another way of gaining access to the images and ways of thinking about them. I encourage readers and viewers to interact with these three texts in whatever ways they find enjoyable and meaningful.

In the late twentieth century, people still come and go from their houses. They still dine with family and friends. People still hang words and images on their walls. They still gather together to enjoy music. And people still sit. All commonplace activities. All ordinary parts of lives. All parts of ordinary lives. All parts of the lives of Victorian Americans too. But Victorian notions of the appropriate goods to frame and enable each of these ordinary acts are no longer ours. The objects they purchased to give appropriate meaning to those activities are no longer produced. When we encounter those objects today, it is likely to be their strangeness that most impresses us. How odd once ordinary things have become. This transformation of the ordinary into the odd is an illusion, however, an illusion made possible by our own ethnocentrism and limited perspective. In fact, the goods were always odd. The beliefs were always odd. And for that matter, the goods of today are odd. The beliefs of today are odd. Like the Victorians, we too live in the fantasy world of culture. Our fantasies are different from theirs, but they remain fantasies, attempts to build convincing and durable bridges across the great darkness, attempts to craft convincing and lasting answers to the great questions, attempts to provide convincing and effective solutions to the great persisting problems of humankind. Looking at Victorian America revealed through the goods in this book brings us to the sobering realization that one society's alleged truths usually become another society's authentic fictions.

1 : First Impressions

First impressions. You can make them only once. An accurate observation, but hardly new. Victorian Americans were acutely aware of the power of first impressions. They knew that what people saw first had a disproportionate impact on the formation of opinions and judgments. It was because they understood so well the importance of first impressions that the Victorians created distinctive forms of material culture to mold and manipulate them.

The modern term for this behavior is *impression management*.[1] When we hear people speak of impression management today, it is usually in the context of the corporate world. The ability to manage people's perceptions can put someone on the road to success in human relations generally and in business in particular. The Victorians had a somewhat different orientation, for while they shared today's commercial values, the current high status accorded to corporate life was only beginning to emerge in the second half of the nineteenth century.[2] In Victorian America the domestic realm was still the major arena for acting out social strategies. The furnishings people put in the hallways of their houses, the first interior spaces visitors saw, played important roles in shaping first impressions and in framing and manipulating Victorians' perceptions of themselves and their relationships to others (1.1). Hall furnishings were widespread and prominent components of the Victorian system of impression management.

It may seem a bit peculiar to speak of hallways and first impressions. Obviously, before visitors even entered a house, they acquired data they could evaluate from the city, the neighborhood, and the exterior of that house. All this information, however, was external to the house and was understood to be superficial, potentially misleading, even suspect. The interiors of people's houses provided more accurate, more authentic information about them. Moving inside a house brought someone into a more intimate association with its inhabitants. Knowing the inner house was something like knowing the inner person. Exteriors of houses and houses unfurnished spoke of architects and builders. But the insides of houses and houses furnished spoke of the life that went on within and the character of those who lived it.

The Four Seasons of Life: Middle Age
Lithograph published by Currier & Ives
New York, 1868
Prints and Photographs Department,
Library of Congress

This chapter is about hall furnishings, the first clues of that inner domestic life in Victorian America. My argument is that these objects, little appreciated today, were once significant parts of a deliberate and pervasive strategy to ceremonialize and ritualize the commonplace activities of everyday life. They played important roles in a style of life that was highly self-conscious and tightly scripted. They were critical components of an elaborate artifactual system that was central to the Victorians' understanding of themselves and their place in the world. They were tools for managing not only impressions but comprehensions, cosmologies.

To understand hall furnishings we need to know something about halls, for these spaces and their relationship to other spaces in houses had some influence on the objects placed within them. I say "some" because I do not want to suggest that architectural or spatial determinism was at work here. Architecture and space enabled a certain mode of furnishing but did not dictate it. Cultural factors were far more important. This becomes clear when we recognize that halls in many nineteenth-century houses were often nearly identical in plan, proportion, and scale to those in eighteenth-century houses. What differentiated the later buildings from the earlier were cultural conventions of use and meaning—and thus of furnishing. One of these was the premise of specialization, a cornerstone of capitalism and a pervasive characteristic of Victorian material culture.[3] In Victorian America, each room of a house was understood to perform a distinctive set of functions. These functions were revealed, served, and advanced by an equally distinctive set of artifacts. Specialization was more frequently demonstrated through furnishings than through any intrinsic properties of the rooms themselves. In other words, unfurnished, eighteenth- and nineteenth-century halls looked pretty much the same; furnished, they looked dramatically different. The movable material culture—that is, culture in visible, tangible, and portable form—made all the difference.[4]

As these comments may suggest, middle- and upper-middle-class domestic building in America has been more notable for continuity than lack of it. A few basic ideas, altered occasionally by ideological, economic, or other factors, underlie the spatial organization of most single-family, free-standing houses.[5] It is possible to assign most middle- and upper-middle-class houses of the nineteenth century to one of two classes on the basis of hall type. The first type of hall, popular into the fourth quarter of the century, was a relatively narrow passage that connected the outside of the house to its interior spaces. This type was based on late Renaissance ideas introduced to this country in the eighteenth century with the Georgian style (1.2). Although frequently obscured by an overlay of complicated ornament or lively asymmetry (1.3), Georgian concepts of spatial organization were perpetuated in Victorian houses; many nineteenth-century plans closely resemble eighteenth-century examples. A characteristic feature of these houses of the Georgian–Victorian continuum was the conceptualization of the hall as a passage. Until about 1880, this was the dominant mode.[6]

In the second and later type of hall, the passage was expanded into a large living space. Derived from medieval great halls and the multifunction rooms of pre-Georgian dwellings in colonial America and associated with the English reform

1.2 *Georgian space in Gothic disguise. The elaborate porch and pierced bargeboards put a fashionable, updated exterior on a concept of domestic spatial arrangement that had been in use for over a century when this design was published. Gothic only on the outside, inside this remains a central hall, symmetrical Georgian house.*

Elevation and plan for Cottage No. 12 John Riddell, Architectural Designs for Model Country Residences *Philadelphia: John Riddell, J. B. Lippincott, 1864* The Winterthur Library, Winterthur, Delaware

Cottage, Nº 12

FRONT ELEVATION.
SCALE

movement, this type was widely published and illustrated in the last quarter of the century and became a prominent feature of many architect-designed houses.[7]

These two hall alternatives can be related to two different conceptual models for domestic structures and domestic life in the nineteenth century. The first was the courtly vision of the house as villa or palace. The second was a more consciously domestic notion of the house as hereditary estate or old homestead.[8] My emphasis here is on the prereform model of the house as palace and the hall as passage. It was for this physical and cultural setting that Victorian America created its most innovative and distinctive hall furnishings.

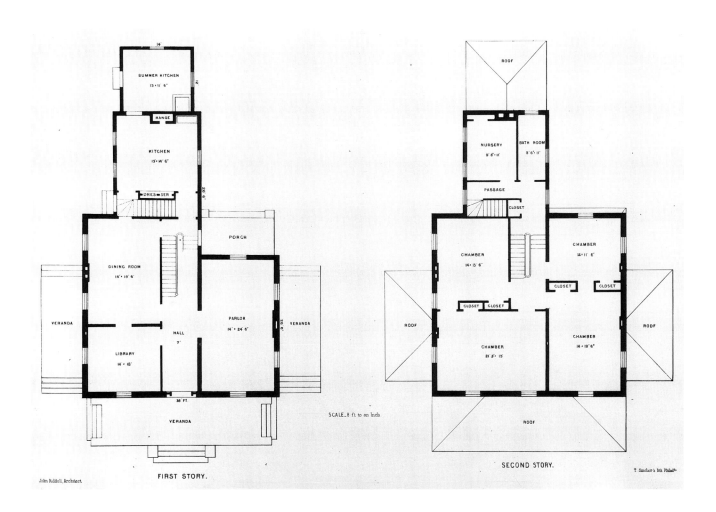

SCALE_8 ft to an Inch

FIRST STORY.

SECOND STORY.

John Riddell, Architect.

T. Sinclair's lith Philad.ᵃ

A typical upper-middle-class house plan illustrates the characteristics of this concept of hall (1.4). The space was usually 6 to 8 feet wide and 12 to 20 feet long, or considerably longer if it ran all the way from the front of the house to the back, as it does here. Its chief architectural embellishments were the framed doorways to parlor, drawing room, library, dining room, or the outside, and the stair and its ornamented newel post (1.5). Little or no communal activity took place in this form of hall. Its shape, dimensions, and placement emphasized its primary functions as connector and separator of rooms. In most houses of this class, people did not enter directly from the outside into one of the living spaces but rather into the hall (or into

1.3 *The picturesque encounters Georgian. An aggressively picturesque house designed by the English-trained architect Jacob Wrey Mould for an affluent American client. Irregular massing, eccentric roofline, and coyly placed front door are new elements, here made compatible with a conventional Georgian "hallway right through," which serves the usual functions of entrance and passage.*

Design 20. House erected for Henry E. Owen on the New Jersey shore
Bicknell's Cottage and Villa Architecture
New York: William T. Comstock, 1881
The Winterthur Library

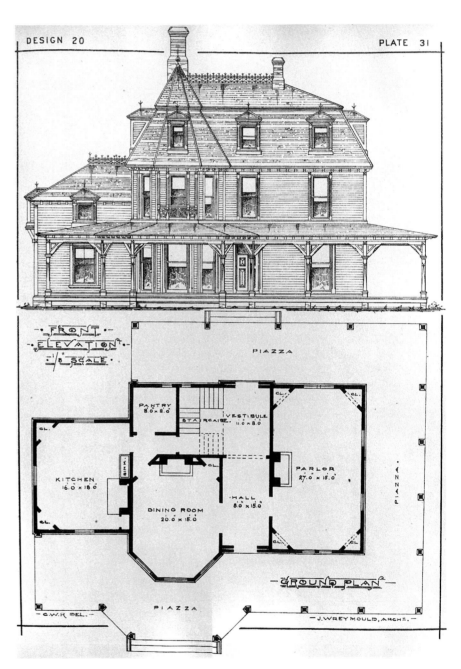

the hall through a vestibule).[9] Although it was possible to move from some rooms to others without entering the hall, it was also possible to enter each room from the hall without passing through any other, thus preserving privacy and the specialized function of each space. With this arrangement, social peers of the homeowners could visit in the formal spaces of the house, while social inferiors remained in the hall or were directed elsewhere and kept from intruding on the family or its guests. In other words, this form of hall emphasized control and hierarchy.

The hall just described might be identified more precisely as a front hall. Many houses with a front hall also had a back hall, which was sometimes an extension of the front hall, sometimes another, smaller corridor adjacent to it. A back hall was not necessarily a discrete space; in some cases, its function was incorporated within another room, as it was in the kitchen shown in the plan in Figure 1.4. To divide the front hall from the back, and formal space from utilitarian, there was usually some real or symbolic barrier—a door, lower ceiling, narrower passage, or change in wall or floor materials or finish. There was also a rear stair, usually narrower and steeper than the front stair and free of architectural pretense. This creation of separate and unequal halls and stairs mirrored the segregation of ceremonial and utilitarian functions within houses and the division of nineteenth-century society into two broad classes: served and servant.

Similar stratification was seen in the way the plans of upper-middle-class houses were conceptually divisible into two units (1.4). The first, larger than the other, was the formal or ceremonial portion of the house. Behind it, performing the mundane duties that sustained the former, was the service section, consisting of kitchen, pantry, and laundry room. The significant difference in the way the two areas were conceived was reflected in their decorative treatment. The front section was architecture as John Ruskin understood it; the rear was only building. Designs for facades of houses appeared in architectural books in great numbers, but backs were rarely shown, for the front belonged to ceremony and first impressions, but the rear only to utility. The front stair was for dramatic and gracious descent to meet family and

1.4 *Hall as passage within a courtly framework. This self-consciously stately and imposing Italian villa appropriately incorporates a hall as passage 7 feet wide and 32 feet long running the full length of the formal block of the house. The floor plan dramatically reveals the hierarchical relationship of the formal front of the structure to its utilitarian back. Like many homes, this one included both front and back stairs.*

*Elevation and plan for Villa No. 2
John Riddell, Architectural Designs for Model Country Residences
Philadelphia: John Riddell, J.B. Lippincott, 1864
The Winterthur Library*

40 FT.
FRONT ELEVATION.
SCALE. ¼ in. = 1 foot

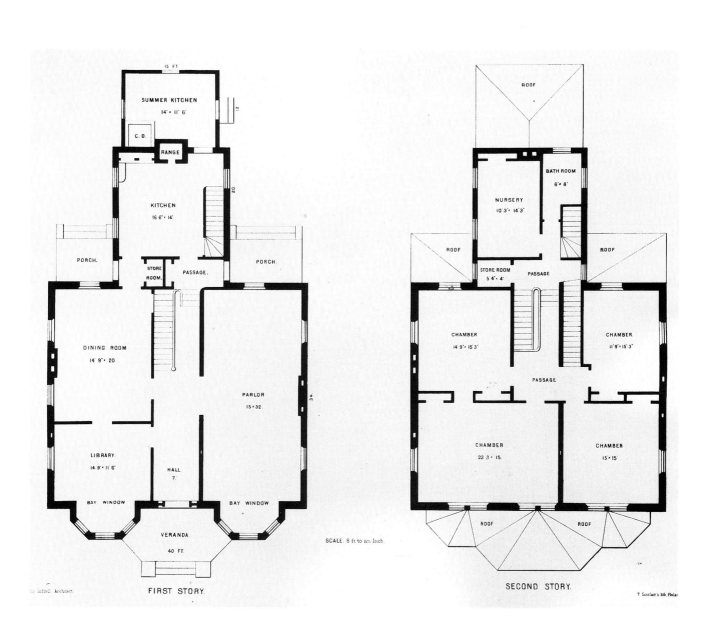

SUMMER KITCHEN
14' × 11' 6"

C. D.

RANGE

KITCHEN
16' 6" × 14'

PORCH.

STORE ROOM.

PASSAGE.

PORCH.

DINING ROOM
14' 9" × 20.

PARLOR
15 × 32.

LIBRARY.
14' 9" × 11' 6"

HALL
7'.

BAY WINDOW

BAY WINDOW

VERANDA.
40 FT.

SCALE. 8 ft to an Inch.

FIRST STORY.

ROOF

BATH ROOM
6' × 8'

NURSERY
10' 3" × 14' 3"

ROOF

ROOF

STORE ROOM
5' 4" × 4'

PASSAGE

CHAMBER
14' 9" × 15' 3"

CHAMBER.
11' 9" × 15' 3"

PASSAGE

CHAMBER
22' 3" × 15.

CHAMBER
15 × 15'

ROOF

ROOF

SECOND STORY.

T. Sinclair's lith. Phila.

1.5 *The constricted space of the hall as passage left little room for furniture. Much of the hall's adornment came from its built-in features: elaborated stairway, balusters, and newel post; wainscotting; doors and door frames; stained glass; lighting fixtures. This image captures the density and compression typical of many halls in the houses of affluent people.*
Front hall in the Joseph R. Walker House
Salt Lake City, c. 1900
Utah State Historical Society, Salt Lake City

guests; the back stair was for servants carrying slop buckets and dirty laundry. This spatial arrangement of Victorian homes documents social realities and distinctions that have largely disappeared in the northern parts of the United States.[10]

HALLSTANDS

Although they were formal and ceremonial spaces, front halls were usually too small for much furniture. Very large front halls sometimes contained a table, stand, or pedestal, and two chairs or a settee or both. Most halls, regardless of size, contained at least a hallstand (1.6). Unlike most furniture of its era, the hallstand has no obvious historical antecedents. It is a nineteenth-century invention, a Victorian original. Appearing around the time of Victoria's accession, the life cycle of the hallstand (1.7 and 1.8) parallels the course of Victorian America. After the middle of the century, the hallstand became more popular and the focus of considerable design attention. It attained its greatest elaboration and monumentality in the 1860s and 1870s, was rethought and reformed in the 1880s, then gradually declined in scale and importance. By 1920, the hallstand was largely extinct.[11] And so was Victorian culture.

Examples of typical hallstands of the late 1870s are illustrated in Figures 1.9, 1.10, and 1.11. Some were manufactured in Grand Rapids, Michigan, noted for quality furniture for the middle- and upper-middle-class markets.[12] The others were made in New York City. Together they show that although the decorative details varied considerably, a high degree of consistency prevailed in the overall concept of the form. Four functional components were generally incorporated: provisions for umbrellas, hooks or pegs for hats and coats, a looking glass, and a small table, often with a drawer and a marble top. Each of these components was conceptually separable from the others, but the synthesis of the four, or sometimes only the first three, into an architecturally conceived whole constituted a hallstand.

1.6 *A formal portrait of a hallstand, part of a furniture salesman's album of photographs. In conventional hallstands, four functional elements—mirror, hooks for hats and coats, umbrella holders, and table or stand—are united and ceremonialized by and within an elaborate architecturelike framework.*

Walnut hallstand
Sales catalog of Nelson, Matter & Co.
Grand Rapids, Michigan, c. 1878
Grand Rapids Public Library

1.7 *A page of British middle-class hall furnishings, from an American edition of an English publication on household furnishing and management.* Top, *hall chairs and benches;* bottom left, *a mahogany hallstand with vertical stem and horizontal crossbars;* bottom center, *a cast-iron hallstand of the central-pole type.* Also shown: *umbrella stands and a foot scraper.*

Thomas Webster and Mrs. Parkes, An Encyclopædia of Domestic Economy
New York: Harper & Brothers, 1845
The Winterthur Library

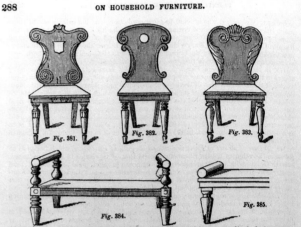
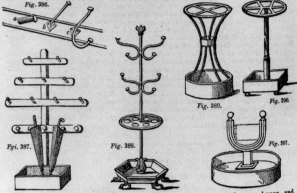

288   ON HOUSEHOLD FURNITURE.

Fig. 381. Fig. 382. Fig. 383.

Fig. 384.   *Fig. 385.*

Fig. 386, *a,* represents pins made of wood, turned and let perpendicularly into a mahogany rail fixed to the wall at a proper height. Cloak pins, *fig.* 386, *b* and *c,* are likewise made of brass and of cast iron, and are screwed on to the rail, their direction pointing upward, the better to secure what is hung on them; another kind has the lower part of it turned upward to hang the hat on. Cloak and umbrella stands are sometimes made of mahogany, consisting of a stem and cross bars, as in *fig.* 387; the lowest rail has large knobs for the umbrellas to stand between, draining into the box, which has a loose japanned tin tray within. The cloaks are hung upon the three upper rails. *Fig.* 388 is a cloak and umbrella stand made of cast iron. *Fig.* 389 is an umbrella-stand made of tin painted; and *fig.* 390 is one that may be constructed of wood.

Fig. 386.

Fgi. 387.   *Fig.* 388.   *Fig.* 389.   *Fig.* 390.   *Fig.* 391.

1181. *Door-scrapers* for the feet are placed at the entrance of every house, and should be in such a situation as to be easily seen. The variety of form is endless, from a simple piece of iron hoop fixed across two uprights of any kind, to those of cast iron, ornamented in various ways, and kept by the ironmongers. They should always, if possible, have a receptacle for the dirt to fall into. A portable scraper, *fig.* 391, which costs only two shillings, is useful, because it may be placed in any situation; as, for instance, in any part of the garden.

1.8 *Hallstand conceived as planar tree with branches. This early version of the form provides nineteen pegs mounted on the central pole, crossbar, and a pair of graduated lyres. Like many early examples in the neoclassical mode, the design of this piece has an open, linear quality.*

Hallstand with mahogany finish
New England, 1830–1840
Dana House, Woodstock, Vermont
Woodstock Historical Society
Gift of Grosvenor Dana

1.9 *Hallstands conceived as extensions of architecture. Here, in place of thin posts and bars, appear fully panelled structures closely resembling doors and doorways, windows and frames, and related components of architectural interiors.*

Walnut hallstands
Sales catalog of Nelson, Matter & Co.
Grand Rapids, Michigan, c. 1878
Grand Rapids Public Library

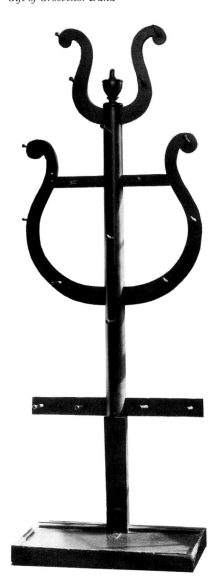

1.10 *As the expense of the hallstand increased, so usually did the area of glass. In this soaring example, representing the top of a major Grand Rapids manufacturer's line, a glass more than 5 feet high fills and dominates a frame nearly 10 feet tall. In an object like this, the glass and its multiple functions take on exceptional prominence.*

Walnut hallstand
Sales catalog of Nelson, Matter & Co.
Grand Rapids, Michigan, c. 1878
Grand Rapids Public Library

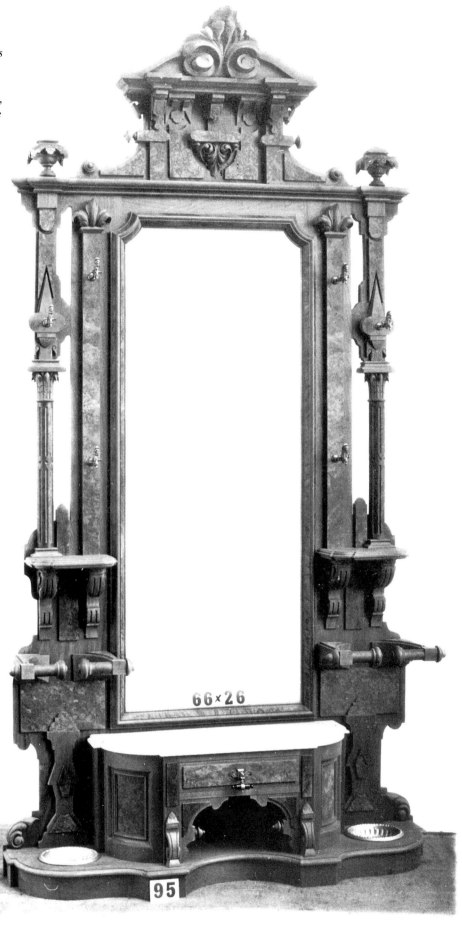

1.11 *How money is manifest in goods. This sheet, advertising a New York manufacturer's line of hallstands, shows clearly how size, amount and kind of materials, and nature, amount, and quality of work all change as one moves up or down the economic scale. No. 1 provides the rudiments of the hallstand form on a small scale, with minimal embellishment and with little costly work. The wholesale price, in 1876, was* $22.67. *At the opposite end of the spectrum, No. 20 offers grandeur of scale, an enormous mirror, and rich and varied ornamentation. The price, wholesale, was* $133.33. *Through the juxtaposition of related goods of different cost, nineteenth-century consumers learned how to appraise informally the material culture around them.*

The two objects in the upper right are experimental hall chairs with compart- ments in their backs designed to serve as umbrella holders.

Page of hallstands and hall chairs
Manufactured by Conrad Eckhardt, New York City
Illustrated on Plate 22 of J. Wayland Kimball, Book of Designs: Furniture and Drapery
Boston: J. W. Kimball, 1876
The Winterthur Library

Plate 22.

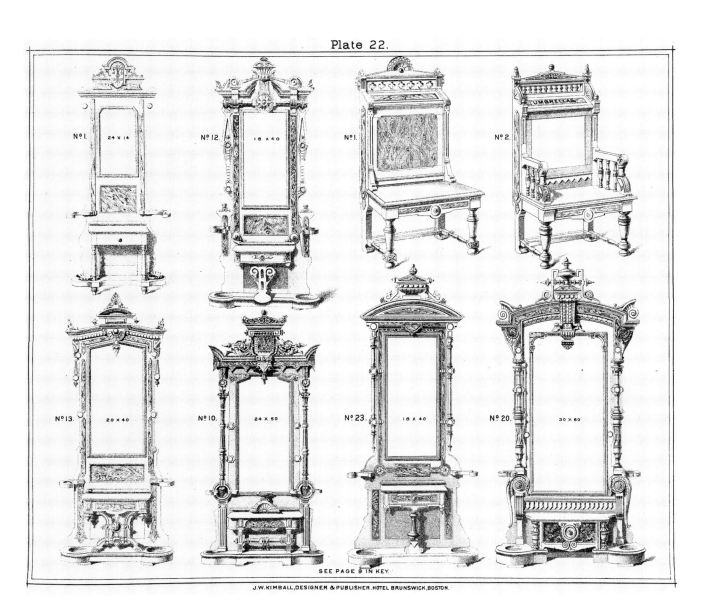

SEE PAGE 9 IN KEY.

J.W.KIMBALL,DESIGNER & PUBLISHER.HOTEL BRUNSWICK,BOSTON.

Provisions for umbrellas normally followed the arrangement shown here. Crook-shaped or armlike devices mounted on each side of the stand at a height of about 25 to 30 inches above the floor supported the upper ends of the umbrellas. In the base of the hallstand, one or two dished receptacles caught and held whatever water might drip from them. Cast-iron pans were the most common. Inexpensive hallstands had thin sheet-metal boxes, but expensive hallstands, particularly those built in as part of the woodwork, had marble dishes. Regardless of the material, all served to protect the floor or carpet and keep the umbrella accessible.[13]

That such an impressive piece of furniture should be designed for such an apparently mundane purpose indicates something about the status of umbrellas. From a twentieth-century perspective, the umbrella might be called the insigne of the Victorian age (1.12). The umbrella's long and eventful history has been recorded by several artifact historians.[14] The umbrella was well known in antiquity in both Europe and Asia, but its modern history stems from contacts between the East and West during the Renaissance. It came from Asia by sea to Portugal and by land to Italy, spreading from these places to others. At the outset, the umbrella was associated with high status; slaves or servants held umbrellas over their owners or employers when they walked in public. By the eighteenth century, the umbrella and a related form, the parasol, had become relatively common. They were depicted frequently in paintings and prints of that period and were mentioned in written documents. The parasol served largely a cosmetic purpose, protecting women's skin from the rays of the sun. Although its use spread through many levels of society, the parasol remained a mark of women of leisure. The umbrella performed a more utilitarian function. It was commonly carried by men after the middle of the eighteenth century. Perhaps because the wealthy owned carriages that protected them from the weather, carrying an umbrella became associated with lesser affluence and, sometimes, republican sentiments. In the nineteenth century, the umbrella became a bourgeois attribute, a portable emblem of respectability. Its prominence reflects a culture pervaded by middle-class values.

1.12 *A familiar scene in the nineteenth century, not only in Paris but wherever bourgeois standards of decorum and presentation prevailed. As a portable shield against rain, the umbrella underscored the period's pervasive concern with maintaining a formal and controlled exterior.*

Paris, A Rainy Day
Gustave Caillebotte, 1877
Oil on canvas
The Art Institute of Chicago, Charles H. and Mary F. S. Worcester Collection, 1964.336
Photograph © 1990, The Art Institute of Chicago. All Rights Reserved

The hallstand's provisions for hats and coats underline the nineteenth-century emphasis on attire and appearance. The popularity of the hallstand coincides with that of the top hat, which in its most extreme form became the "stovepipe" hat of Abraham Lincoln and his generation. James Laver has argued that the top hat was what we would call *macho* today. He further argues that such assertions of masculinity are most extreme at the time of greatest role differentiation between the sexes. He associates the gradual decline of the top hat with that of male-dominated society.[15]

Hats and coats were usually hung on turned wooden pegs on moderately priced hallstands and on small bronzed or gilt metal hooks on more costly pieces. Regardless of material, they rarely projected more than 6 inches or so from the surface of the hallstand. There were generally only six or eight pegs or hooks arranged symmetrically around the mirror. The relatively few attachments for hats, coats, cloaks, or other outer garments make it clear that the hallstand was not intended as open storage. Only a limited number of objects could be placed on it. An analysis of period photographs may help determine what, if any, rules governed the selection. Some homes had storage closets near the hall. Others had closets behind the stair, easily accessible from the hall, yet they still had a hallstand in the front hall.[16] When large numbers of people came to a party, coats were apparently placed on beds in the bedrooms, as they are today. Therefore, there were reasons other than storage for placing garments on the hallstand. I suggest what these reasons might have been after discussing the two remaining components.

The hallstand's third component, the mirror, underlined again the Victorian fixation with personal appearance, but had additional ramifications. Mirrors were a Victorian convention. They appeared where they still do in twentieth-century interiors—on walls in bedrooms and dressing rooms; on chests of drawers, dressing tables, and wardrobes; and adjacent to facilities for washing or shaving—all for obvious reasons. But in the nineteenth century they also appeared on hallstands, étagères, cabinets, and sideboards; over mantels; and extending from floor to ceiling between pairs of windows in formal rooms. The widespread use of mirrors in parlors, dining rooms, bedrooms, and halls of the 1870s reveals the continuing attraction of courtly models for domestic furnishing and, more specifically, the enduring impact of the Galerie des Glaces at Versailles of two centuries earlier and other famous mirrored interiors. Plate glass was still expensive in the nineteenth century, and its prominent display was a sign of wealth and high social standing. Glass was also significant for its ability to reflect forms and light and so expand and illuminate a space. Large glasses were normally placed directly opposite lighting fixtures so that illumination was increased. The mirror also allowed certain visual effects that people enjoyed. When a glass was viewed from an angle, it reflected segments of an interior that changed as the viewer moved, a kinetic phenomenon the art scene exploited as a novelty some years ago but once commonplace in Victorian interiors. The glass in the hallstand was also an ordinary mirror, a dressing glass in front of which people adjusted clothing or hair, brushed off dust or lint, and otherwise groomed themselves before leaving the house or entering one of its formal rooms.[17]

The optional table, omitted from less expensive hallstands, was a convenient resting place for packages, books, gloves, or other small objects. Sometimes a decorative object was placed on it; sometimes it held a card receiver. The drawer was a container for a variety of small objects, including brushes and whiskbrooms for cleaning garments. The table also provided a site for demonstrating the "marble mania" of the age. Like the widespread use of mirrors, marble tops on tables and other case pieces were instances of what Siegfried Giedion called the devaluation of symbols.[18] Marble tops, used in antiquity, were revived during the Renaissance for luxury pieces of furniture. By the nineteenth century, what had been confined to the very wealthy became commonplace, as the vast numbers of surviving objects document. Although marble was heavier, more expensive, and more dangerous to fragile objects than wood, it was very popular. Perhaps the marble on hallstands helped stabilize the great weight of the mirror, but there were other, less expensive ways of achieving this end. It is more likely that the marble surfaces on hallstands, like the clearly dysfunctional slabs on sideboards, chests of drawers, dressing cases, washstands, cabinets, tables, and stands, were largely chosen for their courtly associations.

All four of the functional components I have discussed were combined into a single object by people now largely forgotten. There is no need to turn to what is called folk art to find unsung artisans of the American past; they worked for American industry in the nineteenth century. Their charge was not to express themselves in an uninhibited personal manner but to create a salable product that was similar to but just a little different from others available at the same moment. Surviving artifacts and illustrations in trade catalogs show that these now unknown artisans produced scores of varied designs while adhering to shared notions about symmetry, placement of functional components, projection into space, and consumption of wall area. Because of the hall's limited space, the components had to be combined in a spatially efficient way. Hallstands rarely projected far into the limited space of the hall, usually not more than 12 to 15 inches. But if practical considerations inhibited the consumption of space, there were fewer strictures on the use of area. Most hallstands, including those illustrated here, spread out expansively along the wall to create major focal points in halls and to assert their own significance.

What evidence is there that these objects were meaningful in Victorian America? How do we know that Victorians felt that the purposes of hallstands and the concepts and feelings associated with them were important to their lives? The most obvious clue is the large size of these objects. Their impressive scale demonstrates that hallstands were significant, that they were understood to represent much more than the mere total of their utilitarian functions. The smallest examples, usually of cast iron rather than wood (1.13), were normally about the height of an adult. Wooden examples were more often between 6½ and 8 feet tall. Some of the most costly reached 10 feet. Another clue is that none of these objects was inexpensive; hallstands rarely appeared in lower-class homes. They served, then, as tools for social differentiation. Their very possession was a mark of some social standing. When visitors first set foot in a house, the hallstand—or its absence—helped them locate the owners on the social scale. People's willingness to pay significant sums for hallstands and the obvious expenditure of effort on the design, construction, and finish of these objects all confirm their significance.[19]

The careful placement of the functional and decorative features of the hallstand was also evidence of the object's importance. The functional elements were laid out in balanced and symmetrical arrangements, augmented and emphasized by the decorative elements, which conferred importance on the object and elevated its status. The recurring symmetry so obvious in these items has been mentioned earlier but deserves a few more words. Symmetry is such a common feature of artifacts that it may seem inconsequential, yet this very pervasiveness gives it importance. As

1.13 *Cast iron was one of the miracle materials of the nineteenth century. Once used primarily for relatively crude utilitarian products, technological changes made it possible to create castings of unprecedented detail and fineness. But tradition and cast-iron's earlier associations limited its use as furniture; hallstands were among the very few examples of cast-iron furniture brought into the house. The more common chairs and settees remained outside on the lawn or porch.*

Cast-iron hatrack and umbrella stand
Trade catalog of Wood & Perot
Philadelphia, c. 1875
The Winterthur Library

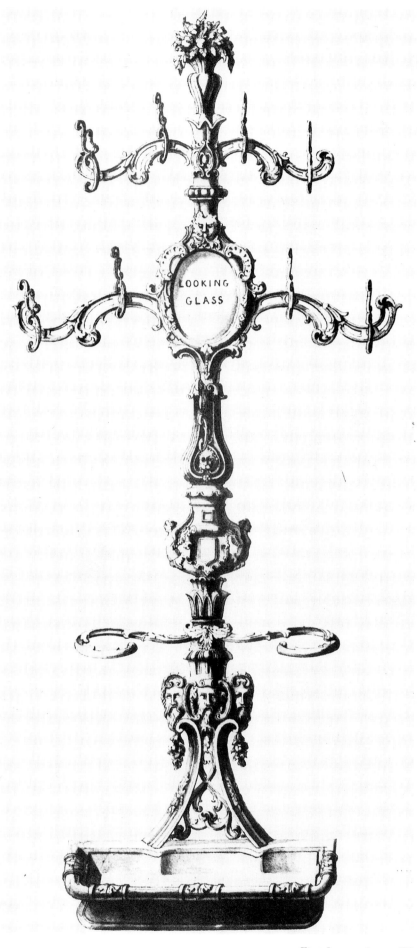

LOOKING GLASS

common as it is, symmetry has nevertheless not been adequately explained. One of the usual arguments is that people make objects symmetrical because they are themselves symmetrical. Others have argued that symmetry is restful and mentally satisfying, fulfilling the mind's search for equilibrium. Symmetry is also a way creative people demonstrate control over their tools and materials. A form created once may be an accident; its exact duplication is not likely to be. An object that is both highly elaborated and symmetrical may then be understood to display an exceptional degree of control and to be a testament to its creator's skill.[20] The emphatic and elaborate symmetry of hallstands reveals that these objects were considered worthy of the considerable design and fabrication effort necessary to create them, that they were appropriate vehicles for the display of high levels of design and artisanal competence.

Like the fact of their considerable size, the extensive ornamentation of hallstands also demonstrated that these pieces met more than utilitarian needs. Much of the wooden frame and all the veneer panels, paterae, pilasters, and other applied and incised decoration were functionally superfluous. The mirrors were often larger than necessary, and the woodwork above them was in every case beyond physical need. The top parts of hallstands served honorific purposes in direct proportion to the cost of the objects. The ornamented upper section was also honorific in another, less direct, more symbolic way. Most examples were capped by an architectural element of some sort—an arch, a pediment, a cartouche, or some combination of these devices. Each of these forms had a long association with status in architectural contexts and probably retained a residuum of that meaning in the nineteenth century. The architectural quality of these hallstands called to mind the facades of temples, churches, and other monumental and meaningful structures, again suggesting that there was more significance attached to these objects than their utilitarian functions would indicate.[21]

A final argument for the high valuation of the hallstand and the activities associated with it was the critical matter of placement. Hallstands usually stood prominently in front halls, immediately visible on entering a house (1.14). There, they

1.14 *Hall as access to the house and hallstand as silent monitor of that access. This photograph shows a glimpse of a drawing room flanked by a hall-stand on the left and a card receiver* *and a marble bust on a pedestal on the right. As was sometimes the case with expensive hallstands, this example bore a monogram (*C *for Corliss) on the cartouche at the top.* *View of the hallway*
George Corliss House, Providence, Rhode Island
Photograph taken 1880–1890
Rhode Island Historical Society

became part of the strategy of impression management. Some people believed that "the hall determines the first impression on entering the house" and that it might be advisable to economize elsewhere in order to create a good effect in the hall. They depended heavily on the hallstand to help achieve the effect they sought.[22] The hall-stand was the major piece of furniture in most halls, and one of the most important visual elements. Visitors could not avoid seeing it, nor could they avoid seeing the hats, coats, canes, or umbrellas on it. Today we use closets to keep garments out of sight because having them in view violates our sense of neatness and order. A century ago, halls were furnished with immense, unavoidable wooden or iron objects that loomed prominently in the semidarkness and were decked out with articles of personal costume. For some who saw them, the scale and stern design of hallstands may have been awesome and intimidating; for others, there was probably a more approachable, human quality about these pieces. To all, a hallstand conveyed something of the spirit or mood of a household and was functional in a variety of other ways. It helped with details of grooming. It communicated nonverbally about who was or was not at home through the objects on or missing from the hallstand. It ceremonialized the coming and going, the entry and exit of the members of the household and their guests and callers. It demonstrated affiliation with the dominant culture. And it served as a setting, a theatrical backdrop for the peculiar ritual of leaving cards, which also took place in the hall.

Clarence Cook probably reflected the views of other Anglophile reformers when he called hallstands of the 1870s "ugly things made of tiresome walnut."[23] Although he and his associates rejected the prevailing form of the hallstand, they did not reject the functions it embodied and ceremonialized. An illustration from *The House Beautiful* shows the hallstand's utilitarian functions performed by objects devoid of the conspicuous grandeur and symbolic allusion suggested earlier (1.15). Yet the image and the caption—"She'll be down in a minute, sir"—are potent demonstrations of the ways artifacts were deliberately used in the nineteenth century as props in the dramas of life. The self-consciousness evident here was as much a component of the reform style as it was of the dominant style. Reformers may have rejected the appearance and sociocultural references of objects in the courtly mode, but they endorsed and embraced the functions those objects performed. The issue was not whether the commonplace acts of everyday life should be celebrated and ceremonialized but which forms and styles were most suitable for, or even worthy of, those purposes.[24]

It may be worth remembering that hallstands were creations of the age of Romanticism. The concept of Romanticism is not much in vogue now, a casualty of changing directions in scholarship and what might be called the new particularism. While such a sweeping term as Romanticism needs to be used with caution, it is useful as a shorthand evocation of clusters of cultural values and traits. The premise of feeling central to Romanticism, the emphasis on affect, emotion, the senses, the self,

1.15 *Hallstand as narrator. Although Clarence Cook disliked the look of contemporary hallstands, he endorsed and embraced their functions. This captioned illustration reveals his understanding of the communicative powers of the hallstand and the role it played in nonverbally conveying information about social life within a home.*

"She'll be down in a minute, sir."
Clarence Cook, The House Beautiful
New York: Scribner, Armstrong, 1878
The Winterthur Library

1.16 *Humorous commentary on Victorian self-consciousness and formality. Disoriented by drink, Mr. Cooley mistakes the reflection of his bright nose in the glass for the lamp at the end of the hall and, in a drunken variation of* Through the Looking Glass, *tries unsuccessfully to walk through the hallstand.*
Illustration by Arthur B. Frost
From Max Adeler (Charles Heber Clark),
Out of the Hurly-Burly; or, Life in an Odd
Corner, *Philadelphia, 1882*

"She'll be down in a minute, sir."

and self-consciousness are all components of the cultural ambience that generated the historical and anthropological curiosities known as hallstands. Two words in particular, self and self-conscious, may be particularly important for understanding these objects. With their great mirrors and receptacles for such extensions of the self as hats, coats, or canes, these objects were agents for self-reflection in both literal and figurative ways (1.16). Courtly society in the eighteenth century was surely self-conscious, but it could not usually see itself. Nineteenth-century society could both emulate eighteenth-century courtly behavior and watch itself doing so at the same time. Few objects provide better insight into the Victorian age's autovoyeurism than the hallstand.[25]

HALL SEATING

The other forms of furniture usually found in the hall as passage were chairs. The wealthy sometimes had leather upholstered settees and matching chairs.[26] The typical middle-class hall chair of the 1870s looked much like those illustrated here (1.17, 1.18, and 1.19). Certain features were characteristic. First, there was the unupholstered plank seat, otherwise unknown in formal rooms of middle-class houses. The plank seat was normally hinged, as it is here, so that it could be raised to give access to a shallow compartment underneath that held gloves, brushes, and other small items. Front legs were usually elaborately turned, stretchers were rare, and the backs were ornamental and expansive so that, like hallstands, these objects commanded and controlled considerable wall area.

The design of the chairs indicates that they were not intended for prolonged sitting, at least not for members of the household or their social peers. The qualities they embodied were visual appeal and utility, not comfort. The plank seat was employed in lieu of upholstery because it would not be damaged by contact with wet or soiled outer garments; because it contributed to the stern, somewhat intimidating grandeur of the hall; and possibly because it was uncomfortable. Under normal cir-

1.17 *The basic middle-class hall chair, intended to create drama at relatively low cost. Hall chairs combine the obvious utilitarianism of a plank seat with equally obvious elements of style, fashion, and courtly allusion. The hinged seat lifts to reveal a storage compartment. The tall back—elaborately shaped, pierced, and molded—gives little support but provides inexpensive grandeur and vaguely armorial associations.*

Walnut hall chair
Eastern United States, 1870–1880
Collection of William J. Wiesand, Jr.

1.18 *Hall chairs often became more architectural as they became more costly, taking on much the same design vocabulary as hallstands. The back of this hall chair closely resembles, on a smaller scale, the configuration of moderately expensive hallstands in the same style.*

Walnut hall chair
Eastern United States, 1870–1880
Stowe-Day Foundation, Hartford, Connecticut
Photograph by E. Irving Blomstrann

cumstances, visiting peers or superiors were quickly shown into one of the formal rooms of the house. The people kept waiting in the hall were socially inferior to the residents of the house, the "messenger boys, book-agents, the census-man and the bereaved lady who offers us soap" condescendingly listed by Clarence Cook, who went on to argue that "as visitors of this class are the only ones who will sit in the hall, considerations of comfort may be allowed to yield to picturesqueness, and any chair or bench that gives us that will serve." When hall chairs were used by people of higher status, they served only as perching places for pulling on overshoes or for similar chores. This purpose, however, seems to have been secondary to their potential for psychological manipulation of social inferiors and to their role in defining the hall as a specialized space.[27]

CARD RECEIVERS

The last important part of the constellation of hall furnishings was a card receiver. Like the other objects discussed, the card receiver is obsolete, or nearly so, for it was intimately linked to a ritual of card leaving little practiced today. The early history of the object is obscure, but it is clear that card receivers were in fashion by the 1860s. The grandest card receivers were elaborate cast-metal stands, sometimes made in France, which rested directly on the floor. More typical were smaller models, ranging from a few inches to over a foot in height, intended to be placed on a table or stand (1.20, 1.21, and 1.22). In all cases, the card receiver was conceived as a dish or tray elevated on a stand that stabilized it and gave it heightened prominence.

Again, it is difficult to fix the point at which calling cards or ceremonial calling became part of middle-class life in the last century. The phenomenon probably derives from courtly behavior of earlier times, for the dual purpose of preserving social status and distinctions and ritualizing interactions recalls protocol for royal audiences and interviews. As with so many other adaptations of earlier conventions, the nineteenth century made certain alterations that we now think of as typical of the era.[28]

Whatever its origins and initial form, the entire card system was well codified by the middle of the nineteenth century and remained largely intact well into the early years of the twentieth. The card ritual fitted neatly into the patterns of conspicuous consumption outlined by Thorstein Veblen, for the task of leaving cards fell primarily, and not surprisingly, to women. A genteel woman was presumed to have time to devote to this activity. In Veblen's terms, the card ritual was evidence of conspicuous leisure and an instance of nonproductive, if gracious, labor. A more sympathetic interpretation might concur on the facts but view calling as important in building and sustaining connectedness and webs of relationship in Victorian society.[29]

It is difficult to know how much credence to give to the normative arguments of etiquette books. In the case of the ritual of cards, the widespread existence of the

1.20 *Card receiver in the cosmopolitan classical manner. The shallow, dish-like receptacle flanked by stylized lion heads holds the cards. The rest of the object literally and figuratively elevates the cards. The classic design elements visible in this photograph culminate within the receptacle, where a portrait medallion of a male head is identified as the Roman emperor Hadrian.*

White metal card receiver finished to resemble antique bronze
Eastern United States, 1870–1880
Height 19″
Private collection
[Objects with no source listed are also from private collections.]

1.21 *Sentimentalizing the card receiver. Whether by intention or accident, relationships could be established, severed, or never even formed through the delicate vehicle of the card, and so card receivers had the potential to play critical supporting roles in the dramas of human interaction. In less formal circles, card receivers often made references to or generated affections and sentiments considered appropriate to friendship and intimacy.*

White metal card receiver finished to simulate gold
United States, 1870–1890

1.22 *The downward mobility of manners and materials. This page from a trade catalog of one of America's major manufacturers of electroplated wares demonstrates dramatically the widening distribution of behavior and material culture once confined to courtly circles. Calling cards and goods seemingly made of silver or gold became accessible to the emerging middle class at about the same time, the first through the dissemination of courtly culture and the second through the process known as electroplating, which deposited a thin layer of silver or gold over the surface of an object made of a less expensive material. This illustration indicates the range of form and taste options available in the 1880s from a single manufacturer. All items were available silverplated or goldplated.*

*Silver- and gold-plated card receivers
Trade catalog of Reed & Barton
Taunton, Massachusetts, 1885
The Winterthur Library*

REED & BARTON
SILVER AND GOLD PLATE.

CARD RECEIVERS.

props and tools—hallstands, card receivers, cards—lends support to the testimony of these books. Since there is agreement about the general contours of card leaving from the earliest books to those of only a few decades ago, it is possible that many who used cards did so in the manner prescribed in these texts.[30]

Most etiquette books stressed that leaving cards was a crucial part of social life (1.23). "Leaving cards is one of the most important of social observances, as it is the groundwork or nucleus in society of all acquaintanceship." Card leaving was a way of entering society, of designating changes in status or address, of issuing invitations (1.24) and responding to them, of sending sentiments of happiness or condolence, and, in general, of carrying on all the communication associated with social life. Not to participate in this ritual, with its strict rules, was to risk being categorized as ill bred, the Victorian euphemism for lower class.[31]

For the most part, cards were supposed to be left in person. Some etiquette books suggested that cards could be sent with a messenger or by mail. Others took a less flexible stance and maintained that it was a breach of etiquette to do anything but deliver them oneself. Certainly not to do so violated the concept of conspicuous leisure and the idea that the relationship was meaningful, for to mail cards or send them with a servant suggested that a woman had household responsibilities or some other activity she valued more highly. Related to the emphasis on leisure was the requirement that cards be left between noon and five o'clock in the afternoon. Since these were normal business hours, it is clear that most men could not be expected to leave cards. They were at work, conforming to the ideology of separate spheres, while their wives engaged in the parallel work of creating and sustaining social bonds.[32]

Cards were critical components of ceremonial calling. This ritual encompassed what we might call primary calling and secondary calling, human interaction and artifact interaction. When individuals were not present, cards sometimes became their surrogates. Since husbands did not normally accompany their wives when they paid calls, the wife could leave her husband's card where she visited. If the lady of the house being visited was at home, the lady visitor could leave two of her husband's cards, one for the lady and the other for her husband. To leave her own card would

1.23 *The ruling-class definition of good taste in calling cards. These seemingly trivial bits of paper were carefully examined for what could be interpreted as flaws of taste or judgment. Plain white or off-white stock with a name engraved in confident, authoritative, but unostentatious type was the norm for those who participated in the dominant culture. To those who did not, cards such as these seemed dull and impersonal. The cards in this photograph vary in their formality and evidence of social rank.*

Calling cards
Used in New York, late nineteenth century
New York State Archives, Albany
Photograph by Craig Williams

1.24 *An "at home" card, distributed to let friends and acquaintances know when they might actually expect a personal encounter with the individual named on the card. Those visiting at other times might have to be content with leaving their cards.*
"At home" card of Miss Harriett Cramer
Used in New York, third quarter of nineteenth century
New York State Archives
Photograph by Craig Williams

1.25 *Cards used by people who were not members of the ruling class and probably did not wish to be. Despite the attempts of tastemakers and pontificators to enforce a monolithic culture, the design of calling cards varied considerably. People outside formal, urban circles often used these more colorful, more sentimental cards, suggesting that, for them, maintaining relationships involved less ceremony, less pretense. These overtly sentimental cards* mocked and subverted what struck many ordinary folks as the impersonality and austerity of ruling-class cards. Needless to say, these lithographed cards were seen as gauche by the dominant culture.
Lithographed calling cards
Used in New York, late nineteenth century
New York State Archives
Photograph by Craig Williams

have been redundant, since she had already seen the lady of the house in person.

If the same woman were paying calls and the woman she intended to visit was not at home, she might leave three cards, one of her own and two of her husband's. The latter two were to be distributed as before, but her card would be left for the mistress of the house; "a lady leaves a card for a lady only." This cult of protecting the virtue of matrons extended to that of maidens as well, for in some circles it was not considered appropriate for a young lady to have visiting cards of her own. Her name was printed beneath that of her mother on the latter's card. The use of *Miss* on a card was often reserved for older unmarried women.[33]

The card ritual associated with ceremonial calling was in many ways a social perpetual-motion machine that, once set going among equals, could not with propriety be stopped unless one party died or moved away.[34] Among social unequals (1.25), it could be halted when the superior ignored the inferior. When there was no intention to visit but only to maintain contact, to sustain a bond, a woman merely handed three cards to a servant, who presumably placed them in the card receiver, the contents of which were later sorted and evaluated.[35] Whatever the intention of the individual—to pay a visit or only a surrogate visit by way of a card—a kind of social code of Hammurabi prevailed: a card for a card, a call for a call. A person of equal or lower social status, visited or called on, was obliged to reciprocate.

Rules governed how and when people of different social status might interact. Calling or only leaving a card could signal differing degrees of intimacy. Among social equals, the law cited here was normally in operation. In cases of obvious social distinction, the situation was different. If a woman of higher social position returned a card with a call, it was considered a compliment. If the roles were reversed and a woman of lower social status returned a card with the more intimate, more familiar call instead of just a card, the gesture could be interpreted as brash or presumptuous.

The use of cards and servants as barriers was extensive in the last century. For example, a man wishing to meet a young woman could arrange to have his card left at her home by a female friend. If the young woman had no interest in meeting him, the solution was simple: His card was not noticed. Similarly, an intended visit could be reduced to the level of a call through the expedient of having the servant announce that someone was "not at home" (1.26). This fiction observed the letter of the social law of calling while acknowledging that other needs might occasionally take precedence over this ritual.[36]

Today, much of the activity associated with calling, with impression management and contact maintenance, takes place in business rather than private life. Telephone calls are our cards, and secretaries—or answering machines—the servants who announce that the important person is at a meeting or cannot be reached. Yet even

1.26 *Genteel avoidance. In this famous painting of an encounter that never takes place, a female figure flees up the stairs to private parts of the house to avoid meeting an unseen caller. Through this polite fiction of being "not at home," unwanted visits were prevented from interrupting time or activities already planned. And this acknowl-* *edged fiction allowed affluent women time to be offstage, away from the stress of formal living and socializing.*
"Not at Home"
Eastman Johnson, c. 1872–1880
Oil on board
The Brooklyn Museum, Accession No. 40.60
Gift of Miss Gwendolyn O. L. Conkling

if some aspects of these rituals survive, contemporary American society no longer cherishes the same set of values the Victorians did or expresses itself in the same ways. The Victorians believed in the ceremonies of daily life as ways to attain elegance and personal nobility, as ways to demonstrate to themselves and others their high level of civilization and their exceptional control over themselves and their world. These self-consciously civilized people embraced social competition while they endorsed social bonding. Yet there was clearly more behind hall furnishings of the nineteenth century than conspicuous consumption, invidious comparison, and self-congratulation. These elaborated objects emphasized and enshrined personal possessions. Hats, coats, umbrellas, and cards were social tools, but they were also tangible pieces of human lives. As such, they touched the emotional, sentimental side of a culture also fascinated by memory and connectedness. Behind these hall furnishings, partly concealed by their courtly, formal facades, were cultural impulses much like those we locate more easily in souvenirs, albums, and popular songs like "The Old Arm Chair," "The Old Oaken Bucket," and "Home, Sweet Home."[37]

If the people who owned the objects we have been discussing could vigorously defend social station and privilege, they could also be moved by associations and relationships with their friends and relatives. The objects they placed in their halls revealed not only these competing facets of the Victorian personality but the very nature of the hall. For it was a space that was neither wholly interior nor exterior but a sheltered, social testing zone that some moved through with ease and familiarity and others never passed beyond. For the latter, first impressions were often final impressions.

2 : Death in the Dining Room

All people need food. About that, there is no disagreement. But when it comes to defining food, opinions differ. What is edible in one society is inedible in another. What is invested with sacred properties or elevated to ceremonial status in one society is taboo in another.[1] Within our own society, some potential foods evoke positive feelings and associations; others provoke disgust and revulsion. Much the same can be said for the etiquettes and environments associated with eating. This chapter is about an environment that contemporary Americans find unacceptably violent and sensual. Their negative reactions to this small fragment of the Victorian material world demonstrate how greatly cultural attitudes and values have changed in a relatively short time. They also suggest that this environment provides access to a side of Victorian culture not usually explored in studies of domestic life, a side our culture finds problematic and disturbing. Perhaps more than any other objects in this book, this environment and the furnishings designed for it complicate our comprehension of Victorian life. Perhaps more than any others, they force us to ponder the ways Victorians were not like us.

There is no accepted name for the phenomenon we examine in this chapter. We could accurately, if not gracefully, call it the mid-nineteenth-century iconography of dining. This iconography is identified and defined by two- and three-dimensional representations of fruits, vegetables, grains, and nuts; of dead rabbits, deer and other mammals, fish, and fowl; of trophies and instruments of the hunt, harvest, and vintage; and of related allegorical figures. My purpose here is not to write a history of this iconography. That would be an immense task, for its roots reach far back in time, to the caves of Lascaux and even beyond to the earliest experiences of humankind.[2] Instead, I want, first, to resurrect for twentieth-century eyes an underacknowledged aspect of Victorian material culture that was both highly visible and significant in its own day. Second, I want to suggest how we might interpret these assertive and expressive goods, these undeniably affecting presences of the Victorian world.[3]

The imagery I have outlined appeared in greatest concentration on sideboards, the most prominent pieces of furniture in nineteenth-century dining rooms (2.1).

2.1 *The sideboard was a dominant presence in the dining rooms of affluent Americans who furnished in the 1850s. This lavishly carved example represented the high end of furniture production of the time. Not only was the design European but the execution probably was as well; elaborately carved furniture of this quality was usually the work of French or German immigrant artisans who settled in major metropolitan areas. All the naturalistic imagery was carved from wood, with the exception of the antlers, which were the real thing. Overall height, nearly 8 feet (92 inches).*

Walnut sideboard with marble slab
Probably Boston, c. 1855
Currier Gallery of Art, Manchester, New Hampshire
Gift of Mrs. Francis MacKay, Accession No. 1981.56

Elements of the imagery were incorporated into the design of French sideboards of the 1840s, but the prime object, the seminal expression of the genre, was an immense walnut sideboard exhibited at the Crystal Palace in London in 1851.[4] This sideboard, at least 12 feet high, was produced by the Parisian firm of Fourdinois. Although now lost, the object was extensively described and illustrated in its day, and its features are therefore fairly well known (2.2).[5] Much of the surface of this sideboard was devoted to an elaborated iconographic program of dining. At the base were six dogs, symbolizing the hunt. Onto a large slab above them tumbled a naturalistically carved deer, game bird, and lobster. Flanking this central composition were panels and roundels of produce. On pedestals above stood female figures representing four continents with what were considered their most celebrated contributions to foodways: Europe with wine, Asia with tea, Africa with coffee, and America with sugar cane. Above these figures were trios of *putti* harvesting wheat and grapes. The upper center of the piece was dominated by a painting of an aloe or century plant (2.3). The entire design culminated in the seated figure of Ceres presenting two cornucopias.

The Fourdinois sideboard occupied and fused two separate design tracks: object–function and ornament. Within the first, it played a key role in the development of the sideboard as a distinctive furniture form. At the middle of the nineteenth century, the sideboard was simultaneously an ancient and a modern object. It was ancient in the sense that case pieces of some sort had been part of the physical context of affluent dining in the West since at least the fifteenth century. These case pieces usually provided some combination of storage and display. The sideboard was also modern in the sense that the sequence to which the Fourdinois example belonged dated only to the late eighteenth century. At that time, many furniture forms were reconceptualized, the sideboard among them. In Britain and France in particular, new arrangements of storage and display functions were articulated. From new beginnings in the 1770s to the middle of the nineteenth century, the lines of sideboard development are quite clear, at least at the level of elite culture.[6]

2.2 *The most authoritative statement in furniture of the mid-nineteenth-century iconography of dining, this immense walnut sideboard was exhibited at the Great Exhibition in London in 1851. Its image was widely disseminated through the many publications that recorded Joseph Paxton's famous Crystal Palace and objects shown in it. Although the Great Exhibition celebrated Britain's economic and political power, the success of the Fourdinois sideboard demonstrated that France still exercised leadership in the arts of elegant living.*

Prize-winning walnut sideboard
A. G. Fourdinois, Paris, 1851
Illustrated in The Art Journal Illustrated
Catalogue: The Industry of All Nations
London: George Virtue for The Art
Journal, *1851*
The Winterthur Library

2.3 *Though the object is now lost, the intricacy and elaboration of the Fourdinois sideboard are still discernible in this period wood engraving. Here, allegorical figures of continents with indigenous products flank a brightly painted picture of an aloe on a mirrored glass surface. The panel below was dominated by the often copied motif of the dead deer.*
Detail of Fourdinois sideboard

The Fourdinois sideboard was a prime object in part because of the success with which it resolved the issue of what a sideboard should be around 1850. That resolution stressed the functions of presentation and display over storage. The Fourdinois sideboard was notable for how little interior space it provided. Because the object does not survive and therefore cannot be examined, it is difficult to be certain, but the Fourdinois sideboard seems to have had no interior spaces at all, except for a row of shallow drawers in the frieze above the seated dogs. While the long horizontal slab could be used for display, the primary function of this sideboard was presentation of itself; that is, of its form and iconography. Its prime object status and the high regard in which it was held in its day rested in part on its power to demonstrate the cultural ideal that consummate objects expressed themselves.[7] Utilitarian functions were subordinate to social, symbolic, or ideological functions. Because for most people household furniture was necessarily utilitarian to some degree, this ideal was rarely attained. As an exhibition piece, however, the Fourdinois sideboard was free from the practical constraints of daily life. It could transcend the limitations of the mundane.

The Fourdinois sideboard was a prime object also because of its ornament, the iconography lathered so luxuriantly across its expansive surface. While the composition was original and innovative, most of the individual components of the composition had long been familiar.[8] The theme of abundant food was popular in paintings produced in the Low Countries in the sixteenth and seventeenth centuries and in France in the seventeenth and eighteenth centuries. References to hunting or foodways were used in Rococo compositions by designers such as Antoine Watteau, Christophe Huet, Jean-Baptiste Oudry, and others, and had been stock elements of *ornemanistes* since the sixteenth century. In the eighteenth century, Parisian townhouses were furnished with carved or painted images of dead game in rooms where dining took place.[9] A thorough survey of design history would locate abundant examples of this kind of imagery.

We can get some idea of how innovative the Fourdinois sideboard was by comparing it with another sideboard that had been publicly exhibited in Paris in 1844 (2.4).

2.4 *The iconography emerges. This sideboard, exhibited in Paris in 1844, possesses in rudimentary form many of the elements that would be more fully exploited seven years later by Fourdinois. These include the clusters of dead game on the doors, the vicious-looking animal heads terminating the scrolls supporting the shelf, and, more visible in the detail, the stylized representation of dogs hunting a stag in the cartouche at the top.*

Oak sideboard in the Renaissance style
Manufactured by Ringuet Leprince, Paris
From Le Garde-meuble album de l'exposition de l'industrie, 1844
Paris: D. Guilmard, 1844
Grand Rapids Public Library, Michigan

This earlier object contained some of the same ingredients but they were handled in a much less assertive way. The piece consequently had much less dramatic impact. The Fourdinois sideboard significantly magnified both scale and complexity. The earlier sideboard had sketched out a rudimentary iconography of hunting and foodstuffs; the Fourdinois sideboard expanded, elaborated, and embellished that iconography. Variations on the 1844 formulation remained typical until 1851, when the Fourdinois sideboard radically elevated and transformed the idiom.

Although exhibited in London's Crystal Palace in 1851, the Fourdinois sideboard was a product of continuing French design hegemony. It was a noteworthy achievement in a long line of noteworthy French achievements. Centuries of royal and state support for the arts of gracious living had helped make France the international center of courtly design. And while French political power was clearly waning, France's cultural authority was still strong. For many people, the mere fact that this object was French gave it cachet. Its selection for a top award by an international panel of judges demonstrated that the French still could not be surpassed in the courtly arts.[10]

As a prime object supported by the cultural power of France, the Fourdinois sideboard generated replications—and replications of those replications—throughout the Western world for well over two decades. Some of them were shown at subsequent world's fairs. At the Centennial International Exhibition, held in Philadelphia in 1876, the German and Spanish sections (2.5) exhibited massive sideboards that were still paying homage to the prototype.[11]

Sideboards were particularly prominent around the middle of the century. In Britain, there was something of a sideboard mania. Hughes Protat, who had designed the Fourdinois sideboard of 1851, was employed in 1853 to design for a country house in Warwickshire another sideboard with similar iconography but laid out in the more horizontal British manner. In the same shire, a few years later, J. M. Willcox produced a highly sculptural sideboard for Charlecotte Park, where it is still on view. Some of the prominent sideboards of the 1850s and 1860s were based on British literature or lore. The most famous of these were probably the Kenil-

2.5 *French international design hegemony. Made in Spain and exhibited in Philadelphia, this sideboard documents the authority of French design ideas. Without the caption, "Spanish Buffet," and the Damascus-style metalwork below, there would be little reason to think this object was not French, or American in the French style, rather than Spanish in the French style. This object and the many others like it produced throughout the Western world are evidence of an international cosmopolitan style that dominated courtly taste in the nineteenth century, as it had in the eighteenth.*

Spanish sideboard exhibited at the Centennial International Exhibition in Philadelphia, 1876
Illustrated in George Titus Ferris, Gems of the Centennial
New York: D. Appleton & Co., 1877
The Winterthur Library

worth sideboard, produced by the Warwick firm of Cookes, and the Chevy Chase sideboard, made by Gerrard Robinson of Newcastle.[12]

The Fourdinois sideboard was swiftly replicated in the United States. In 1853, New York City hosted an international exhibition. Although smaller than the London fair, it too was housed in a Crystal Palace and included exhibits from around the world. The most prominent piece of furniture, if we can judge from the leading catalog of the exhibition, was a massive sideboard loosely modeled on the Fourdinois example. It was exhibited by a New York firm identified as Bulkley & Herter (2.6). Bulkley is unknown today, but Gustave Herter and his brother Christian went on to become leading names in furniture and interior design in the 1870s and 1880s. The sideboard, or "buffet," exhibited by this firm in 1853 was described in the catalog as "truly magnificent," a "noble work," "large in size" and "grand in style." It was illustrated in its entirety on one page and in seven details on the facing page, one of which is shown in Figure 2.7.[13]

The Bulkley & Herter sideboard was not a conventional piece of household furniture. Like the Fourdinois example, it was a specially created exhibition piece, intended to impress with its quality of design and workmanship and great scale. Other sideboards shown in 1853 were more typical of objects in production, albeit at the top of the line. Alexander Roux of New York, already a well-known French immigrant cabinetmaker, exhibited a sideboard (2.8) described in the catalog as "not too large for the use and style of moderately wealthy families."[14] Twentieth-century folk could have made the same pronouncement by analyzing the artifactual record. The Roux sideboard was a fairly standard example of upscale production. Scores of similar and even more elaborate pieces survive today to demonstrate that they were once numerous. Outstanding examples are in the collections of the Currier Gallery of Art in New Hampshire (see 2.1), Yale University Art Gallery (2.9), the High Museum in Atlanta, and the Cleveland Museum of Art (2.10). All follow what seems to have been the prevailing scheme for expensive sideboards. The base of each was divided into four units, all defined by doors. The two center doors were flat; the flanking doors convex. All were adorned with high-relief carving of appro-

2.6 *A blockbuster sideboard for the American Crystal Palace in 1853. Like its English model, the New York City international exhibition was housed in a bold and innovative glass structure and included an exceptional sideboard that attracted considerable attention. More than any other example of the period, this piece blurred the distinction between furniture and architecture, introducing design allusions to a chapel and altar into an object presumably intended for a domestic dining room.*

Sideboard by Bulkley & Herter exhibited at the New York Crystal Palace in 1853 Illustrated in Benjamin Silliman and C. R. Goodrich, eds., The World of Science, Art and Industry Illustrated
New York: G. P. Putnam & Co., 1854

2.7 *A rare instance of violence. Most sideboards presented the outcome or aftermath of violence, rather than scenes of actual death or dying. But Bulkley & Herter prominently placed a scene Silliman and Goodrich described as "The Death of the Stag" as the focal point of their intensely altarlike sideboard.*

"The Death of the Stag"
Carved centerpiece of the Bulkley & Herter sideboard

2.8 *The basic sideboard of affluent Americans of the 1850s. This example, manufactured in New York by the firm of French-trained immigrant Alexander Roux, is typical of expensive production. The four-unit base with curved ends and the three-stage back are recurring elements. This rather staid sideboard owes less to the Fourdinois tour de force of 1851 than to the sideboard illustrated in Figure 2.4. Scores of similar sideboards still survive.*

Sideboard by Alexander Roux exhibited at the New York Crystal Palace in 1853
Illustrated in Benjamin Silliman and C. R. Goodrich, eds., The World of Science, Art and Industry Illustrated
New York: G. P. Putnam & Co., 1854

2.9 *This sideboard, by an unknown firm, closely resembles several exhibited at the New York Crystal Palace.*

Black walnut sideboard
Probably made in New York, c. 1853
Yale University Art Gallery, New Haven
Jos. Earl Sheffield Collection
Height 102″

2.10 *One of the most elaborate American sideboards from the 1850s, this lavishly carved example adroitly manipulates key elements of French-derived design vocabulary, even nationalizing the design through the addition of a pair of Native American hunters. Like other very heavily ornamented sideboards, this one allows little surface for the display of other objects. Its major display is of itself.*

Walnut sideboard with marble top
Possibly made in Philadelphia, c. 1855
Cleveland Museum of Art, Purchase from the J. H. Wade Fund, 85.72
Height 114"

2.11 *This carved figure of a Native American hunter, one of a pair, plays an ambiguous role in the iconography of this exceptional sideboard. Nineteenth-century ethnocentrism and racism enforced the tendency of Western ruling culture to associate Native Americans and other people of color with the natural world and themselves with civilization. Thus, in a crude equation, white folks were understood to be people, but others were animals. This double standard survives today in some museums, where the past of white people is exhibited as history, but the past of Native Americans is natural history.*

Detail of walnut sideboard shown in Figure 2.10

Photograph courtesy of Peter Hill, Inc., Maplewood Manor, East Lempster, New Hampshire

priate imagery. Above the doors were drawers; two were flat and two convex. A large horizontal slab, of either wood or marble, provided a surface for display and visually terminated the lower section.

On this lower section of four units rested an upper section of three units. Conceptually, the central pier or dividing element of the lower section was eliminated in the upper in order to create a broader expanse. The three examples shown here display varying treatments of this basic formula. They also demonstrate the alternatives for the crest on top of the piece. Some combination of pediments, scrolls, cartouches, and stag's head were typical.

Wood engravings in exhibition catalogs, however detailed and accurate, provide little clue to the visual impact of these sideboards. Seeing these massive and aggressive objects firsthand in domestic settings or art museums is a memorable experience. Their large-scale, high-quality workmanship, and, above all, explicit imagery, make them powerful, assertive, even commanding. All the examples listed here repay careful examination. The Cleveland Museum of Art's sideboard provides a particularly rich sculptural program. Figures of Native American hunters (2.11) flank a roundel filled with fruits and vegetables (2.12). Above the roundel is a vigorous sculpture of dead game (2.13), clearly derived in its conception from the Fourdinois sideboard of 1851. The entire design is crowned with an impressionistically carved hawk holding a bird it has just caught and is about to devour (2.14).

The most lavishly decorated midcentury sideboard currently on public view is owned, perhaps appropriately, by the Museum of Fine Arts in Houston (2.15). Laid out according to an alternative scheme of a three-part base, all but a few surfaces of this sideboard are densely covered with exceptional carving. On the center door are trophies of the hunt, including a gun, pouch, powder horn, and hunting bugle, bound to oak branches by a crinkled ribbon (2.16). On the left door is a seafood medley, composed of two fish, an eel, and a lobster, all garnished with cattails and bound by another ribbon (2.17). The right panel is ornamented with gamebirds in similar fashion (2.18).

2.12 *A composition of selected produce. There may be meaning in the fact that all the foods depicted are associated with plant reproduction. Fruits, nuts, berries, grapes, melon, corn, peas, and the pineapple either are seeds or contain them. This carved imagery, then, perpetuates long-standing conventions of fertility and abundance. For if flowers offer the possibility of sexual union and fertilization, fruits are evidence that both have taken place.*

Detail of walnut sideboard shown in Figure 2.10
Photograph courtesy of Peter Hill, Inc.

2.13 *The dead stag and other victims of predation carved in black walnut, the wood used for furniture masterpieces of the French Renaissance of the sixteenth and early seventeenth centuries. Within a shallow niche, the prototypical dead stag is joined by two game birds and a rabbit, the whole composition unified and contextualized through naturalistically carved branches, vines, and grasses. The architectural frame for this intensely sculptural composition is further enriched with naturalistic touches, making it clear that artifice controls nature and nature ornaments artifact.*

Detail of walnut sideboard shown in Figure 2.10
Photograph courtesy of Peter Hill, Inc.

2.14 *Where do predation and death come from? Sometimes they swoop down from above, catching their victims by surprise. This extraordinary sideboard culminates in an image of a bird of prey and its catch, an image* *that can be interpreted literally and in more metaphoric terms. The carving is not minutely detailed, but evokes plant and bird forms through the loosely handled, impressionistic style admired at the time.*

Detail of walnut sideboard shown in Figure 2.10
Photograph courtesy of Peter Hill, Inc.

2.15 *More carving per square inch than any other mid-nineteenth-century sideboard in the public domain. One of the most startling artistic accomplishments of Victorian America, this densely ornamented sideboard presents a rich and intricate synopsis of the major features of the iconography of dining. The entire composition and its complex web of meanings and associations are nationalized and endorsed by the American bald eagle and shield at the top. The introduction of the American emblem and totem commingles natural order with national order, natural predation with national predation.*

Carved walnut sideboard
Made in a major East Coast city, c. 1853
Museum of Fine Arts, Houston
Museum Purchase with funds provided by Anaruth and Aron S. Gordon
Photograph courtesy of Peter Hill, Inc.
Height 106″

2.16 *Signs of human predation. Carved in walnut, the pouch, gun, bugle, and powder horn are transformed from tools to symbols and ornaments. Such artful arrangements of parts of the material culture of daily life reach back as far as the sixteenth century and are long-standing parts of French design vocabulary.*

Center door of carved walnut sideboard shown in Figure 2.15
Photograph courtesy of Peter Hill, Inc.

2.17 *Food from the sea. Lobster, fish, and eel, garnished with cattails, the whole carved in walnut.*

Left door of carved walnut sideboard shown in Figure 2.15
Photograph courtesy of Peter Hill, Inc.

2.18 *Food from the sky. Two water birds, tied together and hung as trophies.*

Right door of carved walnut sideboard shown in Figure 2.15
Photograph courtesy of Peter Hill, Inc.

Elaborate as it is, the base of the object seems sparsely decorated when we turn to the upper section, which presents an intricate composition of hunting dogs (2.19), fox heads, small mammals, and seemingly endless naturalistic, Mannerist, and Baroque forms. The largest and most assertive section depicts a dead stag hanging head downward, one leg bound by a rope fastened through the scrolls of a foliate cartouche (2.20). Like the Cleveland example, the whole design is capped by a bird of prey. Here, however, the bird of prey is an eagle grasping, not a victim, but a shield emblazoned with the stars and stripes. A European design concept has been explicitly Americanized.

2.19 *As in the Fourdinois sideboard, dogs serve here not only to sustain the reference to hunting but to support and guard display surfaces. Unarguably animals, in the hunt dogs act as human agents and serve human purposes. Dogs might be described as the soldiers of fortune of the animal world.*

Carved dogs, parts of a carved walnut sideboard shown in Figure 2.15
Photograph courtesy of Peter Hill, Inc.

2.20 *The ritual sacrifice of the stag.
The designer of this sideboard drew on
venerable traditions in crafting the ceremonial centerpiece of this extraordinary
sideboard. The captured stag, bound by
one foot, hangs head downward in front
of an aedicule, a doorwaylike or arklike
form long used to convey significance
on objects or figures placed within it.
By being located within this canopied
architectural form, this little temple,
this shrine, the stag becomes sacralized.
On the facades of Gothic cathedrals and
in Renaissance paintings, saints stood
within similar honorific and symbolic
structures.*

*Carved stag, centerpiece of walnut sideboard
shown in Figure 2.15
Photograph courtesy of Peter Hill, Inc.*

These sideboards represented a highly visible cultural phenomenon around the middle years of the nineteenth century. Originating in France and empowered by French cultural authority, the concept was widely and swiftly emulated. For nearly two decades, sideboards such as these were prominent at international exhibitions. Surviving examples allow us to experience their powerful presence. While they induce in us a certain degree of awe, we tend to see them as alien, foreign, decidedly odd. On one level, they are fascinating; on another, slightly repulsive. Today it is difficult for many to believe that normal, well-socialized people in Victorian America voluntarily put these boldly expressive objects in their dining rooms and ate daily in their presence. Evidence suggests that Victorians not only tolerated these objects but found them desirable. We wonder why. What did these sideboards mean to them? How are we to interpret them?

First, they have meaning purely as sideboards. If we strip away the lavish carving, we still must contend with the form and, even more, the immense scale of these objects. Even after the midcentury iconography of dining was out of fashion, sideboards remained large and imposing. Part of their significance as sideboards was related to the process of specialization that restructured nineteenth-century domestic life. Begun earlier at the courtly level, this specialization required that each room have its discrete functions and that these functions be articulated and enabled by the furnishings in that space. Put into practice, this usually meant that in homes of affluent people, the distinctive function of each room was signaled by equally distinctive decor. It often turned out that in each room one object was especially magnified, as if to take lead responsibility for defining the function of that space. In the hall it was the hallstand; in the dining room, the sideboard.

Like hallstands, sideboards glorified the functions that took place in their presence and contributed to the self-consciousness of their users.[15] Like hallstands, sideboards were large precisely because dining was understood to be of extraordinary significance. To nineteenth-century minds, dining was important because it was basic and because it simultaneously provided an occasion for the display of highly civilized behavior. Here was a charged, even sublime set of realizations. Eating linked nineteenth-century people to all people, of every time and place. Taken one step further, it also linked them to all living things, past or present, that were known to eat—or be eaten. Transforming the commonplace and even bestial act of eating into the civilized ceremony of dining elevated Victorians above all other creatures and most other human beings. These were large ideas, powerful realizations, and they deserved appropriate artifactual recognition.[16]

Yet clearly what stands out to, and offends, twentieth-century eyes is less the size of these objects than their explicit and highly sensual references to foods of all kinds and, above all, to dead animals. I do not intend to determine why these naturalistic carvings of dead rabbits, fish, or deer offend twentieth-century sensibilities, intriguing though the question may be. My goal is to figure out why such imagery seems to have engaged people in the 1850s and 1860s.

Some of the answer may be found in attitudes toward violence, a prime ingredient of the Romanticism of the last century. Violence pervaded literature and design. The imagery on sideboards has many close cognates in contemporary artistic expression. In France, at about the same time that the Fourdinois sideboard was being designed, Eugène Delacroix was painting some of his most violent, most Romantic lion hunts, tiger hunts, and other exoticized scenes of predation (2.21).[17] At that time, too, Antoine Louis Barye was crafting his small but intensely powerful bronzes of lions, bears, pythons, and other carnivores locked in deadly combat (2.22).[18] In Britain, Sir Edwin Landseer was painting stag hunts and other well-received scenes of animal conflict (2.23).[19] These were only the most visible participants in a far broader phenomenon.[20]

But these were, as I have suggested, only close cognates. Compared to the work of Delacroix, Barye, and Landseer, the images on sideboards seem tame and subdued, the violence occurring offstage, so to speak. With rare exception, the creatures on sideboards are dead, rather than engaged in fatal struggles. These carved wooden images, then, are not meant to evoke the same excitement or passion as the scenes of conflict. Nor are they presentations of gratuitous violence. Their meanings are more subtle and more complex.

2.21 *Violence and aggression exoticized. For nineteenth-century Europeans, the Islamic world constituted a major "other," a world against which Europeans defined and measured themselves and onto which they projected their fantasies. This swirling and unlikely scene of vicarious combat was created by a privileged Parisian painter. Within a barren and untamed landscape, wild, colorful, exotic, and terrifying animals struggle with people most Parisians probably would have defined in similar terms.*

The Lion Hunt
Eugène Delacroix, 1860–1861
Oil on canvas
Courtesy of The Art Institute of Chicago
Mr. and Mrs. Potter Palmer Collection, 1922.404
Photograph copyright 1990, The Art Institute of Chicago. All Rights Reserved.

2.22 *The violence of nature. The naturalness of violence. Or so it might seem. But Barye's small and powerful bronzes often bring together in deadly struggle two species that either do not normally interact or are not normally enemies. Thus Barye's own proclivity toward violence, and that of the larger society around him, become problematized. This sculpture is less about the violence characteristic of the animal world than about the violence that marks human relationships, the violence that lurks just behind most human beings' "civilized" facades, and the particular potential for violence that seethes within males of the species.*

Lion with Foot on Serpent
Bronze sculpture by Antoine Louis Barye, 1851
Philadelphia Museum of Art, W. P. Wilstach Collection
Photograph by A. J. Wyatt, Staff Photographer

2.23 *The stag hunt was a familiar image and concept in the nineteenth century and was rendered in many media. This version was painted by an artist better known for creating that enduring icon of animal nobility, the famous* Monarch of the Glen, *still used in the advertising of a major insurance company. This scene, if less famous, is more typical of midcentury attitudes toward the animal world.*

The Hunted Stag
Sir Edwin Landseer, before 1833
Oil on canvas
The Tate Gallery, London

They seem to be, for one thing, statements about the relationship of humankind to the natural world, expressing and endorsing a highly human-centered vision. The repeated depiction of bountiful displays suggests that the entire produce of the world was understood to be at humanity's service. Most of the animals, fruits, and vegetables on American sideboards seem to have been indigenous, but the Cleveland sideboard clearly depicts a pineapple, suggesting a wider purview (see 2.12). The Fourdinois sideboard was the fullest expression of what might be called alimentary imperialism, with its allegorical representations of four continents and representative products (see 2.2).[21]

These sideboards reaffirmed an ancient view, recorded as far back as the Book of Genesis, that humankind should have dominion "over the fish of the sea, and over the fowl of the air, and over the cattle, and over all the earth, and over every creeping thing that creepeth upon the earth."[22] These objects expressed that enduring comprehension in wholly secular terms, yet religious underpinnings, not usually visible, gave added resonance to their pronouncements.

Here again, the Fourdinois sideboard, perhaps because it was the most elaborated expression of this mode, provides the most insights. As noted, the Fourdinois sideboard culminated in a figure of the Roman goddess Ceres flanked by *putti,* those on one side harvesting wheat, the others harvesting grapes. These references seem universal, alluding to all food and drink, yet specific, suggesting the staples of French foodways, bread and wine. Yet bread and wine are basic to many other foodways as well, and for that reason central to the Christian ritual sacrifice of the Mass. This association could not have been lost on nineteenth-century observers, nor could they have failed to note, as have many in the twentieth century, that a large number of these sideboards strongly resemble the altarpieces of Catholic churches. Sideboards seem to be altars of profusion, abundance, prosperity, plenty. In a secular view undergirded by religious texts and allusions, these objects celebrated the sacrifice of "every creeping thing" in the service of humankind.

Celebration of sacrifice is one way of defining the meaning of these objects. Celebration of predation may be another, more skeptical way of describing it. Death on these sideboards has not simply happened; it has been brought about by agents. Where those agents are identified, they include animals, *putti*, or figures in historic or exotic garb. Predation expressed in this form was simultaneously muted and transformed into symbol and ceremony. Hounds attacking a stag, Native American hunters, or *putti* are all "natural" (or supernatural) and outside the normal daily experience of "civilized" Parisians and urban Americans. Even the hunting attributes on the central panel of the extravagant Houston sideboard (see 2.15) only imply a human agent. As far as I know, no figures of nineteenth-century Europeans or European Americans appear on any of these sideboards.[23] Although the figures that do appear are naturalistically rendered, because they are remote from experience, violence is also made remote, or abstract, and therefore more acceptable. In fact, instead of violence itself, we witness the outcome of violence. Often the animals look more asleep than dead. They are artfully arranged and balanced. There are no mangled, twisted bodies, no partially dismembered or devoured corpses. We are in the realm of symbol and symbolic language here. The more closely we examine this "natural" composition, the more self-consciously artificial it becomes. This elevated, artful presentation of ends coupled with the concealed, understatement of means sets up a dynamic tension between ends and means, effects and causes, repose and action, safety and danger, purity and defilement, art and life, and finally death and life—and life and death.

Although actual scenes of death are not common, and although we are more likely to encounter images of the dead than the dying, these objects still celebrate and enshrine predatory activity. Expressed in naturalistic terms, this predation seems part of the natural order, simply the way things are. We have to wonder, however, if the celebration of predatory activity is confined to human assaults on the edible inhabitants of the natural world or whether these sideboards were also conscious metaphors of Western social patterns around the middle of the century. "Conscious" may be the key word here. Intentions are difficult to demonstrate. Predation was surely a major theme of Western society in the nineteenth century. Perhaps it is enough to suggest that these objects celebrate a predatory impulse that was at the very heart of nineteenth-century society and that this impulse found major expression in two other broad areas of behavior. First, it sustained the wide range of human depredations of the natural world. However else these may be interpreted, the continuing rape of the landscape, the unthinking slaughter of creatures and extermination of species, and the short-sighted consumption of nonrenewable resources, in short, the consistent elevation of economic and stereotypical masculine values above all others, were all grounded in a predatory mentality. Second, this predatory mentality was incorporated into a social structure and a culture that allowed powerful people to prey, not only on the animal world, but on members of their own species. In its most dramatic form, this meant colonization. In only slightly less dramatic form, it meant control of capital and labor. If these sideboards were artifacts of the age of Delacroix, Barye, and Landseer, they also belonged to the world of Friedrich Engels and Karl Marx. Exploitation of the natural world and exploitation of labor are related behaviors, grounded in the same values, the same hubris. Men were still hunters, but their predatory activity took place within the allegedly civilized world of business, industry, and national expansion. Mark Twain recognized the dubious claims of civilization and expressed in Huckleberry Finn a critique of the ascent of man. Just as Huck gave up his wild ways to become civilized and join Tom's band of robbers, nineteenth-century capitalists relinquished their struggles with the animal world to become civilized and prey instead on their fellow human beings.[24]

Yet predation is hardly the only theme or association of these complicated and assertive objects. It is difficult, for example, to speak of predation without also speaking of gender, of conventional Victorian understandings of what masculinity was all about. According to Victorian stereotypes of masculinity, stereotypes still widely held today, these sideboards would have been considered masculine.[25] They were masculine in the roles they played, the functions they performed. These sideboards enshrined the conventional masculine roles of hunter and provider. In the nineteenth century, provider might have been understood as a culturally created role, but man as hunter was considered as inseparable from certain conceptions of "natural" masculinity as it is today. Men are supposed to hunt. Men are supposed to kill. Sideboards with dead game and hunting trophies could only be male. But style as well as content were interpreted as masculine in these objects. These sideboards were masculine because they were bold, strong, forceful, assertive, aggressive. They had a powerful and commanding presence. In the Victorian mental inventory of gender attributes, all this added up to masculine goods. Few pieces of household furniture have been as clearly or as emphatically masculine since.

As early as the 1840s, references to stag hunts appeared on sideboards. It is obvious that these endorse pursuit, predation, and human domination of the animal world. It may be less obvious that they carry class allusions as well. These class allusions may be obscured by historical and cultural differences between Europe and America. In both regions, the stag holds a privileged position among the hunted. Its high valuation rests in part on what might be called aesthetic factors and in part on mythic and mystical associations. In Europe, these associations were augmented by the identification of deer hunting with royal prerogative. In the Middle Ages and Renaissance, deer were kept in royal game preserves. In later years, the wealthy had deer parks. Throughout, the possession of deer and the right to hunt them were identified with royalty, power, status (2.24).[26] While some of these allusions may have been lost or altered in the land of the Deerslayer, in Europe the presence of the stag or the stag hunt on these sideboards indicated their links to the courtly vision of the ideal life. The courtly references on sideboards were consistent with the pattern prevailing at mid-century. For much of white, urbane Western society, the vision of the good life was derived largely from European monarchical and aristocratic lifestyles of the past. Yet these objects bear a curious relationship to their courtly antecedents. The reference to the stag hunt may have been considered necessary at the time to give these objects courtly associations, for while mid-century sideboards incorporated historical design vocabulary, their form did not replicate any known historical modes. Although courtly in scale, presence, and cost, they also departed from historical precedent in their heightened and unequivocal allusions to stereotypical masculine associations and values. In short, the nineteenth century did not

2.24 *The royal prerogative of the deer hunt, transferred to an American context. In this imaginative image from the mid nineteenth century, America's uncrowned monarch rests as his catch is being weighed, while Martha, alias Jean Étienne Liotard's* La Belle Chocolatière, *enters bearing refreshments. Here, key figures of the eighteenth century are reconfigured into a dramatic vignette understandable to and congru-* *ent with Victorian taste and values. The image also suggests that the hunt, the dead stag, and the meal all had latent sexual dimensions that later Victorians repressed. George's eyes are not on the stag, but on Martha as she brings drink to supplement the meat he has provided. If money is an aphrodisiac in the twentieth century, an abundance of food—money expressed in more immediately sensual terms—was an aphrodisiac* *in earlier times. This erotic aspect was potentially heightened when the food was obtained by hunting, understood as a ritual affirmation of masculinity.*

Home from the Hunt
Engraving by Henry Bryan Hall after A. Henning, 1855
Courtesy of Fraunces Tavern Museum, New York

attempt to replay or relive the past but to interact with and draw from it, much as it did with the natural world.

When sideboards appeared at international exhibitions or were illustrated in trade catalogs, they usually stood alone, in isolation. Neither function nor physical context was indicated. But sideboards were intended for dining rooms. There, they provided a theatrical backdrop for the ritual of dining. During the meal, bottles of wine, bowls of vegetables, and platters of meat were often placed on them. In these situations of actual use, another set of meanings emerged. Much as the iconography of the piece and its use by elite society played on the continuum and dissonance of savagery and civilization, sideboards in use revealed the dialectic between the raw, depicted on the sideboard, and the cooked, presented in the meal. Humankind was the agent for the transformation from the raw to the cooked, from natural to artificial, from nature to artifact. Civilization could be in part demonstrated at a meal by the number of these transformations and the distance between the two poles. Raw was a fixed category, but the cooked could be elevated and embellished to exquisite levels of subtlety, delicacy, and refinement.[27]

The nineteenth-century ritual of dining has been capably discussed elsewhere.[28] Here I want to underline, not the structure or organization of the meal, but its ritualistic dimension. Rituals are deliberately repeated acts or events that order and control. Rituals reaffirm cosmology, assure people of the way things ought to be.[29] Many human activities, however seemingly ordinary or bizarre, can be ritualized; consider those that took place in nineteenth-century halls. The ritualization of eating, however, is commonplace. Eating is a core component of the rituals of many societies. Across the anthropological and historical record, people have created eating rituals to initiate and maintain human relationships. In Victorian America, a dinner was also at some level a ritual of bonding. Eating the same foods from matching dishes with matching silverware bound diners to one another in one set of ways. Dining in the presence of the sideboard, and therefore absorbing and endorsing the cluster of cultural values expressed on it, bound them in another. As they dined, they sat in the presence of a rich and intricate nonverbal text that spoke of the struggle for existence and the subordination of groups to other groups; of the interrelatedness of all living things; of order, hierarchy, domination, and survival; of history and progress; power and gender; of the inescapable truth that some must die for others to live. As they dined they affirmed the truism that life depends on death.[30]

These remarkable sideboards were products of the time of Delacroix, Barye, and Landseer, of Engels and Marx, and, of course, of Charles Darwin. I have held until last the name many would have listed first in order to propose that the conventional ordering may not be quite accurate and to suggest, as do these sideboards, the interrelatedness of cultural behaviors and ideas. It is important to recognize that these objects antedate Darwin's major publications. Although their messages are sometimes ambivalent, they demonstrate without ambivalence the period's heightened attention to natural order. The sideboards are not Darwinian texts in another medium. They are evidence that the society in which Darwin and others worked was alive with questions and assertions about hierarchy, dominance, progress, and the relationship of humankind to the rest of the world, present and past.

Sideboards, particularly those shown at international exhibitions, presented the most assertive and startling examples of the mid-century iconography of dining. But they were by no means the only examples of that manner. Similar designs were widely used in association with food and dining. The iconography could on occasion be spread around an entire dining room. One of the best surviving examples of this decor is in the Henry Lippitt House in Providence, Rhode Island. There, between 1863 and 1865, a highly fashionable dining room was installed. Furnishings included a sideboard, side table, dining chairs, dining table, lounge, and mantle, all *en suite* and all ornamented with appropriate imagery. The walls were hung with a variety of still-life paintings that underlined and reiterated the basic themes of bounty and domination. Other houses around the country retain woodwork, ceiling paintings, etched glass, or other architectural elements embellished with this once widespread imagery.[31]

French design books of the nineteenth century included suggestions for dining room chimney-piece paintings of stag hunts and window shades adorned with images

2.25 *Spreading the iconography around the room. This image, from a French collection of designs for window treatments, shows a window shade with decoration appropriate for a dining room. The balustrade with pot of flowers and the benign landscape in the background are generic, but the assortment of fruit and the jug of wine in the foreground give the image dining room specificity. The window cornice, garnished with a cluster of fruit, is "in keeping," as they would have said in the period.*

Design for a dining room window
From Le Garde Meuble Collection de Tentures
Paris: D. Guilmard, c. 1855–1860
Bibliothèque Forney, Paris

Collection de Tentures

Croisée de salle à manger

of fruits and vegetables (2.25). Wallpapers suitable for dining rooms were also manufactured. The most lavish of these were French. One notable example depicted a stag hunt. Another pattern, known as "Décor Chasse et Pêche," displayed a complicated pseudo-architectural setting with illusionistic wall brackets supporting stag hunts, a fox killing a fowl, wild boar hunts, fishing allegories, and other relevant imagery, all treated in a vigorous neo-Renaissance style (2.26 and 2.27).

By far the most prevalent instances of this imagery, however, were still-life paintings and prints. Prints were more numerous, for they were mass produced and inexpensive, while paintings were handmade and more costly. We are so familiar with paintings hanging in art museums that it is easy to forget that most were originally purchased for other settings. Still lifes, according to the conventions of the period, were usually considered dining room pictures. Prints of still-life themes were

2.26 *One of the most extraordinary dining room wallpapers, produced, appropriately enough, by a major French manufacturer. Like the famous Fourdinois sideboard, the iconography extends throughout most elements of the design. In the horizontal panels at the top, putti dangle dead birds before hunting dogs. These panels alternate with images of predatory birds with dead rabbits. Each of the illusionistic piers is adorned with trophies of dead game and supports allegories of hunting or fishing, posed before ceremonial niches like the dead stag on the Houston sideboard.*
Wallpaper in "Décor Chasse et Pêche" pattern
Designed by Wagner
First manufactured by Lapeyre, Paris, 1846 or 1847
Musée des Arts Décoratifs, Paris

sometimes advertised as fruit pieces, but just as often as dining room pictures. Depictions of dining rooms, inventories, and surviving environments all demonstrate convincingly that these images were polychromatic extensions of the imagery carved on sideboards.[32] Parallels with sideboard imagery suggest nonverbal ways in which linkages were made between paintings and sideboards. One notable feature was an emphasis on volume and density. Just as the most expensive sideboards seemed nearly to overwhelm with the sheer volume of carving, some still-life paintings were packed with foods and related utensils. Paul LaCroix's *Nature's Bounty* is emphatically bountiful (2.28). Large clusters of grapes, lush green leaves, a mixture of other fruits and nuts, and a champagne bottle and glass are pulled together in a luxurious image of abundance. A similar quality is apparent in the work of other mid-century painters in this country, most notably Severin Roesen.[33]

2.27 *Violence on the wall. Central panel from the "Décor Chasse et Pêche" wallpaper showing the abstraction or trivialization of death through the use of* putti—*secular cherubs—who blow bugle horns, lead hunting dogs, and spear stags. When combined with the emphatically Mannerist design vocabulary of the illusionistic wall bracket, death becomes a decoration, a motif.*

Panel of putti *killing a stag*
Illusionistic central panel from "Décor Chasse et Pêche" wallpaper
Designed by Wagner
First manufactured by Lapeyre, Paris, 1846 or 1847. This example produced by Desfosse et Karth, Paris, after 1865.
Cooper-Hewitt National Museum of Design, Purchase, Friends of the Museum Fund, 1955-12-10A, Smithsonian Institution/Art Resource, New York

2.28 *Homage to the grape, the juice of the grape, and assorted fruits and berries. The architectural supports for this scene of profusion are all but invisible beneath the lush cascades of grapes and other evocations of nature's bounty. In this image, nature predominates but is joined by and perhaps elevated by the artificial. The high degree of visibility given to the bottle and the glass suggests that champagne was understood to represent the most lofty attainment of the grape.*
Nature's Bounty
Paul LaCroix, c. 1860
Oil on canvas
From the collection of the New Britain
Museum of American Art, New Britain,
Connecticut
Alix W. Stanley Foundation Fund
Photograph by E. Irving Blomstrann

Sometimes the subject matter of still-life paintings was nearly identical to the carved imagery on sideboards. Emanuel Leutze's 1860 painting of dead game (2.29) seems little more than a colored, two-dimensional version of the central panel of the Fourdinois sideboard (see 2.2 and 2.3). Sometimes even the format of painted images recalled the structure of a sideboard. Many of Roesen's fruit pictures were enclosed within oval frames, making them visual cognates to the carved doors on sideboards (2.30). A. F. Tait's 1853 painting of dead gamebirds hanging by their feet (2.31) could have been suggested or at least reinforced by seeing carved versions of the same theme on the doors of sideboards at the New York Crystal Palace.

Outside the home, this same imagery was part of the foodways of the dominant culture. It appeared on the covers and frontispieces of cookbooks (2.32). A mid-

2.29 *A painted version of the center-piece of the Fourdinois sideboard. This composition of dead game was produced by Emanuel Leutze, better known for* Washington Crossing the Delaware, Westward the Course of Empire Takes Its Way, The Storming of Teocalli, Mexico, *and other grand and ambitious history pictures. Seen from the perspective of the middle of the nineteenth century, this scene of dead animals also dealt with a grand and sweeping theme, a theme that reached back deep into the mists of human history, a theme as mysterious and profound as life itself.*

Game
Painted by Emanuel Leutze to the order of Robert L. Stuart (sugar refiner, philanthropist, and committed Presbyterian) in 1860
Oil on canvas
Courtesy of The New-York Historical Society New York City

2.30 *Why were people of the nineteenth century so infatuated with the oval frame? Oval-framed panels on sideboard doors. Oval-framed panels on book covers. Oval-framed paintings, prints, daguerreotypes. An oval frame for this fruit piece by Severin Roesen. Was it the degree of difficulty that drew admiration, or was there some metaphysical meaning to the shape itself? Whatever the underlying motivation, oval frames unified much of the pictorial world of Victorian Americans.*

Fruit
Severin Roesen, 1850–1860
Oil on canvas or board
Present location unknown
Photograph, The Winterthur Museum

2.31 *Painted in the year of the New York Crystal Palace exhibition and its extensive display of costly sideboards in the French style, this small oval oil offers a technicolor rendition of the theme of dead birds hanging head downward. Very similar compositions, usually monochromatic and more impressionistically rendered, were stock ornaments on most of those sideboards.*

Paintings such as this were typically hung in the dining rooms of the wealthy, where they augmented and extended the iconography of the sideboards.

Dead Game Birds
Arthur Fitzwilliam Tait, 1853
Oil on canvas or board
Present location unknown
Courtesy Kennedy Galleries, New York

2.32 *The imagery of sideboards became the imagery of foodways and cookbooks. This ornamental title page offered a Germanic version of mid-century iconography. While the fantasticized architectural setting, the bizarre shield, and the frenzied banner were self-consciously derived from German design of the sixteenth century, the arrangement of dead game, fish, and vegetables were familiar parts of a design idiom generated in France and disseminated throughout Europe and the Europeanized world.*

Ornamental title page
J. Rottenhöfer, Neue vollständige theoretisch-praktische Anweisung in der feineren Kochkunst
Munich: Braun und Schneider, c. 1880
The Winterthur Library

2.33 *Embossed cover of a nineteenth-century edition of one of the world's most famous books on food. Here the raw and the cooked were laid out together in a lavish display before a figure of omnivorous humankind, the whole design conceived as a rustic-Mannerist wall bracket or ornament.*

Cover design
Jean Anthelme Brillat-Savarin, Physiologie du goût
Paris: Furne et Cie., 1864

2.34 *The all-consuming human mouth and a sampling of the range of foods it devours. This whimsical visual anthology combines truth and fiction and people and foodways from far and near in a mock-serious homage to nourishment. The image is not totally random. Within the period's preferred oval configuration, there is not only sym-*

metry but hierarchy. Cannibals occupy the bottom of the image and the bottom of the human order. A modern chef, presumably French, occupies the top.

Les Alimens
From Jean Anthelme
Brillat-Savarin, Physiologie du goût
Paris: Furne et Cie., 1864

century edition of Jean Anthelme Brillat-Savarin's *Physiologie du Goût* contained witty and humorous adaptations of the imagery, cleverly combining and juxtaposing the raw and the cooked (2.33). In the manner of the age, the book included a number of more or less allegorical plates. Some of these illuminated issues that were treated more obliquely on sideboards. In one image, entitled *Les Alimens*, a large and satisfied mouth presided over a complex composition of tiny figures engaged in delivering or producing a wide range of foods. Ironic references to struggle and survival appeared at the bottom of the page, where human legs could be seen disappearing into the mouth of a crocodile while a family of dark-skinned people chewed on the arms and legs of a European (2.34).

Dining imagery became a shorthand way of identifying restaurants. The notice of O. S. Hulbert's Dining Hall in Rochester, New York, is fairly typical (2.35). When restaurants were put on wheels and made part of rail service, the imagery went along. The trade card for the Chicago & Northwestern Railway probably dates from the 1880s but shows that even a generation after the imagery had flourished in East Coast domestic settings, it was still useful and meaningful in other contexts (2.36).

Victorian sideboards became obsolete long ago, but another, perhaps more subtle artifact of the mid-century's heightened attention to dining and dining rooms endures. This is the American holiday of Thanksgiving (2.37).[34] Like many other artifacts, holidays are complex cultural creations. They are by intention coercive, manipulative. Their purpose is to interrupt the regular flow of life to focus a society's attention on a specific set of values or at least a shared set of behaviors. They serve to enforce conformity and promote unity, solidarity, and a shared view of purpose and origins. For example, Thanksgiving has sometimes been interpreted as a symbolic expression of the North's victory over the South in the Civil War. Thanksgiving gave primacy to New England ancestors rather than Virginian ancestors. In cosmological terms, it affirmed that America's beginnings and its appropriate models were to be found in Puritan New England.

Thanksgiving was a relic of yet another struggle, the struggle between emerging secular views of creation and the cosmos and traditional views grounded in bib-

2.35 *Dining room iconography becomes synonymous with the iconography of restaurants. Here a medley of game, fruits, oysters, wine, and other familiar forms provides a nonverbal clue to Hulbert's line of business, much as shop signs did before the age of literacy. Expensive restaurants and the dining rooms of hotels and steamboats offered levels of opulence and amounts of extravagant food that could rarely be equaled in private homes.*

Advertisement for O. S. Hulbert's Dining Hall, Rochester, New York
From The New York Central Gazetteer for 1873 and 1874
Rochester: M. L. Flynn & Co., 1873
The Winterthur Library

2.36 *The iconography of dining on wheels. The first railroad dining cars were conceived as mobile restaurants. Thus it is not surprising that advertising stressing the quality of railroad dining would use much the same imagery as conventional restaurants. In this trade card, a roundel in the upper left provides a glimpse of the elegantly appointed, clerestory-lit dining car, with its white linen, elaborately set tables, and other trappings of gentility. The rest of the image is dominated by more loosely associational imagery suggesting the abundance, variety, and freshness of the food and attentiveness to its preparation and service.*

Trade card for the Chicago & Northwestern Railway
Lithographed by Heffron & Phelps, New York and Chicago, c. 1885

2.37 *The imagery revised and transformed for the American holiday of Thanksgiving. This postcard provides an apparently conscious dialogue with and critique of mid-century dining imagery. Instead of the familar convention of dead birds, feathers intact, tied with ribbon or cord and hanging head downward, the designer of this image presents a solitary turkey, plucked and naked, dangling before a nearly empty panel. The panel's shape and the position of the turkey recall compositions on the doors of sideboards in the 1850s. Here, however, the ribbon is colored red, white, and blue and is draped about like bunting, stressing the heightened patriotic content of Thanksgiving.*

"Thanksgiving Greetings" postcard Published by A & S, postmarked Arlington, New Jersey, November 25, 1908

lical texts. Here the victory belonged unequivocally to the forces of tradition, for Thanksgiving institutionalized giving thanks to God in a society that was increasingly skeptical about owing God anything, if indeed there even were a God.

Thanksgiving was an effective and little-recognized manifestation of the Victorian domestic religion so capably described by Colleen McDannell. The key feature of this domestic religion was the fusion of traditional religious symbols with domestic values. The religious dimension was apparent in the expression of gratitude to the deity. On Thanksgiving Day, the "people of plenty" gave thanks for nature's (God's) bounty. The domestic values were manifested in the gathering of generations of family members within the home. Thanksgiving was an ideal product of this domestic religion in the way it built upon widely shared understanding of the bonding powers of a shared meal and institutionalized linkages of history, home, and church. As McDannell put it, domestic religion "bound together what was truly meaningful in Victorian society." [35]

In recognizing the link between Thanksgiving and domestic religion, we also recognize Victorian gender politics at work. Thanksgiving provided a formal, institutionalized context for the assertion of stereotypical feminine values and experiences. The emphases on nurture, on communion and community, on family, on togetherness, connectedness, were congruent with genteel female values. In nineteenth-century America, as now, women were responsible for making Thanksgiving happen. Males played cameo roles as carvers of the ceremonial turkey, but women prepared the meal, women served the meal, women cleaned up after the meal. And women pressed to make Thanksgiving a national holiday. Although it was Abraham Lincoln who issued the first national Thanksgiving Proclamation in 1863 and William Seward who wrote the text, most students of the holiday credit Sarah Josepha Hale, novelist and editor of *Godey's*, with leading the campaign to nationalize the holiday. For over thirty years, she agitated for this moral cause. And it was Lydia Maria Child who wrote "Over the river and through the woods, to grandfather's house we go."[36] Thanksgiving became a feminized event, a celebration of connectedness and intimacy within a setting of abundance and nurture.[37]

As a holiday, Thanksgiving gave a religious benediction to, and transformed, the mid-century glorification of dining. Seen from this perspective, the similarities and differences between sideboards and the holiday are illuminating. Both were products of a value system that pervaded the West in the nineteenth century. While grounded in the biblical conception expressed in Genesis, sideboards were props for a worldly lifestyle that celebrated sensory life and elevated it to a high level. Sideboards were products of elite culture and were grounded in courtly, largely secular values. They were parts of settings for formal dining among social peers. And they were emphatically masculine as the age understood that construction, celebrating abundance through violence and domination. Thanksgiving, in contrast, was explicitly religious, albeit Protestant, and was built on middle-class values. It provided an occasion for ceremonial but not necessarily formal dining in which multigenerational bonding became paramount. Mid-century sideboards and Thanksgiving were alternatives and phases of a larger cultural expression. Thanksgiving was an American, middle-class accommodation and assimilation of a courtly, elite-culture concept. As such, it provides a fascinating instance of the mutability of culture.

The elements of nationalism in Thanksgiving identify an emerging conflict between cosmopolitanism and localism, between a world vision and a national vision. Born as a national holiday during the Civil War, Thanksgiving can be seen as an early artifact of the Colonial Revival, transforming and naturalizing cultural expressions generated elsewhere that, for a time, had been part of cosmopolitan culture (2.38).[38]

Material culture reveals the link between the iconography of dining and Thanksgiving. An illustration of Thanksgiving Day dinner in *Harper's Weekly* of 1858 shows that domestic ritual taking place in a dining room adorned with characteristic mid-

2.39 *The imagery and the holiday collide. In this 1858 illustration of a Thanksgiving dinner, a dining room furnished in the cosmopolitan mid-century style serves as the setting for the nationalized celebration. The emblems of the holiday—turkey, celery, wine—grace the table, while the iconography of dining—pictures of dead game and a stag—adorns the walls.*

Thanksgiving Day—The Dinner
Engraving after Winslow Homer
Harper's Weekly, *November 27, 1858*
The Winterthur Library

century dining room pictures (2.39). A more revealing image is the dining room of Louis C. Tiffany as it looked in the 1880s (2.40). The radical winds of the Aesthetic Movement have swept through the space, leaving it spare, planar, and very tasteful. Nothing that was defined as fashionable in the 1850s can be seen. Instead, above the mantel hangs a rather startling Americanized version of the dining room picture. No stag hunts, hanging rabbits, or dead fish here. In their place, a large tom turkey and ripe pumpkin loom up between sere stalks of corn. Here in Tiffany's dining room are all the pictorial conventions of modern Thanksgiving. Today, when Americans celebrate Thanksgiving, they rarely recognize it as an invented tradition.[39] They assume, as they were meant to, that they are part of a practice that reaches back without interruption or alteration to the days of the Pilgrims. Few realize that they are acting out a scenario that reveals far more about Victorian America than it does about the people of Plymouth in the seventeenth century (2.41).[40]

2.40 *The aesthetic of the self-consciously artful in the 1880s, bringing with it a new blend of cosmopolitanism and pretentious unpretentiousness. Unassuming furniture, either old or in old styles; old woodwork updated; and a strong Asian feel to the walls and ceramics are all part of a taste generated in England and disseminated through what today might be identified* *as the art culture avant-garde. What is not English or Asian about this installation is the prominent iconography of American Thanksgiving over the mantel. As it turns out, this decoration never became popular in painted form, but pumpkins, corn stalks, and turkey have been ritually reinvoked ever since as essential elements of the holiday celebration.*

Dining room of Louis Comfort Tiffany
From Artistic Houses; Being a Series of Interior Views of a Number of the Most Beautiful and Celebrated Homes in the United States
New York: D. Appleton, 1883–1984

2.41 *The triumph of American Thanksgiving. This postcard employs allusions to triumphal chariots and parade floats, metaphorically harnessing traditional conceptions of abundance and bounty to American energy, under American direction. Here, the*

cosmopolitan, the international, the supranational become nationalized as part of the evolving iconography of America as land of abundance, land of plenty, and home of the people of plenty. "Thanksgiving Greetings" *postcard German or American, c. 1910*

The iconography of dining explored in this chapter was dominant until the late 1860s, when it was challenged by an alternative vision. This new vision was part of a major shift in cultural hegemony in the West. It came not from France but from Britain. Its historical references were not Renaissance or Baroque but Gothic or more generally medieval. Sideboards in this new style were still massive, still richly adorned, but their affective and cognitive impacts were dramatically different.[41] A sideboard made in Grand Rapids in the late 1870s well represents the new genre (2.42). No carving, only incised decoration. Nothing mimetic, everything stylized. Nothing aggressive, nothing distasteful. In 1878, the year this sideboard was probably made, Harriett Spofford wrote: "The perpetual reminder of dead flesh and murderous propensities is not agreeable at table."[42] A year earlier, Rhoda and Agnes Garrett attacked pretentious and vulgar productions . . . which are usually covered with a profusion of ornament in hideous caricatures of every animal and vegetable form. Monsters besmeared with stain and varnish grin at you from every point, and you cannot even open a drawer or a cupboard without having your feelings outraged by coming into contact with the legs or wings of a dead bird or some other ghastly trophy of man's love of slaughter.[43]

Modern spectators may applaud, relieved that not everyone in the nineteenth century was deluded; at least a few had the wit to recognize how offensive these sideboards really were. To take this view is to miss the point entirely, I think. In 1851, these sideboards were accepted enthusiastically. In 1877, they were rejected in disgust. The goods had not changed, the culture had.

How to evaluate this change? Like so many other cultural changes, it seems equivocal. The critics quoted above were women. We can suspect that even more of the home had become feminized by the late 1870s than had been in the 1850s. The dining room had become female territory, a place where violence was rare and relationships appeared safe. Explicit references to constructed masculinity had disappeared, replaced by an environment reflecting the values of constructed femininity. How we feel about that depends on our politics. To my mind, celebrations of the decline of the mid-century idiom are a bit misguided. The act of introducing an alternative mode was not a gesture of cultural boldness but yet another example of genteel avoidance. These objects were indeed distasteful in dining rooms of the 1870s, not because they were, in any objective way, ugly or vulgar but because their imagery was too truthful, too provocative, and ultimately too disruptive. The issues these objects raised, the questions they asked, if pushed far enough, threatened to force the rethinking of major tenets of Western culture. Easier to avoid than rethink.[44]

A shift in the paradigm for the home supported this retreat from confronting major questions. By the 1870s, a more bourgeois vision of the home had become wide-

2.42 *At the least, the furniture of avoidance. For reformers in the 1870s, dining and dining room furniture were important. What the reformers rejected was the prevailing style, imagery, and iconography of that furniture. Sideboards continued to be prominent, but they were stripped of mimetic decoration. References to the natural world were eliminated. Function became ornament. Indeed, this furniture goes beyond avoidance. This is the furniture of Prohibition. This is the furniture of the Comstock Act. This is the furniture of repression.*

Walnut sideboard in the English Reform style
Sales catalog of Nelson, Matter & Co.
Grand Rapids, Michigan, c. 1878
Grand Rapids Public Library

spread. The utopian retreat Kirk Jeffrey identified years ago was not an appropriate place to be forced to confront major questions about the relationship of humankind to the natural world. If anything, it was a place where one could escape from the cares and difficulties, problems and conflicts of the outer world. When these sideboards became popular, the courtly model of domestic life was still prominent. In this model, public and private aspects of life were freely intermingled. In the succeeding model, these two were more effectively segregated. The mid-century iconography of dining had become offensive precisely because it violated the emerging belief that homeyness meant and required seclusion from troubling aspects of the outside world.[45]

The Aesthetic Movement has often been hailed for rescuing the Victorian world from pretentiousness and vulgarity. Surely it changed the appearance of that world, but who is to say that anyone is better for it. In general, I am suspicious of aesthetic and moral crusades. They generally do more harm than good, avoiding, denying, or suppressing difficult social and cultural issues instead of bringing an open mind to problems and encouraging workable solutions. There are parallels between what amounts to the suppression of these sideboards and the Prohibition movement of the nineteenth century.[46] Both were attempts to control behavior and culture. An even closer parallel may be the Comstock Act of 1870, which regulated and effectively suppressed public discussion of sexual matters in America for more than a generation. Sexual problems were not resolved, merely avoided. Advances in personal and public health, birth control, understanding the nature of sexuality, and many other matters were severely inhibited by the Comstock Act. Because sexual information was suppressed, ignorance was promoted.[47]

In like manner, the cultural if not legal suppression of these sideboards had a deleterious effect. These objects raised serious questions about the relationship of humankind to the natural world and about hierarchy and domination. These questions were connected to others about exploitation of land and human labor. Pushed far enough, these objects might also have led to inquiries into unequal distribution of resources and the very structure of society. With the new style, these questions evaporated. These same questions may have been asked in the outer world, but they could be safely avoided at home.

In fact, few if any of the issues raised by mid-century sideboards were resolved in the nineteenth century or have been resolved in our own time. Cultural segregation makes it easy to spend more of life avoiding thinking about them or working toward solutions. Many twentieth-century people who react so negatively to these sideboards probably eat meat and believe in the American version of capitalism, yet see no irony in these stances.

What, then, do we finally make of these objects, these dramatic and affecting presences of Victorian dining rooms? They are products of an undeniably romantic and self-conscious age, but today, in our own time of segregation and avoidance, it is their realism that stands out. The people who designed these sideboards acknowledged the earthly origins of the foods they ate and the relationship of humankind to the rest of the animal kingdom. They knew that life depended on death. In short, they understood, or tried to understand, where they fit into the big picture. And they were moved by the immensity and sublimity of what they saw. Considering the state of our own world, it is difficult to fault them for that.

3 : Words to Live By

Home Sweet Home. Jesus Loves Me. Forget Me Not. Consider the Lilies. God Bless Our Home. Abide with Me. No Cross No Crown. Old Oaken Bucket. Rock of Ages (3.1). A motley array of sentiments, titles, aphorisms, invocations, maxims, and references. What do they have in common? For one thing, they are all short, terse, curt. They are easily memorized, easily recalled. For another, these compact texts and more than a hundred others like them (3.2) were prominent in American domestic interiors in the last third of the nineteenth century (3.3). Some were commercially printed. More were embroidered by hand in colorful yarns on perforated cardboard. All were usually hung high on a wall (3.4), sometimes over a door. There they kept in constant view words to live by.[1]

The needlework mottoes commonplace in the 1870s and 1880s were products of a dynamic, nationwide culture. Although they were parts of the lives of ordinary people, mottoes also testify eloquently to cultural forces in Victorian America that transcended individual lives. Through these small, frail, and perishable objects, powerful currents once surged. In these small, frail, and perishable objects, powerful truths endure.

Embroidered mottoes are relatively simple as artifacts go: a text or script worked in thread on a supporting ground of perforated cardboard (3.5). Words on a thing. A message in one material wrought upon another. Messages and mediums. But as Marshall McLuhan pointed out years ago, mediums are also messages.[2] The most obvious message of a motto is its verbal text, but the materials from which and on which the words are wrought contribute meaning as well. In mottoes, text and materials interact, each affecting the meaning of the other. In attempting to understand the meanings people in Victorian America made of commonplace embroidered mottoes, I want first to discuss one of the materials, then the texts. Finally, I try to show how these seemingly insignificant artifacts provide a window not only on the complexities and contradictions of Victorian culture but, more broadly, on all of American culture.

3.1 *The basic object. This is a "standard" size embroidered motto in its original marbleized frame. As is conventional in these objects, the words are few but powerfully evocative. "Rock of Ages" is the title of a popular hymn written in England about 1775 by Augustus Montague Toplady.*

Embroidered motto
Thread on black perforated cardboard
Eastern United States, 1870–1890
Photograph by John Yost
[Objects with no source listed are from private collections.]

Like so many other inventions of the nineteenth century, the introduction of perforated cardboard was brilliantly imaginative on one level and obvious on another, startlingly novel yet deeply grounded in tradition. Perforated cardboard replaced and in some ways improved on the various natural woven fabrics that had long served as foundations for needlework. This was new. For much of their history, however, textiles and paper had been closely linked. Paper and paperboard had been traditionally made from cloth rags. And sometimes paper products had been used as substitutes for textiles. During the nineteenth century, wood pulp replaced rags as the major ingredient of paper products. The manufacture of paper and paperboard became increasingly independent industries propelled by their own developing lineages of invention and experimentation. Perforated cardboard was one of the new products of the nineteenth-century paper industry, but it drew on a long-standing and venerable association.[3]

I have not been able to determine exactly when perforated cardboard was first introduced. Both artifactual and written sources indicate that it was available by

3.2 *Mottoes were part of the explosion of wall ornament in the second half of the nineteenth century. Bowen & Lee, a typical wholesaler, provided both chromolithographed and perforated cardboard mottoes. This page, from one of the firm's trade catalogs, gives an idea of the range of texts available.*

Page advertising chromo mottoes and other goods
Trade catalog of Bowen & Lee
Chicago, 1881
The Winterthur Library

BOWEN & LEE, CHICAGO. 73

8 1-2 x 21 Chromo Mottoes.

List of Chromo Mottoes.

On Assorted Colored Grounds, with Gilt and Colored Letters.

PRICE. Per doz
8½ x 21 .... $0 85

Home, Sweet Home. With border.	After Clouds, Sunshine.	Forget Me Not.
Home Sweet Home. Without border. Two styles.	Christ is Risen.	Grace, Peace and Mercy.
God Bless Our Home. Without border. Two styles.	Peace Be unto this House.	There is no Place Like Home.
God Bless Our Home. With border.	What is Home Without a Mother.	Friendship, Love and Truth.
Rock of Ages Cleft for Me. Two styles.	Pray Without Ceasing.	Malice Toward None, Charity for All.
Remember Thy Creator.	God is Our Hope.	Praise God, from Whom all Blessings Flow.
In God We Trust.	Live Peaceably with all Men.	Praise the Lord.
Remember Me.	Children, Obey Your Parents.	Labor Has Sure Reward.
Welcome Home.	Love Thy Neighbor as Thyself.	Sweet Rest in Heaven.
The Lord Will Provide.	Saviour, Like a Shepherd Lead Us.	The Lord is my Shepherd.
Consider the Lillies.	With Joy We Greet You.	Our Saviour, Our Hope.
God is Love.	Humbly at Thy Cross I Bow.	Happy New Year.
Thou Art My Hope.	Love One Another.	Merry Christmas.
Faith, Hope and Charity.	God Bless Our Sunday-School.	Pope Leo XIII.
	The Fear of the Lord is the Beginning of Wisdom.	And many others.

If you are in need of Motto Frames, be sure and examine the various styles we illustrate on other pages of this Book.

Floral Mottoes.

On Chocolate Background, very handsome. Size, 8½ x 21.

God Bless Our Home.	Love One Another.
No Place Like Home.	In God We Trust.
Home, Sweet Home.	Remember Me.

PRICE.
Per Dozen $1 75

Perforated Card Board and Mottoes.

PRICE. Per Doz
8½ x 21 .... $0 25
17 x 21 60

Perforated Card Board.

PRICE. Per Doz.
17 x 21—Plain $0 35
17 x 21—Silvered 60
17 x 21—Silvered Embossed 65
17 x 21—Checkered, Fancy 1 10

Tin Foil.

8½ x 21, for Backs of Mottoes.
PRICE.
Per dozen $0 30

Photographs of Celebrities, Etc.

PRICE. Per hundred.
Cabinet size .... $ 5 00
Promenade size 10 00

Comic Photographs.

PRICE. Per hundred
Cabinet size $5 00

8 x 10 Photographs on Tinted Mounts.

These are Photographs of Fine Paintings
PRICE.
Per dozen $1 00

Chromos on 9 x 11.

Tinted and Lined Mounts.
PRICE.
Per hundred $1 35

Chromos in 8 x 10.

Fancy Mats.
PRICE.
Per hundred $1 35

3.3 *The motto in a typical environment. High on the wall, above the tall chest of drawers with mirror, a chromolithographed motto, God Bless Our Home, constitutes the only prominent verbal element within an otherwise nonverbal domestic composition.*

Photograph of a bedroom of an unknown house
Probably New York City, c. 1890
New York State Museum, Albany
Photograph by Craig Williams

the 1840s and that it was initially used for small items. The most common seem to have been bookmarks. The needlework portion of these was roughly the same size or a little larger than contemporary calling cards and awards for merit. Intrinsic and extrinsic data place many of these in the period from the 1840s to the 1860s. Sewing boxes, envelopes, decorative and commemorative pictures of many kinds (3.6), and samplers were worked on this material as well, often in wool but also in silk, hair, and other threads. Most of these objects were also comparatively small. Before 1860, needlework projects on perforated cardboard rarely measured more than 12 inches in their longer dimension.[4]

Perforated cardboard was regularly, if briefly, mentioned in needlework texts of the 1840s and 1850s. Because these texts were often pirated, the same commentary appeared in volumes published over a period of several years. The most frequently repeated passage noted that needles too large would break the holes, that small designs should be worked in silk and large in either wool or silk, and that the work was "beautiful and highly ornamental."[5] An 1859 volume indicated that perforated cardboard could be bought in whole or partial sheets and could be used for many ornamental articles. It was described as easy to work, nearly equal to fine canvas work in its effect, and appropriate for children. The authors of a volume published in 1875 wrote that they had not known about perforated cardboard until a few years earlier, except for "the plain white variety, of which our mothers formed bookmarks, with a text, motto, or some device wrought upon it, with colored silk or silver, gold, or even steel beads."[6]

The first phase in the development of perforated cardboard can be described as tentative and experimental. A second phase, emerging by the 1870s, was characterized by simultaneous standardization and diversification of the product line. The standardization can be seen in the emergence of the familiar motto as a discrete form. The motto assumed a standard size of 8½ by 21 inches, with a larger size, called a full sheet and measuring 17 by 21 inches, also available. About 80 percent of the surviving mottoes are the standard size or the standard size slightly cut down

3.4 *There is probably a correlation between the motto's high elevation on the wall and a belief that its message was equally elevated. The motto's lofty placement implied that it was above the more earthly surrounding artifacts. Grace flowed downward from the motto to the people and objects below it in the room. The location of the motto over the mirror was also significant. Someone looking into the mirror simultaneously saw herself and the words God Bless Our Home and thereby comprehended herself as part of a religious universe. The photographs of relatives or friends and the small reproduction of a Raphael Madonna flanking the mirror indicated the importance of relationships and maternal love. The print over the mantel, depicting the story of Dante and Beatrice, alluded to romantic love. Thus the motto presided over and blessed a network of relationships and affections.*
Detail of photograph shown in Figure 3.3

3.5 *Simple in concept but visually intricate. This intricacy was achieved in part through eccentric calligraphy, in part through elaborated outlines and flourishes, and in part through the use of variegated thread. The changing intensity in the lettering visible here is due to systematic color variation of the thread, which is shaded from light pink through red to red-black and then back. The text, Thy Will Be Done, is from the Lord's Prayer.*

Embroidered motto
Thread on perforated cardboard
Eastern United States, 1870–1890
Collection of Gail J. Ames

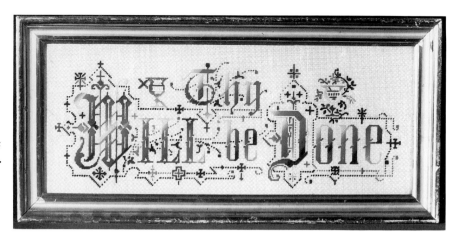

3.6 *Perforated cardboard was initially used for small items, such as this memorial picture, which is only about 7 inches high. The design was not printed on the cardboard. The needleworker created her own composition, attaching cloth flowers in the corners and a curl of the infant's hair in the middle.*

Embroidered memorial picture
Thread, cloth, and hair on perforated cardboard
Eastern Pennsylvania, c. 1865
Collection of Gail J. Ames

or trimmed. Another 10 percent are the full-sheet size.[7] Standardization occurred not only in the perforated cardboard itself but also in frames. Trade catalogs for the frame industry for the 1870s and 1880s routinely listed motto frames, explicitly identified as such and consistently described as measuring 8½ by 21 inches. Most mottoes that survive today are still housed in their original frames, which were, like the mottoes themselves, inexpensive yet flashy.[8]

The diversification characteristic of this second phase led to the production of cardboard stock in a variety of colors and even textures. Most mottoes were worked on white or off-white stock, which was the cheapest, or on black (3.7), which cost a little more and was less common. Trade catalogs indicate that several other options were available, often at two or three times the cost of plain stock. These included half a dozen different tints and textures, the fanciest of which were silver, silver embossed, gold, and even checkered cardboard.[9] Occasionally the cardboard was enriched with techniques like spatterwork or stenciled decoration (3.8). Perhaps because of their higher cost, these more elaborate cardboards were not widely purchased and are rare today. Their availability in the period, however, reveals how the industry attempted to diversify its product line and expand its market.

There were also efforts in the nineteenth century to promote perforated cardboard as a multipurpose craft supply. The solids between the perforations could be cut away to produce designs of considerable delicacy and intricacy. These designs could be glued on top of one another to create shallow relief sculptures. Books and magazines published patterns and directions for a wide variety of items, including handkerchief boxes, wall baskets, lamp shades, portfolios, and a few things that seem particularly odd or "cute" today: an elaborate vase or urn for cigars, a tape-measure holder in the shape of a coffee mill, and a container for various unidentified small objects in the form of a miniature Swiss cottage.[10]

Despite these imaginative suggestions, some of which were followed, to most people in the 1870s and 1880s perforated cardboard meant mottoes. And perforated cardboard mottoes sold very well. Low cost, ease of use, and the fact that the ma-

3.7 *Black cardboard was less common than white or off-white, but it produced a more dramatic effect. Many lithographed mottoes were also printed on black backgrounds. In this vertically oriented motto, the words The Lord Is Risen flank a cross decorated with several varieties of flowers, standard Easter iconography of the period. This motto still retains its original frame and pine backing. The latter bears the penciled inscription, possibly written by the framer: "Mrs. L. H. Bromley, Pawlet, Vt."*

Embroidered motto
Thread on black perforated cardboard
Possibly Vermont, 1875–1885
Photograph by John Yost

3.8 *With little or even no embroidery, this motto could be decorative, if a little drab. Much of the surface is printed in light gray, in imitation of stencilwork. The needleworker apparently decided to embroider only the words, although she could have also embellished the flowers, leaves, ferns, and Bible if she chose to. This motto is enclosed in an artificial walnut frame enriched with ebonized moldings and a prominent gold liner.*

Embroidered motto
Thread on perforated cardboard printed to resemble stencilwork
Eastern United States, 1875–1885
Collection of Gail J. Ames

terial was novel had much to do with their appeal. Domestic interiors of that period were furnished with a disproportionately high number of patented or otherwise novel products, disproportionate at least when compared to other periods. People then seemed to share a sense that anything could be improved upon by technology. Faith in the doctrine that the mechanical mind could overcome the limitations of traditional materials reached deep into most industries. It is difficult to find a field that did not, at some point, believe that chemical, mechanical, or technological knowledge had made possible the attainment of new levels of excellence.[11] Perforated cardboard was hardly the most dramatic expression of that vision, but it was a pervasive one. With perforated cardboard, traditional woven textiles were replaced by pressed and perforated wood pulp. The functions this artifact performed remained traditional, but both the object and the processes behind it were revolutionary. People of the period knew that.

But, as I have suggested, few inventions are wholly new. The idea of perforating had been around for centuries. Artisans had long recognized that materials could be pierced or perforated for two very different and usually mutually exclusive purposes. A material was normally perforated in order to contain or secure one substance or material while allowing some other substance or material to pass through it. Pierced metal panels on food safes protected food but allowed air to pass through. Pierced metal sheets shaped into lanterns shielded flames from wind and rain but allowed light to pass through. In the form of colanders and sieves, they held solids but let liquids run off. Piercing the seat rails on chairs made it possible to pass thin strips of cane through the holes and weave natural fiber seats that supported people but allowed for flexibility and ventilation (3.9). When those holes were drilled too close together or when the pressure on the seat was too great, however, the seat rails tended to break along the line of perforations. From the point of view of a chairmaker or a chair owner, this was undesirable. But the failure in the first application pointed the way to a second function of perforations after postage stamps were introduced in the 1840s. Early stamps had to be cut apart by hand, a tedious, time-consuming process. Perforating machines, introduced in 1857 in the United States, were hailed

3.9 *Decreases before the invention of perforated cardboard, the seat rails of wooden chairs were pierced so that cane could be woven through them. This photograph shows the underside of the front seat rail of a caned-seat chair of the 1870s. A row of holes, all of the same size and placed at regular intervals, has been drilled in the rail and around all four sides of the seat. Through these holes, a "chair bottomer" wove thin strips of cane to create a light and inexpensive seat. The most common* *pattern for seat weaves, shown here, produced a regular gridwork of evenly placed, identical holes. From a distance, caned seats look something like perforated cardboard.*

Underside of the front seat rail
Child's folding chair with caned seat
Marked "Collignon's Patent/July 11, 1871" (the patent applies to folding, not perforating)
Collignon Bros., Closter, New Jersey, c. 1875

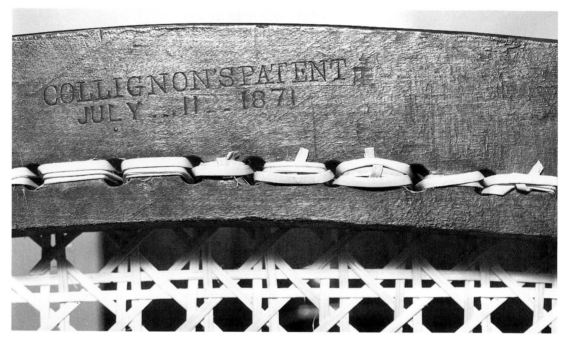

as "the invention of which almost everyone has daily cause to be thankful." One description of the perforating machine muses, "Simple as this machine is, no one hit upon it for years after the introduction of stamps."[12]

Where did the idea come from? In the process of invention, lateral transfer from one medium to another is often part of the answer. Perforated cardboard antedates the perforation of postage stamps, probably by at least two decades. The effect sought in postage stamps had often been inadvertently attained in perforated cardboard needlework by using needles that were too large, as needlework books had warned for years. What had been a fault in one context became a virtue in another.

As I noted earlier, the replacement of woven textiles with perforated cardboard seems obvious on some levels—as obvious as perforating postage stamps—but it reveals and is based on a significant reconceptualization of structure. Traditionally, natural fibers had been woven at right angles to each other to create a textile that served as a background or grid on which needlework (3.10) could be executed. In

3.10 *From a distance, a woven fabric may seem to be a single structure. Up close, we can see that it is actually constructed of hundreds or even thousands of threads running at right angles to each other, the cross or weft threads alternately passing over and under the warp threads. The result is an interwoven grid. Look closely at this late-eighteenth-century sampler and the* *grid becomes apparent. It is through the openings in this grid that the needleworker drew the colored threads to embroider the sampler.*

Embroidered sampler
Silk thread on linen
Abigail Purintun, Reading, Massachusetts, dated 1788
The Winterthur Museum

order to be worked, this textile had to be stretched tight, like a drumhead, over a supporting frame. The needleworker's threads normally passed between the woven warp and weft strands. If the fabric was tightly woven, these had to be pried apart to create an opening. Many needlework projects required painstaking counting of threads to regulate the design.

Perforated cardboard, however, was not woven but pressed. It was not a pliable, multicomponent structure, like a weave, which could be disassembled merely by pulling the strands apart, but a firm material that retained its shape without a frame. Perforated, it had the gridlike character of a woven textile. Unlike that woven textile, however, perforated cardboard revealed few if any signs of the process by which it had been manufactured. While it could be cut or torn, it could not be unraveled into its original components. With the advent of perforated cardboard, a product created through the additive or constructive process of weaving was replaced by one created through compression or fusion. Many discrete and separable components were replaced by a single, structurally integrated sheet.

There were analogs in other industries. For example, something similar happened in the innovative furniture construction developed contemporaneously in New York by John Henry Belter (3.11) and his competitors.[13] Belter and others supplanted the traditional additive process of furniture construction by introducing plywood. The conventional method of constructing the back of a wooden chair required the joining of individual pieces of wood, normally verticals and horizontals meeting at right angles, through the use of mortise-and-tenon joints, pegs, or some similar elements. In a sense, the verticals and horizontals, analogs to posts and lintels in architecture, were also analogs to warp and weft threads in weaving. Belter eliminated this form of construction, in which process was usually at least partially visible on the surface, when he used plywood, which he often pierced in intricate designs. While the true paper-product analogy is pasteboard—that is, both plywood and pasteboard are sheets glued together to produce a boardlike product—the construction of plywood is invisible on its face. Only by examining edges of sheets or cut surfaces can we see the individual layers that constitute the material. More to the point, in its handling, plywood is analogous to cardboard. Both are worked as if structurally integrated. And neither can be readily returned to its preproduction state.

An even closer analogy can be found in the perforated wooden chair seats produced after 1872 by Gardner & Co. of New York (3.12), a similarity noticed at the time.[14] W. R. Reid's catalog of frames and pictures for 1880 advertised on the same page mottoes on perforated cardboard and perforated chair seats.[15] In the case of Gardner's three-ply veneer chair seats, a glued and pressed wood product competed with and replaced cane seating, a weave of natural fibers. The similarities went even further, for Gardner's plywood was not merely pierced but perforated in ordered configurations. For the most part, the perforations were arranged to form decorative geometric patterns, but the company perforated texts as well.[16] Most of these were names of some sort, either of persons or places (3.13) or of organizations or institutions (3.14). On rare occasions, Gardner & Co.'s perforated plywood spelled out exactly the same text that was available on perforated cardboard (3.15).

The exact duplication of texts, however, is less important than the realization that in the nineteenth century ideas appeared in and crossed back and forth through many mediums. An idea may seem unusual or even unique within the context of a single line of goods, but examination of a broader range often reveals similar activity elsewhere. All the goods I have been discussing—and many others as well—were products of an industrial or technological mindset that reached across and informed many apparently unrelated trades and manufactures. These goods were the result of a distinctive and pervasive industrial culture that shaped the ways things were thought and made. They were the products of an aggressive, competitive, dynamic, rationalized, male-dominated industrial culture that valued technological innovation and change.

This novel product of male industrial culture—cardboard, mechanically perforated—became the standard ground for a standard artifact of the Gilded Age, the embroidered motto. A motto is a short sentence or phrase, usually attached to an object—a coat of arms, a sundial, a coin, a college seal—and expressing a reflection or sentiment considered appropriate. It can be a maxim, a guiding principle, a

3.11 *New technology and piercing. The upper portion of this sofa was made from laminated rosewood, a kind of up-scale plywood. By gluing thin sheets of wood together at right angles, the manufacturer was able to create a single-piece back that could be pierced in an intricate foliate design. The result was stronger than a similar design produced by traditional additive construction. The idea of piercing or perforating is also suggested by the upholstery. While the indentations of the tufting do not pass through the object, the regular pattern of concavities closely resembles the visual effect of perforations.*

Laminated rosewood sofa
Factory of John Henry Belter, New York City, 1850–1860
The Winterthur Museum, gift of The Manney Collection

3.12 *Plywood and perforations. The back and seat of this doll's chair are made from a single piece of bent plywood. Like the cardboard used for mottoes, the plywood has been perforated. Unlike the cardboard, the perforations are not laid out in a grid but are arranged to create a design and to spell out words.*

Walnut doll's chair with perforated plywood seat and back
Gardner & Co., New York City, 1875–1885
Collection of Gail J. Ames

3.13 *Like the tin sheets of pie safes, the plywood on Gardner & Co. settees was often perforated with decorative devices and texts. Here the text, Otsego County, serves largely to designate place and ownership, although it might also have been a statement of local patriotism. This settee and several others like it were purchased to furnish a county courthouse.*

Settee with perforated plywood seat and back
Gardner & Co., New York City, 1875–1885
Otsego County Courthouse
Cooperstown, New York

3.14 *The pervasiveness of perforating. The concept of perforating was widespread throughout Victorian material culture. It invaded even the domain of the unworldly. This modern view of perforated settees made for the Mount Lebanon Shakers shows that even people who held many of the world's baubles at arm's length were seduced by the appeal of the perforated word and design.*

Chapel benches
Manufactured by Gardner & Co., c. 1880
Mount Lebanon Shaker Village, New Lebanon, New York
Photograph by Paul Rocheleau

3.15 *Talking furniture. One of these Gardner & Co. perforated plywood settees admonishes one to Visit the Sick. The other calls out Friendship, Love and Truth, a text that also appeared on perforated cardboard embroidered mottoes. These settees are mottoes one can sit on, mottoes one can physically engage and bodily absorb.*

Settees bearing texts, bent plywood perforated
Trade catalog of Gardner & Co.
New York City, 1884
The Winterthur Library

rule of conduct. In a literary context, a motto can be a few words at the beginning of a text summarizing or indicating contents, theme, or conclusion. A motto is necessarily brief. It is a compression, a condensation. As a form, it reveals the workings of human cognition and memory. A few words stand for, evoke, or initiate a longer text. Little stands for much. *Multum in Parvo.* Mottoes may be reductionist and simplistic—clear, concise texts positing order and reason in a chaotic and irrational world. Or they may be associational or synecdochic—small parts standing for larger wholes. However they function, they are conventionally concise, compressed expressions of larger ideas, principles, ideologies, or values.[17]

While mottoes have an extensive history, they seem to have been a nineteenth-century compulsion. They appeared in a variety of contexts. They adorned the title pages and beginnings of chapters of countless volumes.[18] They were emblazoned across the facades of public and university buildings. Sometimes they were carved into the woodwork or furniture of halls and dining rooms. Most of the time, when they appeared in household interiors, they were of the portable, framed variety, sometimes lithographed, more frequently worked in thread on perforated cardboard (3.16).

In theory, the needleworker was free to embroider any verbal text she chose. Plain perforated cardboard was cheap and readily available in dry goods stores and frame shops. The designs or texts she might create on these blank sheets were limited only by imagination and convention. In actual practice, however, convention severely constrained imagination as it so often does. Indeed, imagination in text selection was hardly the point. Surviving examples indicate that most buyers chose cardboard sheets with texts already printed on them. Usually the contours of the letters and some decorative elements were printed in blue, black, or gray. The needleworker could then decide exactly how much of the surface to fill in and with what colors and stitches (3.17).

When it came to texts, purchasers had well over a hundred to choose from. As unrestrictive as that number might seem on the surface, a tabulation of the texts

3.16 *Centered on the wall, on axis above the dressing case, this embroidered motto, Jesus Loves Me, presided over a densely furnished bedroom in an eighteenth-century house. This image shows how placement contributed to and revealed a motto's power. In a book, placement on a title page or at the head of a chapter exploited the principle of primacy. In a room, placement high on a wall exploited the principle of hierarchy. Harriet Gould occupied this room in May 1882, when this photograph was taken. When she looked into the mirror on the dressing case, she could see her reflection beneath the reassuring text. As she saw herself she also saw Jesus Loves Me. With the self-consciousness characteristic of the age, she could simultaneously assess both her outward, physical state and her inner, spiritual condition.*

Photograph of the northeast bedroom at Cherry Hill
Albany, New York, taken May 1882
Collection of Historic Cherry Hill

reveals that they fell within a fairly limited cultural and ideological range. The texts on mottoes tended to be sentimental and culturally conservative. Humor occasionally appeared (3.18 and 3.19), but radical or alternative views were not, as far as I know, among the choices of printed texts (3.20). Few if any mottoes were drawn from the writings of liberal thinkers. No Thomas Paine. No Voltaire. No Charles Darwin. No Robert Ingersoll. Most of the mottoes seem either linked to or at least consistent with evangelical Protestantism of the period. They expressed the values of the conservative center.

3.17 *Perforated cardboard mottoes with designs printed on them were mass produced and mass distributed. Yet few surviving mottoes are exactly the same, even when embroidered on identical sheets. This detail shows why. The lightly printed design usually provided only general guidelines for the embroiderer. The likeness of Lincoln shown here was simply superimposed on the perforated grid. The needleworker had to decide for herself how to transform the printed image into needlework.*

Detail of an embroidered motto
Thread on perforated cardboard
Eastern United States, 1876–1890
Collection of Gail J. Ames

3.18 *Mottoes may not have been humorous, but Victorian humorists sometimes used mottoes for comic effect. This card offers an ironic commentary on two popular texts. The ubiquitous God Bless Our Home in its rustic frame hangs high on the wall of this domestic space. Yet the message is mocked by the main action of the card, as Mother beats her screaming and kicking child with a hairbrush or kitchen implement. In this context, the motto at the bottom, What Is Home Without a Mother? takes on new and altogether quite promising meanings.*

Engraved comic card
Eastern United States, 1875–1890
The Winterthur Library: Joseph Downs Collection of Manuscripts and Printed Ephemera, No. 71 × 247.18

3.19 *What Is Home Without a Mother-in-Law? is an authentic motto text. The fact that comic cards usually give an ironic twist to conventional pieties suggests that the motto might not have been intended as humorous. In this card, the text There Is No Place Like Home presides over a scene of role reversal. Father struggles unsuccessfully to quiet two crying children, while Mother peacefully reads a book and Mother-in-Law peruses a feminist newspaper. These comic cards remind us that the pieties expressed by the mottoes may have had little correlation with the realities of the everyday lives of those who lived in their presence.*

Engraved comic card
Eastern United States, 1875–1890
The Winterthur Library: Joseph Downs Collection of Manuscripts and Printed Ephemera, No. 71 × 247.18

What is Home Without a Mother?

WHAT IS HOME WITHOUT A MOTHER-IN-LAW?

There were some exceptions. Along with the predominant, standard half-sheet and full-sheet mottoes distributed throughout Protestant culture, mottoes with clearly Catholic iconography also turn up (3.21). These usually differ in format and even materials. Ribbons, cording, dried flowers, and celluloid saints and angels are often worked into these artifacts. Texts are sometimes in English, more frequently in German, occasionally in Polish or some other eastern European language. These products of Catholic culture bear clear structural and functional relationships to the mottoes of the Protestant culture. They point to a world that was similar in some of its material aspects but different in its conception of religion and iconography.[19] There are no celluloid saints or angels on the mottoes of mainstream and conservative American Protestants. The long Protestant tradition of iconoclasm or, more exactly, iconophobia, was generally followed here, albeit with some interesting variations.

A survey of more than one hundred fifty texts compiled from several hundred mottoes used by the dominant Protestant culture reveals the following pattern: About 10 percent of the mottoes can be identified as patriotic. A significant portion of these commemorate the centennial of American Independence of 1876 (3.22). Another 15 percent or so display a variety of secular sentiments or are associated with fraternal organizations such as the Masons (3.23) and Odd Fellows or with the Temperance movement. A third group of about the same size includes texts referring to the home or to some member of the family, or texts that evoke memorial or nostalgic themes (3.24). The largest category by far is composed of mottoes with an identifiable Christian orientation. About 60 percent of the texts surveyed were drawn from the Bible, both Old and New Testaments; from the first lines or titles of hymns, both traditional and gospel; or otherwise conveyed an explicitly Christian message (3.25). Determining the frequency with which given words occurs leads to the same conclusion. The most frequent references are to God and then to house or home. The most common motto by far is God Bless Our Home (3.26).

God Bless Our Home was embroidered on perforated cardboard thousands of times by American women and children in the last century. A deceptively simple text, it was usually expressed in the charged and energized calligraphy of the Victo-

3.20 *A text never seen embroidered on perforated cardboard. It is not clear today whether this boldface SIN was meant as condemnation, invitation, or merely notification.*

Sample typeface
From the trade catalog of William H. Page & Co.
Greenville, Connecticut, 1874
The Winterthur Library

3.21 *Same process, different culture. The embroidery is still on perforated cardboard and still follows printed contours. But the German text, which can be translated as "Saint Joseph, helper in all distress, intercede for us," is dramatically different from those of mainstream American Protestantism. In many German examples, as here, the words are joined by images of saints or angels in pressed paper, celluloid, or some other material. Strictly speaking, this is not a motto but a prayer.*

Embroidered prayer to Saint Joseph
Thread, metallic cord, dried and artificial flowers and leaves, and celluloid on perforated cardboard, imitation walnut frame
United States or Germany, 1880–1910
Photograph by John Yost

3.22 *Motto with patriotic text and imagery. Produced to commemorate the centennial of American Independence, this motto combines a portrait of Abraham Lincoln and two American flags with the dates 1776 and 1876 and two phrases from Lincoln's Second Inaugural Address.*

Embroidered motto
Thread on perforated cardboard
Eastern United States, c. 1876
Collection of Gail J. Ames

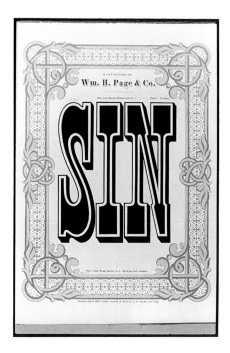

3.23 *Motto with Masonic associations. The text, Trust in God, occurs frequently on mottoes. Here it is surrounded by explicitly Masonic iconography: the pair of columns topped by globes and the familiar compass and square superimposed on the Bible, opened to Chapter VII of the Book of Amos. The chapter was understood as meaningful to Masons: "and, behold, the Lord stood beside a wall made by a plumb-line, with a plumb-line in his hand. . . . Then said the Lord, Behold, I will set a plumb-line in the midst of my people Israel."*

Embroidered motto
Thread on perforated cardboard
Eastern United States, 1870–1885
Museum of Our National Heritage, Lexington, Massachusetts, gift of Charles V. Hagler
Photograph by John Hamilton

3.24 *Motto with a nostalgic theme. This text, The Old Arm Chair, is derived from the title of a popular song by Eliza Cook. The song begins, "I love it—I love it, and who shall dare to chide me for loving that old arm chair?" As explained in the song, the chair serves as a prod to memory, for it was in the old arm chair that the narrator's beloved mother died ("I saw her die in that old arm chair"). Thus the chair evokes profound memories and emotions. While the motto has a specific literary reference, it can also be seen as a continuing invitation to personalize, sentimentalize, and even sacralize the material culture of everyday life. "A sacred thing is that old arm chair."*

Embroidered motto
Thread on perforated cardboard
Eastern or midwestern United States, 1875–1890

3.25 *Motto with a religious message. "The Lord is my Shepherd" is the opening line of the Twenty-third Psalm. While many versions of this common text were embroidered on cardboard following printed contours, this example was created without such guidance. The regularity of the lettering, the tightly controlled and balanced design, and the subtle colors (gold, buff, and russet) suggest that this motto was created later than some of the others by a needleworker with artistic training.*

Embroidered motto
Thread on perforated cardboard
New England or New York, 1880–1900
Photograph by John Yost

3.26 *The most common motto of all, God Bless Our Home. Also very popular were Home Sweet Home and There Is No Place Like Home. The latter were derived from an aria from* Clari, or, The Maid of Milan, *an opera written by an American, John Howard Payne, and first performed in London's Covent Garden in 1823. Compared to these, God Bless Our Home is much more explicitly a prayer, an invocation. The text appeared in many configurations; this is one of the most frequently found.*

Embroidered motto
Thread on perforated cardboard
Eastern United States, 1875–1890
Strong Museum, Rochester, New York

3.27 *Giving power to words. The elaborated typefaces so characteristic of the Victorian age may be understood as visual rhetoric, as ways of making the drama of oratory visible.*

Title from the preface page
Benjamin Silliman and C. R. Goodrich, eds., The World of Science, Art and Industry Illustrated
New York: G. P. Putnam & Co., 1854
The Winterthur Library

rian age (3.27). This calligraphy represents a cultural phenomenon in its own right. One of its purposes presumably was to give power to whatever words were so presented (3.28). The most obvious historical antecedents for this lettering were the embellished initial letters (3.29) of illuminated manuscripts of the Middle Ages. As I show shortly, this medieval association was purposeful.

In the recurring embellished recitations of God Bless Our Home, important traits of Victorian culture were fused. On the one hand, the objects demonstrated the culture's attraction to potent condensations of meaning.[20] On the other, they showed, particularly in their dramatic style of lettering, a fascination with hyperbole. Howard Mumford Jones, among others, was struck by the Victorians' inclination to hyperbole, to exaggeration.[21] The bold and powerful lettering on mottoes was not confined to those objects but was stylistically in accord with typefaces used throughout the culture (3.30), particularly in public and ceremonial contexts (3.31). In a more abstract way, the general design qualities of exaggerated form, heightened contrast, diversified surface and palette, intricacy, and complexity were found throughout many classes of design, ranging from architecture and furniture (3.32) to silver

3.28 *Two powerful and resonant words, here not merely adjacent to each other but conjoined, interwoven.*

Cover design, gold lettering embossed on green cloth
Elisha Charles Hussey, Home Building. A Reliable Book of Facts, Relating to Building
New York: Leader & Van Hoesen, 1876
The Winterthur Library

3.29 *The illuminated initial letter revived. The beginnings of chapters or sections of Romanesque and Gothic illuminated manuscripts were often dramatized and ceremonialized by embellishing the first letter of the first word. Sometimes these embellished letters occupied most of the page. Often they displayed great imagination and wit. This initial A from the middle of the nineteenth century documents the reintroduction of that practice.*

Initial A *from the preface page*
Benjamin Silliman and C. R. Goodrich, eds., The World of Science, Art and Industry Illustrated
New York: G. P. Putnam & Co., 1854
The Winterthur Library

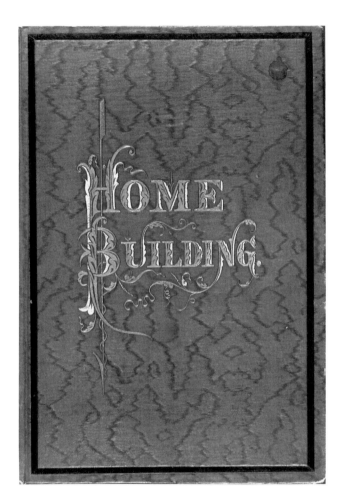

3.30 *Psychic resonance made visible. On this dedication page, the key words, "Home Loving" and "Home Building," are elaborated, embellished, so that they seem to expand, to radiate beyond their own boundaries. The sense of agitation, of movement, of inner life or energy conveyed by this system of embellishment has many parallels in the art of illuminated manuscripts.*

*Dedication page
Almon Clothier Varney,* Our Homes and Their Adornments
*Detroit: J. C. Chilton & Co., 1882
The Winterthur Library*

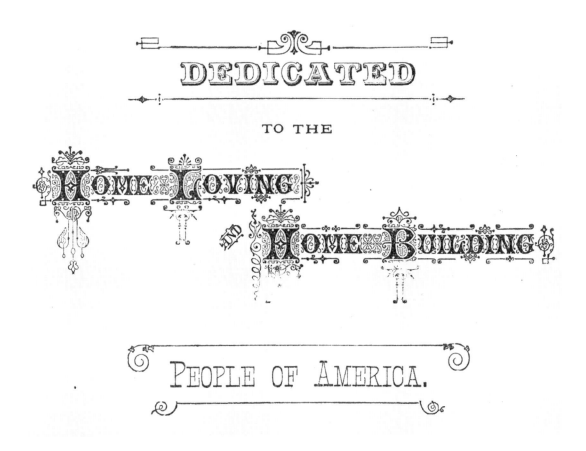

DEDICATED

TO THE

Home Loving

and

Home Building

PEOPLE OF AMERICA.

holloware and jewelry. The peculiar qualities of Victorian design of this period have been noted repeatedly. Carroll Meeks's description of this visual manner as the high point, the most extreme statement, of the aesthetic of picturesque eclecticism is valid enough but lacks explanatory power.[22] We still do not really know why this culture chose to give its material culture exaggerated form. Why is the lettering on mottoes so elaborated, so complicated?

One accurate if not wholly satisfying answer may be that these mottoes were presented in elaborate calligraphy because so much else of the period was too. In other words, the calligraphy served to mediate and locate the text. Victorian motto texts were brief, clear, concise—and derived from a wide variety of historic sources. Although the meanings of these words were usually unambiguous, the same can-

3.31 *Ceremonial lettering for a ceremonial text. This complicated artifact consists of an elaborated and ceremonial testimonial surrounded and elevated by an elaborated and ceremonial frame. The text is a statement of appreciation presented on December 31, 1869, by the Board of Aldermen of New York City to its President, Thomas Coman. The testimonial uses over a dozen different typefaces, some of which are very difficult to read.*

Elaborately framed testimonial to Thomas Coman
New York City, 1869
Museum of the City of New York

3.32 *An aesthetic of exaggeration and studied awkwardness. Victorian design of the 1870s was dominated by a calculated gracelessness. Carroll Meeks attributed this to the dominance of picturesque values, to a preference for visual surprises, for lines and contours that varied suddenly and in unexpected ways. This marble-top table is typical of this mode of design at the middle- and upper-middle-class levels. Compare the contours of its legs to the shapes of letters on contemporary mottoes.*

Walnut table with white marble top
Possibly Grand Rapids, Michigan, c. 1875
Collection of John H. Noyes

3.33 *The text is not overtly religious, but the style of the letters links it to earlier religious texts and, more generally, to venerability. Current admonitions in old lettering may seem to be old admonitions. Emphasis on the word* Learn *also ties the motto to larger cultural currents in Victorian America. One could learn taste. One could learn manners. One could learn to do good. The initial* L *is particularly complicated and resonant here.*

Embroidered motto
Thread on perforated cardboard
Eastern United States, 1875–1885
Collection of Gail J. Ames

3.34 *Elaboration in the secular world. The cover of this book of natural history for young people includes two extraordinarily embellished letters. Yet the book is completely secular. Despite its religious origins, in the nineteenth century the elaborated mode was employed in both sacred and secular spheres. And if this fusion could be interpreted to mean that religion was infiltrating secular thought, it could just as readily be interpreted as showing that religious symbolism was being devalued. The cover of* Ingersoll's Lectures, *containing the thoughts of "the great agnostic," was embellished with an elaborated* I *and* L. *Yet few popular books of the nineteenth were less religious. Sometimes a style is just a style. Its purpose may be to make temporal or cultural linkage, not to promote ideology.*

Cover design
Black and gold embossed on green cloth
Olive Thorne, Little Folks in Feathers and Fur and Others in Neither
Hartford: Dustin, Gilman & Co., 1875
Photograph by Craig Williams

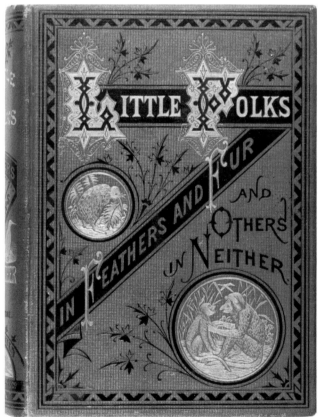

not necessarily be said for their temporal location or association. What time or times were they meant to evoke? The moment they were first spoken or written? The present? Eternity?

The evidence of the calligraphy suggests that in some cases the answer was all of the above. The self-conscious medieval style of lettering linked the texts of mottoes to script normally associated with Bibles and other sacred writings (3.33). Indeed, many motto texts had biblical origins. The style of calligraphy illuminated or underlined those origins. Yet the visual properties of this lettering—embellished, intricate, and even sometimes visually confusing—were also characteristic of the dominant secular design aesthetic of the period (3.34). Thus the calligraphy bound the texts to Victorian culture and Victorian life. In so doing, it demonstrated the basic locating function of style. Consider an analogy: American automobiles of 1937 and 1957 are much the same in their working elements; they are both products of the same "normal technology."[23] But they are dramatically different on the outside. Anyone with elementary design literacy will be able to distinguish between the two. One major function of the external differences is to locate the artifacts in time. In like manner, the style of script helped Victorian culture "possess" these texts, whether they were contemporary, eighteenth century, or even biblical in origin. Finally, the calligraphy linked these texts, these condensed alleged fundamental truths, to eternity. This linkage was again achieved largely through visual references to biblical or sacred style. If the Bible and other religious texts expressed supposed eternal verities, then one might generalize that words rendered in that same style, whether of biblical or of some other origins, could also potentially transcend time.

For many in the nineteenth century, then, God Bless Our Home was not merely a linear arrangement or arabesque of words conveying information. It was a charged composition of vibrant and visually resonant words bringing to mind equally charged and resonant concepts, values, and beliefs. In these needlework mottoes, understatement and overstatement were fused. The verbal message was short, tight, concise, understated. It was expressed in hyperbolic visual terms, in a bold, aggressive, explosive overstatement that suggested something of the glory, majesty, and enduring importance that the concept of the home, the divinity, and their association held for believers. God Bless Our Home was a powerful thought, a fervent invocation, expressed in a calligraphic form that underscored its significance and rendered it both timely and timeless.

Sometimes images of houses appeared in conjunction with the words. When this occurred, words and images enriched each other. From a historian's point of view, these images are helpful in explicating more clearly the predominantly conservative and retrospective orientation of these artifacts. Compare, for example, a full-sheet God Bless Our Home motto with a house embroidered on it (3.35) to a Currier & Ives lithograph, *American Country Life: May Morning* (3.36). The motto probably dates from 1870 to 1880 and was embroidered by an unknown person. The lithograph dates from 1855 and was drawn by the prolific Frances Palmer.[24] Both images are products of nineteenth-century popular culture. Both are products of the same general ideological stance. Yet they show shades of meaning and references that differ significantly. Each reflects a different attitude toward worldliness. Each is grounded in different historical or, more particularly, art historical visions. Rather than undercutting or fragmenting the prevailing ideology of domesticity, however, they reveal some of the richness and variation possible within it.

In both of these images, houses figure prominently. In both, the houses are seen from a three-quarter view, a mode of presentation that became common around the middle of the nineteenth century. While eighteenth-century architectural images normally showed a building starkly from the front as if it were two-dimensional, nineteenth-century architectural presentations turned the building on its axis in order to reveal its volumetric subtleties and the interactions of its masses, considered important in architecture at the time.[25] Both buildings depicted here were grounded in the later visual and conceptual convention. Both houses are nestled in nature and surrounded by trees, but references to nature and the outer environment are extensive in the Currier & Ives print and rudimentary in the motto.

3.35 *The American, middle-class domestic ideal embroidered on perforated cardboard. A single-family, free-standing house, surrounded by its own plot of land, isolated from the corrupting influences of the city and of fashion. The wellsweep on the left is meant to convey tradition and old-time values, although the conservatism of the house form does so as well. This motto is backed with gold foil, which can be seen shining through the perforations, giving the entire image a golden hue.*

Embroidered motto with picture of a house
Thread on perforated cardboard backed by gold foil
Eastern United States, 1870–1880
Collection of Gail J. Ames

Other differences seem more important. The Currier & Ives image belongs to the Renaissance tradition of pictorial illusion. It is conceived as a window on the world, as a continuation of the viewer's own physical space. The lithograph includes a variety of familiar conventions for enabling viewers to enter its pictorial space conceptually, the most noticeable being the road winding from the foreground into the background. While reduced in scale, the image is wholly mimetic, grounded in traditions that sought to represent convincingly the three-dimensional world on a two-dimensional surface.

3.36 *Both worldly and ideologically correct, this famous normative image provides a concise introduction to the doctrine of separate spheres. Males outside it, women within, the fence serves as a powerful metaphor of American gender distinctions. While these folks are ideologically orthodox, they are also worldly and fashionable, as can be seen from their clothing, the scale and magnificence of their lands, their newly built and probably architect-designed Tus-* *can villa on the crest of the hill, and the obvious presence of hired farmhands. If wealth legitimizes, then the obvious wealth depicted here legitimizes the ideology and confirms its correctness.*

American County Life: May Morning
Lithograph, drawn by Frances Palmer and published by Currier & Ives
New York, 1855
Library of Congress

AMERICAN COUNTRY LIFE.

The motto, in contrast, perpetuates pre-Renaissance or medieval ideas. It looks more like a Trecento icon on a gold background than a rationalized Renaissance projection of space. The house embroidered on its surface has intimations of volume, but the brief, two-dimensional, symbolic landscape flanking it does not fill the pictorial field. The objects in the motto image are more iconic than mimetic. In this nineteenth-century version of a pre-Renaissance concept, word and image are interwoven on a surface that is largely two-dimensional. The gold foil behind

3.37 *Upright-and-wing house in thread. The concept was introduced with Greek Revival architecture. Turning the gable end toward the street, architects placed columned porticos on costly houses. For cheaper versions, builders suggested Grecian architecture by attaching pilasters at the corners. The needleworker who embroidered this* image captured the pilasters and a suggestion of a complex doorway, possibly adorned with sidelights.
Detail of house shown in Figure 3.35

the perforated cardboard gives the motto a gleaming, reflective surface much like a panel from an altarpiece or a page from an illuminated manuscript. The similarity to sacred manuscripts is further heightened by the Romanesque and Gothic lettering mentioned earlier.

Both of these are products of the ideology of domesticity, but they occupy different positions on the continua of sacred to secular and of traditional to modern. Palmer's design, rich in normative dimensions, effectively packages a constellation of ideas about domesticity and separate spheres, but the world it depicts and perhaps addresses is largely secular and urbane. The motto, on the other hand, more closely resembles a prayer. Its world is more visibly conservative and religious.

The architectural structures in these two images underscore this point. The Currier & Ives print first appeared in 1855. The exact date of the motto on perforated cardboard is not known. It is probably later than 1870, yet the house it depicts is earlier in style than the house in the 1855 lithograph. The Italianate villa of Fanny Palmer's design was the height of fashion in 1855, and similar images are widespread in leading books on domestic architecture of that period. Palmer's picture shows a fashionable house inhabited by fashionable people living fashionable lives.

The motto depicts a house type perceived as conservative by 1870 (3.37). The form, known to students of vernacular architecture as an "upright and wing house," was apparently codified in the 1840s in the East, then spread westward with Yankee culture (3.38).[26] It was replicated across the northern states as a conservative and, sometimes, less expensive alternative to the more worldly, flamboyant Italianate villas. Such a house fits into the middle-class plain tradition, an alternative repeatedly hymned in culturally conservative literature. The following passage from New England Unitarian minister John F. W. Ware is fairly typical:

A house standing alone, roomy, convenient, should convey immediately . . . the idea of home. . . . No wasted decoration, no useless expense. . . . It should be the centre of gentle but permanent influences. . . . Well-ordered, thrifty, and hospitable. . . . Such homes there have been, and by the blessing of God such homes shall ever be.[27]

Mottoes sometimes depicted more fashionable houses but most of those embroidered on perforated cardboard represent conservative, idealized images. The strong current against worldliness and fashion running through these elaborately scripted objects parallels the strictures against fashion, worldliness, and gaudy life found abundantly in the moral crusade literature of the period.

3.38 *The upright-and-wing house moves west. This photograph by Andrew Dahl shows a family sitting in front of their recently built upright-and-wing in the vicinity of Madison, Wisconsin. Here, explicit references to Greek Revival architecture have disappeared. Only* the upright-and-wing configuration endures. *The sense of propriety or moral conservatism suggested by the style of the house is echoed in the furniture, which also looks new and follows styles considered conservative or orthodox in the late 1870s.*

Photograph of a family in front of their house
Vicinity of Madison, Wisconsin
Andrew Dahl, c. 1875
State Historical Society of Wisconsin, Madison

The medievalism of mottoes is clarified by another God Bless Our Home. In this example the concept of the blessed home is expressed through its external form (3.39). In the usual manner of these mottoes, the text floats above an evocation of an undatable house, presumably the eternal Christian home, apart from and un-affected by worldly concerns and fashions. In one possible reading of this image, the ideal Christian home is as timeless as the heavenly home. The short strip of fence, the four rudimentary and nearly symmetrical trees, and the patch of grass that dis-appears into the cardboard void, all, in their cursory two-dimensionality, assert the primacy of idea over object, of symbol over substance. In this motto, spiritual truth is expressed through matter it simultaneously transcends.

This rural, ideal Christian home, this utopian retreat from the outer world, is de-picted without concession to Renaissance perspective (3.40). Gable ends and two intervening walls are pressed flat onto the surface. The structure is simplified, its fenestration minimized. The dominant gable has a door flanked by windows in a balanced, symmetrical, tripartite composition. At the top of this gable is a form un-common, if not unknown in domestic architecture: a belfry like those found on parish churches in rural England and introduced here in the early phases of the Gothic Revival.[28] In this image the Christian home becomes synthesized with the Christian church. An even more explicitly ecclesiastical element appears on the other gable, where a small but discernible cross rises (3.41). Although nearly lost in the tree behind it, the contrast of brown thread against green makes it impossible to mis-take this object. Possibly suggested by an illustration of the Christian house in the Beecher sisters' *The American Woman's Home* of 1869 (3.42), this image reflects not outer physical reality but an ideal.[29] Like medieval icons, the motto depicts spiritual truths rather than earthly truths, religious reality rather than the concrete, objective experience of visible and tangible life. This is an image of the invisible. This is a statement of faith.

Although the words embroidered on mottoes are usually few in number, they re-sound with meaning. Equally compressed but charged and meaningful expressions appear in the cemetery and with other material culture associated with death. These texts echo some of the same sentiments, the same rhythms—and sometimes even the same words (3.43)—thus linking house and cemetery, life and death, earthly home and heavenly home.[30] Inscriptions in stone of Heaven Is My Home (3.44), Missed at Home, Gone Home (3.45), or Called Home, confirm the identification or linkage of these two "homes." Similarly, mottoes embroidered with Sweet Rest in Heaven are obvious counterparts to At Rest (3.46), Resting, or Resting from Their Labors in the cemetery, whether on tombstones or coffin hardware.

The two spheres were often linked by images as well as words. The image of a pair of clasped hands, which appeared on mottoes with the text Remember Me (3.47) was frequently replicated in stone (3.48).[31] The motto text, No Cross No Crown, was balanced in the cemetery by carving the words or by carved or cast likenesses of these two objects (3.49). Words and images were interchangeable parts of a wide-reaching religious comprehension that stretched from the church to the home, from the home to the cemetery, and from the cemetery to the afterlife.

These mottoes offer some intriguing correlations with the larger religious world of which they were a part. The evidence of the objects suggests parallels with evangelical religious movements of the later part of the nineteenth century and the general "softening" perceptible throughout most forms of Protestantism. Even as Calvinistic a denomination as Congregationalism, the original New England Puritan church, went through dramatic transformations.[32] So did needlework.

Qualities that distinguish late eighteenth- and early nineteenth-century samplers from these later mottoes are roughly analogous to those distinguishing Calvinist Protestantism of the earlier period from Evangelical Protestantism of the later.[33] Sandra Sizer, outlining these transitions within religion, showed how conceptions of people's relationship to their god changed markedly during the nineteenth century. The traditional Calvinist view was that people were low, vile, unworthy creatures, guilty of sin and in need of atonement. Over time, emphasis shifted from peoples' sins to their salvation. Whereas Calvinist doctrine of the eighteenth century had defined people

3.39 *Homes depicted on mottoes often represented abstractions or concepts and were not intended as mimetic images. The house shown here clearly is one that never existed on earth. The denial of perspective underscores its symbolic function.*

Embroidered motto
Thread on perforated cardboard
Eastern United States, 1870–1890
Collection of Gail J. Ames

3.40 *The carefully controlled needle-work follows a printed pattern now largely invisible beneath the thread. Like the final embroidered image, the printed design eliminated perspective and pressed both gable ends flat.*
Detail of Figure 3.39

3.41 *Spiritual reality made visible. Among the small* X *shapes in green meant to evoke trees rises an unmistakable cross in brown thread. The home in this motto is thus unequivocally Christianized. Less unequivocal is the way the needleworker made meaning from the pattern printed on the cardboard.*

This motto is unusual in that the design has been abstracted into a pattern of squares, apparently color coded. Both the belfry and the cross were printed on the cardboard and were not inventions of the needleworker.
Detail of Figure 3.39

as depraved sinners, gospel religion viewed them as passive victims of evil and impersonal forces. Early hymns were full of admonitions to be strong and appeals to an all-powerful, vindictive God. Gospel hymns, on the other hand, emphasized heaven and the afterlife, stressing Jesus rather than God. This Jesus had become a friend who carried people across rivers, walked with them, guided them down paths, or stood at the door and knocked. He was no longer, in Sizer's words, "the active king-conqueror or the lawyer-advocate of Watts." The hymns and the religion in general expressed a new sense of intimacy, devotion, and emotional relationship with Jesus (3.50). His help and salvation had become eminently accessible. In hundreds of homes across America, one could look up on the wall and be reminded that Jesus Loves Me (3.51).[34]

3.42 *The daughters of a Congregational minister preach the gospel of Christian domesticity. The Beecher sisters'* American Woman's Home *is often praised today for its emergent pragmatism and feminism, but less often acknowledged as a religious tract. The book was in large part a sermon to women. This image appears at the head of the second chapter, which opens with the words, "In the Divine Word it is written, 'The wise woman buildeth her house,'" and ends with "Christian example and influences." A similar house appears on the title page but without the three very visible crosses that adorn it here.*

A Christian House
From Catharine E. Beecher and Harriet Beecher Stowe, The American Woman's Home
New York: J. B. Ford and Co., 1869

3.43 *A selection of texts appropriate for the cemetery. Although few of these occurred as embroidered mottoes, they closely resemble mottoes in grammatical structure, number of words, and cognitive function. Like mottoes, these texts offered simple, even simplistic explanations for or responses to profound, perplexing, and deeply troubling events.*
"Brief Epitaphs"
From Thomas E. Hill, Hill's Manual of Social and Business Forms
Chicago: Hill Standard Book Co., 1882

3.44 *Heaven Is My Home could be seen in embroidered form in domestic interiors and in carved form in cemeteries. We now recognize that it was in these two arenas, the domestic and the funerary, that Victorian society made some of its most emphatic and distinctive cultural statements. It has been less often noted that the two arenas were closely linked and were shaped by and promoted congruent ideologies.*
Heaven Is My Home
Inscription on a marble gravestone
New Castle County, Delaware, c. 1880

II.

A CHRISTIAN HOUSE.

Brief Epitaphs.

Father.	Our Mother.	Charlie.
All is Well.	Gone Home.	Christ is my Hope.
Darling Sister.	Gone, but not Forgotten.	The Morning Cometh.
We will Meet again.	Rest, Darling Sister, Rest.	Dying is but Going Home.
Over in the Summer Land.	In after Time we'll meet Her.	There shall be no Night there.
Absent, not Dead.	Gentle, Sweet little Freddie.	They are not Dead.

3.45 *A simple explanation for the mystery of death. A simple account for an absence that will last forever. A simple statement of faith in something beyond. A simple statement of resignation, of hope, of peace.*

Gone Home
Inscription on a marble gravestone
South central Wisconsin, c. 1880

3.46 *If one can believe in a God, one can also believe that there is no death. A denial of death was a prominent component of verbal texts in mainstream Protestant cemeteries of the late nineteenth century. At Rest was a common denial—or euphemism. The words were often inscribed on headstones or, as here, made the message of a footstone. In some ways, this footstone resembles a motto. It is relatively small, has a brief but resonant text, and by using rustic letters implies that it is grounded in the natural order. For the same reason, mottoes often had frames in the rustic style.*

At Rest
Carved marble footstone
Laurel Hill Cemetery, Philadelphia, c. 1880

3.47 *An invitation to remember. And an opportunity to ponder the power of these reductionist artifacts called mottoes. Remember Me is simple enough, straightforward enough. Only two words. But whose memories can be contained within two words? What human being can be comprehended by the monosyllable Me? Deceptively direct, this text holds a potential personal Pandora's box of memories, sentiments, and associations. The text is, in the end, manipulative. It issues a directive, a command, or perhaps a plea. Whatever the case, the onus is on the recipient or the viewer to remember and to make meaning of the image of two hearts and two hands conjoined.*

Detail of an embroidered motto
Thread on perforated cardboard
Eastern United States, dated 1880
Collection of Gail J. Ames

3.48 *Two hands joined is a motif that appears frequently in cemeteries. The detail here is from a double stone dedicated to a husband and wife, Dominecus and Barbara. The little bit of clothing visible is gendered so that we will know that the hand on the right is his, the hand on the left is hers.*

Detail of a carved marble gravestone Savannah, Georgia, 1882 or 1892

3.49 *Coffin plates are nameplates for coffins. The name of the deceased was engraved in the blank area beneath the text. Texts on coffin plates often closely resembled those found on gravestones, which in turn resembled embroidered mottoes. No Cross No Crown was a popular motto text. One might see it one day in a household and the next day on a coffin plate at a funeral or on a grave-* *stone in the cemetery. Thus an extensive cultural system linked life and death and sought to use the power of each to extend its domain over the other.*

Two silver-plated coffin plates
Trade catalog of Columbus Coffin Co.
Columbus, Ohio, 1882
The Winterthur Library

3.50 *The softening or feminization of Protestant Christianity. Gone is the hellfire and damnation. Gone is the angry, vengeful God. Large letters on the wall at the front of the Water Street Mission Room in New York City spell out the proclamation God Is Love. The same assertion was embroidered on perforated cardboard hundreds and perhaps even thousands of times. The name of Jesus appears on the mission's walls prominently and repeatedly. The text For God So Loved The World was available on perforated cardboard.*

Interior of the Water Street Mission Room
From Helen Campbell, Darkness and Daylight; or, Lights and Shadows of New York Life
Hartford: A. D. Worthington & Co., 1892

THE PLATFORM FACING THE AUDIENCE IN THE WATER STREET
MISSION ROOM.

3.51 *Jesus walks with me. Jesus talks with me. And above all, Jesus Loves Me. Neither musically nor rhetorically distinguished, this saccharine hymn, written by Anna B. Warner in 1859, became popular in the late nineteenth century, particularly in Sunday schools. Better than many documents, it demon-strates the period's promotion of cloying sweetness and sentimentality, of passivity, smug egocentrism, and infantile credulity.*
Detail of a photograph of the northeast bedroom at Cherry Hill in Figure 3.16

"Accessible" is a key word here. The accessibility of both Christ and salvation in nineteenth-century gospel religion parallels the accessibility of the mottoes themselves. The mottoes were physically and visually accessible, placed within Christian homes where family members and sometimes guests could see them on a daily basis. It makes sense that mottoes were most common when the belief in environmental determinism was strongest. Those who philosophized and moralized about houses and their contents maintained that objects like mottoes worked stealthily to infuse good messages, good thoughts, into the hearts and minds of those who were daily in their presence.

Mottoes were accessible on another level as well. The ease with which they could be crafted was a critical factor in their popularity. In the eighteenth century, needlework samplers were slowly and painstakingly created, the hundreds and sometimes thousands of stitches requiring care and precision. The completed product was the result of substantial time, effort, attention, and energy. With mottoes on perforated cardboard, the inclination, a little bit of money, and only a modicum of time and effort were sufficient to produce these bright and often dramatic statements of commitment to the community of the faithful. Like salvation in the gospel hymns, the values expressed on the mottoes were accessible to those who sought them. Ease of salvation within a religious context was roughly equivalent to the ease of execution of these mottoes. No trials, no long bouts of self-denial or meditation were necessary. With just a little work, a wondrous thing could be wrought. With just a little conviction, one could be saved. Perforated mottoes were not expensive. Nor were they difficult to embroider. As the objects themselves reveal and as writings about needlework noted, even children could work them and produce passable results. A satisfactory outcome did not depend on extensive training or imagination. Because the texts were usually preprinted, the needleworker had only to follow a few simple directives. Good followers could craft good mottoes. These mottoes made it easy to be a moral mother and a moral child. It was easy to create and enshrine words to live by.

Whether or not this correlation of accessibility is legitimate, it is beyond question that with these objects, allegedly iconophobic Protestants kept in their homes expressions of religious faith that were at odds with a long tradition of repression or avoidance of explicitly religious material culture in the domestic sphere. If some of the changes in Protestantism can be attributed to a feminization of the religion, the appearance of these mottoes can also be seen as a Catholicization of Protestantism (3.52).[35]

These mottoes lead to yet other conclusions, however, with more far-reaching ramifications. These perforated mottoes brought together in uneasy union within a single artifact quite different and contradictory orientations. On one hand, the perforated cardboard was a modern, innovative product, grounded in reason and the aggressively rational, masculine world of technology. It reified the doctrine of progress, for at the time of its introduction it was understood to be superior to its various antecedents. In this sense, mottoes were products of technological modernism.

The texts that women and children embroidered on them, on the other hand, were grounded in premodern comprehensions. In many cases they were long-enduring, unexamined assertions about the fundaments of Christian life: Christ Is Risen. He Leadeth Me. Heaven Is My Home. Jesus Loves Me. Labor Has Sure Reward. The Lord Will Provide. Safe in the Arms of Jesus (3.53). In this way mottoes were thus also culturally premodern. In short, the objects were culturally modern and premodern, masculine and feminine, radical and conservative, challenging and accepting, reasoned and beyond reason. In these mottoes, reason served nonreason, reason served what was beyond reason. For in the end, the most basic articles of faith, of belief, indeed, the guiding laws of culture itself, lie beyond the explanatory powers of reason.[36] Put in other words, few categories of human endeavor depend on reason more than technology and few depend on it less than religion. Both realizations were celebrated in these Victorian artifacts.

These seemingly simple mottoes are, then, artifacts of a specific time, place, and culture—Victorian America (3.54)—and statements about deep-seated and endur-

3.52 *Catholicism Protestantized. Protestanism Catholicized. This image served as the frontispiece to a popular collection of sentimental and normative poems and short texts. The book included an introduction by the prominent Presbyterian minister Theodore Cuyler. This image was titled* Mother. *Beneath the title appeared the additional statement: "From a Photograph of the original Painting 'The Holy Family' painted for the Empress of Russia by*

L. Knaus." The ordering of these words suggests that the specific religious origins—and meanings—of this image, while partially acknowledged, were less significant than the more universal and, for the Victorians, far more compelling concept of motherhood.

Frontispiece
Golden Thoughts on Mother, Home, and Heaven
Philadelphia: Garretson & Co., 1878–1882

3.53 *Antirationalism. Antiintellectualism. Conflicting cultural currents converge in this artifact. If perforated cardboard was a product of the male world of invention and industry, of innovation and technical problem solving, the text embroidered on it was a product of feminized religion and domestic culture. If the material, the method of printing on it, the production and packaging of yarns and threads, and the merchandising of these mottoes all depended on varied and even extensive technical expertise, the text itself was a statement of childlike credulity, requiring neither expertise nor even intelligence to accept. In part, the suggestion of childlike faith reflected the period's high valuation of childhood and childhood innocence. And, in part, it suggested orthodox hostility to intellectual freedom and inquiry. From a rationalist's perspective, this motto was a lie to live by.*

Embroidered motto
Thread on perforated cardboard, in original rustic frame
Eastern United States, 1875–1885
Collection of Gail J. Ames

3.54 *The Christian capitalist family. Is the profit motive America's true god? An extended family is gathered together within a luxurious interior. In this setting, the motif of the extended family means morality and virtue. The motto on the wall indicates that these people live by conventional religious beliefs. They pray Give Us This Day Our Daily Bread. And behold. Miller's Baking Powder is a sign, an answer to their prayer. This is a happy household. They are happy because they have an expen-* *sive house, a piano, a fancy mantelpiece, an elaborate clock, and a servant. And they are happy because they subscribe to social, economic, religious, and probably intellectual orthodoxies. Woe be to those who do not.*

A Happy Household.
From Asher and Adams' New Columbian Railroad Atlas and Pictorial Album of American Industry
New York: Asher and Adams, 1876–1877
The Winterthur Library

" A Happy Household."

ing tendencies in American thought and culture. The material aspect of mottoes captures American fascination with technical expertise, with narrow pragmatism, with the dream of technological progress, with compulsive conquest of the concrete. Perforated cardboard is the product of inquiry, of exploration. The texts, on the other hand, reveal the limits on inquiry imposed throughout much of society, limits that determine which parts of the world can be problematized and which cannot. Although they were presented as promptings to a spiritual life, we can see that many of the alleged truths of these texts were and still are authentic fictions. They are doctrinaire if gentle lies and delusions that mock human intellect and close off inquiry into and debate about the larger questions and issues that confront humankind are doctrinaire. To the mentality that embraced these mottoes, as Robert Ingersoll noted a century ago, unbelief was a crime, investigation sinful, and credulity a virtue.[37] That mentality still survives today and is still prominent. Thus these mottoes shed light on enduring cultural constraints that continue to inhibit American intellectual life at the end of the twentieth century. They shed light on persisting American avoidance and denial of big questions and big issues. They shed light on American anti-intellectualism.

For many Victorians, these mottoes expressed great truths. From our perspective today, we can recognize that the truths they expressed were greater than the Victorians knew.

MOTTO TEXTS

The following is a compilation of motto texts drawn from extant mottoes and period trade catalogs. This listing includes mass-produced, pre-printed texts only.

Abide with Me

Absent But Not Forgotten

After Clouds Sunshine

As Thy Days So Shall Thy Strength Be

Auld Lang Syne

Be Not Weary in Well Doing

Be on Thy Guard

Be True in Heart

Bless This House

Blessed Are the Pure in Heart

By Industry Thrive

Call Again

Charity Never Faileth

Christ Is Risen

Come unto Me All Ye That Labor

Come Ye to the Waters

Consider the Lilies

Dare to Do Right

Do Right and Fear Not

E Pluribus Unum   1876   United We Stand

Eat Drink and Be Merry

Faith Hope and Charity

Feed My Lambs

For God So Loved the World . . .

Forget Me Not

Friendship Love and Truth

Give Us This Day Our Daily Bread

God Bless Our Daily Bread

God Bless Our Home

God Bless Our School

God Bless the Old Folks at Home

God Is Love
God Is Our Refuge and Our Strength
Good Morning
Good Night and Pleasant Dreams
Grace Peace and Mercy
Hail Columbia   Liberty   1776–1876
Hallowed Be Thy Name
Happy New Year
He Leadeth Me
He Shall Give His Angels Charge
   over Thee
Heaven Is My Home
Holy Angels Guard Thy Bed
Home Sweet Home
Honor Thy Father and Thy Mother
I Am the Bread of Life
I Am the Light of the World
I Am the Vine
I Know That My Redeemer Liveth
I Need Thee Every Hour
In God We Trust
In God We Trust   1776–1876
In Honor Shall Wave   1776–1876
Jesus Loves Me
Kind Words Can Never Die
Kindness Makes Friends
Knowledge Is Power
Labor Has Sure Reward
Lead Kindly Light
Lead Us Not into Temptation

Learn to Do Good
Liberty   1776–1876
Little Church Around the Corner
Little Deeds of Kindness . . .
Live and Let Live
Lord Keep Us Through This Night
Love Thy Neighbor As Thyself
Malice toward None   Charity to All
Merry Christmas
Mizpah
Nearer My God to Thee
Ninety and Nine
No Cross No Crown
No Place Like Home
Nothing but the Leaves
Obey Your Parents
Old Arm Chair
Old Oaken Bucket
Onward and Upward
Our Betsy
Our Father Who Art in Heaven . . .
Peace Be Still
Peace Be unto This House
Praise God from Whom All
   Blessings Flow . . .
Praise the Lord
Pray Without Ceasing
Remember Me
Remember Thy Creator
Rock of Ages

Rock of Ages   Cleft For Me

Safe in the Arms of Jesus

Savior Like a Shepherd Lead Us

Shall We Gather at the River

Simply to Thee I Cling

Simply to Thy Cross I Cling

Sweet Rest in Heaven

The Lord Is My Shepherd . . .

The Lord Is Risen

The Lord Will Provide

The Old Oaken Bucket

The Ten Commandments . . .

There Is No Place like Home

Thou Art My Hope

Thou God Seest Me

Thy Will Be Done

To My Dear Sister

Touch Not   Taste Not   Handle Not

Trust in God

Tune Thy Harp to Songs of Praise

United We Stand   1776–1876

Walk in Love

Watch and Pray

We Meet upon the Level

We Mourn Our Loss

Welcome

Welcome Home

Welcome to All

Well Begun Is Half Done

What Is Home Without a Baby

What Is Home Without a Father

What Is Home Without a Mother

What Is Home Without a
   Mother-In-Law

What Is Home Without a Wife

Wisdom Is Strength

With Joy We Greet You

Work For the Night Is Coming

Work Out Your Own Salvation
1776–1876

4 : When the Music Stops

M usic. There is nothing else like it. Powerful. Compelling. Beyond translation into words. Music takes us into ourselves and beyond ourselves. It bonds us to others. It enlivens and gives meaning to our present. It evokes and confirms our past. Music is a central cultural form. Those who create or perform music enjoy high status. Music makers are living gods.[1]

We know ourselves through music; we know our times through music. It stands to reason that we might also know other people and other times through their music. This chapter is an effort to know some of the people of Victorian America better, in part through their music and in even greater part through an instrument for that music, the parlor reed organ (4.1).

Parlor reed organs may seem quaint or old-fashioned today, but they were once prominent and valued parts of Victorian lives. Indeed, parlor organs were distinctively Victorian musical instruments. The first examples of the form appeared early in the nineteenth century. Although production of reed organs for domestic use remained low until the 1840s, patent records reveal a dramatic shift in attention to this instrument around the middle of the century. Between 1818 and 1846, a total of only seven patents were taken out for reed organs. But between 1848 and 1856, the number leaped to thirty-four, with eight patents in 1856 alone. By the late 1860s, the annual production of reed organs in the United States had reached over fifteen thousand instruments, a figure that continued to grow until about 1890, the high point of popularity for this form. After that date, pianos and then phonographs gradually took over the major music-producing functions in American homes.[2]

Parlor organs are large objects. Like pianos, they take up a good deal of space in a room. Like pianos and unlike violins or harmonicas, they are always in place, always on view (4.2). When the music stops, the parlor organ is still there. But while pianos and parlor organs are both keyboard instruments and might seem to have much in common, there is good reason for distinguishing between them. To begin with, there are significant differences in sound. The piano is basically a hammered harp. In the conventional square and grand pianos of the nineteenth century, the graduated metal strings of the harp were laid out horizontally and struck by hammers; sound was created through mechanical impact.[3] The reed organ, in contrast, might be thought of as a graduated set of woodwinds. Sound was created by pushing air over or along reeds fastened at one end and free at the other. In parlor organs, this air was normally generated by bellows pumped by the player's feet at the base of the instrument.

If pianos and parlor organs differed in the sounds they made and the way those sounds were produced, they also differed in the nature of the music that could be performed, in the demands they placed on players, in their case design, spatial requirements, cost, class associations, and, in subtle ways, in the values they represented. For example, although the parlor organ was well suited to playing chords and melodies, it lacked the rapid response and easy dynamics of the piano. The piano was, in a sense, the star musical instrument of the nineteenth century. It was the electric guitar of the Victorian age. Frédéric Chopin, Franz Liszt, and Artur Rubinstein were the B. B. King, Jimi Hendrix, and Eric Clapton of their day. They were virtuosos, and the piano was a virtuoso instrument. Some of the period's greatest music was written for piano.[4] In contrast, the music written for the parlor organ, whether original or adapted from other sources, was usually relatively simple, easy to play, and free of pyrotechnics. The instrument could produce pleasant harmonies and graceful melodies, but it could not equal the dramatic range of the piano. The effort of constantly pumping the foot pedals to generate air for the reeds also made playing the organ a different and in some ways more awkward experience than playing the piano. And, as I have indicated, the sounds of the two instruments could never be confused.[5]

The appearance of these two musical instruments also normally differed. The parlor organ's case was elaborate and intricate (4.3), whereas the typical contemporary piano's woodwork was conceived primarily as a protective enclosure for the works (4.4). Although elegant in design, fabricated from high-quality materials, and finely finished, it remained subservient to and closely related to the internal workings of the instrument.[6] The lower portion of the parlor organ's case was also primarily a

4.1 *The parlor reed organ provided both sound and dramatic presence. The lower section of the case concealed and protected the works. The upper section provided theater. It performed no musical function but added significantly to the object's height, visual impact, and ability to dominate a space. Both sections were heavily ornamented, for parlor organs were as much furniture as musical instruments. This example, more or less in the English-inspired Modern Gothic style, is capped by a small canopy. The canopy is associational, linking the organ to the medieval past, and honorific, symbolically protecting and enshrining people and activities beneath it.*

Parlor organ
Chromolithographed trade card of Newman Bros.
Chicago, c. 1885
The Winterthur Library: Joseph Downs Collection of Manuscripts and Printed Ephemera, No. 71 × 247.13, Album No. 35

STYLE NO. 110 CASE.

FRENCH BEVEL EDGE MIRROR IN THIS CASE EXTRA.

DIMENSIONS.
Height, 78 inches; Length, 50 inches; Depth, 23 inches.
Weight, boxed, about 380 pounds.

4.2 *Always on view. Unlike some other musical instruments—harmonicas, cornets, violins—parlor organs remained in place when not in use. This fact in part explains why parlor organs were conventionally ornamented like furniture. And like large pieces of furniture, parlor organs often became focal points of the rooms they furnished.*

Parlor of the Firestone farmhouse
Restored to c. 1885
Henry Ford Museum & Greenfield Village,
Michigan
(Negative No. B93778)

4.3 *Elaboration and intricacy. The case of this Estey organ is embellished with fretwork, spindles, finials, and incised floral and abstract decoration. Like much furniture and architecture of the period, it has eccentric contours and an agitated skyline. In an attempt to give this middle-class object upper-class associations, the manufacturer called it a "drawing room organ."*

"Estey Drawing Room Organ"
Estey Organ Co., Brattleboro, Vermont, c. 1885
Hagley Museum and Library, Delaware

4.4 *The most common Victorian piano was the so-called square type illustrated here. Although parlor organs are relatively easy to date, assigning dates to square pianos is much more difficult. Square pianos were produced with relatively little exterior change for most of the second half of the nineteenth century. The instrument shown here, for example, with its rounded case design, C-scrolled lyres, and massive cabriole legs, was informed by neo-Rococo design ideas of the 1850s, but it was still being advertised and sold in 1880.*

Square piano
Trade catalog of Chickering & Co.
New York, 1880
The Winterthur Library

STYLE 1.—Rosewood. 7 Octaves. SQUARE. Front Corners large round. Square Back. Double Mouldings on Plinth. New Patent Agraffe Bridge throughout. Handsome Fret Desk and Carved Legs.

protective enclosure for standardized, mass-produced works and was consequently fairly consistent in configuration, but the musically superfluous upper section was another matter. Often architectural in form, it frequently rose high on the wall, contributing to the verticality of the object and its ability to dominate a room visually (4.5); like hallstands and sideboards, parlor organs were often the most prominent object in a room.[7] This upper section included shelves, brackets, and niches for displaying a variety of objects, and sometimes a mirror as well. Thus, while the piano remained largely a musical instrument handsomely cased (4.6), the parlor organ was both a musical instrument with an elaborate enclosure and a piece of furniture. Its upper section incorporated functions associated with the mantel, the étagère, and the whatnot.

Such syntheses or compressions of functions extended beyond portable objects. A similar pattern can be seen in designated room use in nineteenth-century America, where it usually correlated with economic factors. Middle- or working-class people often compressed into a single room—the parlor, for instance—artifacts and activities for which the affluent created several specialized spaces. The wealthy installed tiers of paintings in clerestory-lit galleries in their mansions,[8] but people of moderate means hung a few chromolithographs on their parlor walls and selected an image of special significance for display on a fabric-draped easel. While the affluent might place a Steinway or Chickering grand piano and a richly carved étagère in the same spacious drawing room (4.7), those with limited means and small spaces synthesized musical and display functions in the more spatially efficient organ and installed it in the bourgeois parlor. The organ occupied only about one-third of the floor space taken up by a conventional square piano and even a smaller proportion of the greater area required for a grand piano. It is a historical irony that because of its synthesis of functions, the parlor organ, in some ways the product of limited means, has become a richer object for today's historians to interpret than the once more prestigious piano.

Despite its fancy woodwork, its shelves and brackets, the parlor organ cost less than the piano. Organ works were so inexpensive that in the 1870s and 1880s the

4.5 *A shrine within a shrine. This is the parlor of the Henry Ford Birthplace as installed at the Henry Ford Museum. The practice of enshrining birthplaces of the great reveals the unconscious at work, the perpetuation of some unreasoned cosmology that operates deep within our culture. The cult of birthplaces demonstrates the enduring attraction of origins, of beginnings. Visiting these sites, these shrines, becomes an act of renewal. The focal point and visual culmination of this secular shrine is the parlor organ. In its own day a shrine to domestic virtues, this parlor organ is now the centerpiece of a shrine to the powers and forces that begat Henry Ford.*

"New Salon" parlor organ
Manufactured by Estey Organ Co., Brattleboro, Vermont, c. 1885
Parlor of the Henry Ford Birthplace
Henry Ford Museum & Greenfield Village, Michigan
(Negative No. B2393)

4.6 *A space for the arts. In the homes of the affluent, whole rooms were often set aside for music and collections of paintings and other artworks. In this drawing room, an entire wall was adorned with a broad band of oil paintings, each dramatically set off by its own massive, gilded frame. Centered on the wall, ceremonially draped with fabric, was a square piano like that illustrated in Figure 4.4. For much of the century, the natural habitat of the square piano was the upper-middle-class home.*

Photograph of a square piano and oil paintings
Drawing room of the Richardson House, Oswego, New York, c. 1890
Oswego County Historical Society Collection

4.7 *The grand was the top of the piano line. It was the most expensive; it produced the fullest sound; and it occupied the most space. Grand pianos were prestige items. Their occurrence in a domestic setting was evidence of considerable affluence.*

Photograph of a Steinway grand piano in its elegant setting
Drawing room of the George Price Crozer home, "Netherleigh"
Upland, Pennsylvania, c. 1880
The Winterthur Library: Joseph Downs Collection of Manuscripts and Printed Ephemera, No. 76 × 86.7

average parlor organ, even with extensive casework, sold for less than half the price of an average piano.[9] Parlor organs were also more closely linked to changing styles and fashions (4.8). It is often difficult to date a piano by looking at its case. Square and grand pianos in the style of the 1850s were still in production in the 1880s and, in some instances, as late as the turn of the century. By resisting changing fashions, the piano, like some other high-culture artifacts, both past and present, conveyed a sense of stability, permanence, and timeless good taste. The parlor organ, in contrast, was a sensitive barometer of style in popular furnishings; its casework today aids rather than hinders attempts at dating.[10]

This emphasis on stylishness points to a second irony of the parlor organ: Although the styles of organ cases were worldly, the object itself had persisting ecclesiastical associations.[11] Thus the parlor organ combined the sacred and the profane. If the piano was largely an instrument for secular music in secular contexts, both by sound and history the organ was linked with the church. Parlor reed organs were descendants, albeit distant, of church pipe organs. The parlor organ may then be said to represent the intrusion of the church into the Victorian home. It was a major material culture component of the religion of domesticity. Finally, cost, size, religious associations, documented original ownership, and other factors indicate that the Victorian parlor organ was primarily a part of middle-class culture. Its examination enriches our picture of bourgeois America in the last century.

When people purchased a parlor organ (4.9), they could not have foreseen all the subtle ways it would alter their lives, nor could they envision all its communicative possibilities. They may have had a vague sense that it would in some way mark a milestone in their lives, compartmentalizing and marking time. Buying a prominent object like a parlor organ might initiate a new chapter in a group of interrelated lives by providing not only a new way to use time but also a new tool to measure time. In later years, the object would serve to remind its owners of the day it first entered their home, of the time that had passed since then, and of memorable events that had taken place. It would not only structure their present but their perceptions of their own past.[12]

4.8 *Of its time. The design of this trade catalog cover and the organ illustrated on it share the same aesthetic. Both were aggressively modern compositions when created. Unlike pianos, which changed relatively slowly over time, the exteriors of parlor organs changed rapidly and visibly during the peak years of the object's popularity. Although pianos were understood to transcend fashion, cheaper parlor organs exploited stylistic change to promote sales.*

Cover
Colored wood engraving
Trade catalog of the Packard Orchestral Organ
Fort Wayne Organ Co., Fort Wayne, Indiana, 1884
The Winterthur Library

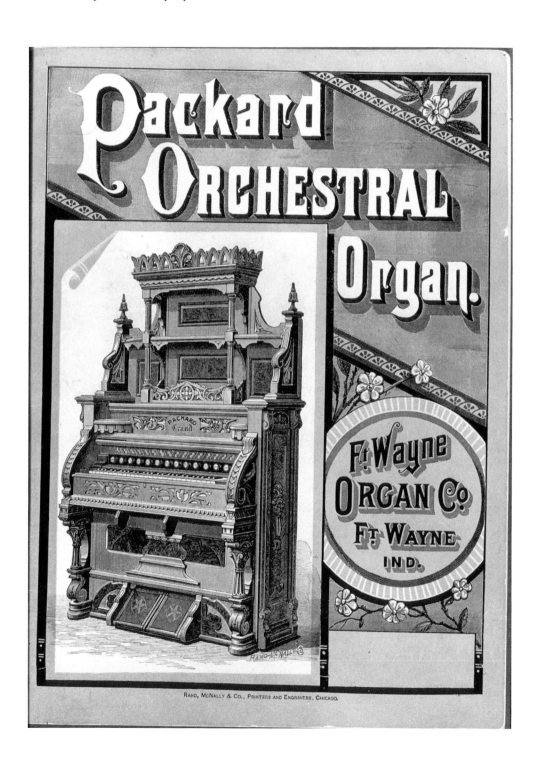

4.9 *The magic moment of transformation. A parlor organ is delivered, and a new chapter opens in someone's life. The purchase of such a major item facilitated or even necessitated a redefinition of self. People who acquired this desirable object were different and in some way superior to those who did not, at* *least in their own eyes. With the arrival of this object came not only a change in status but also a whole range of new opportunities, ranging from making music, socializing, learning, and setting new goals and objectives to merely rearranging furnishings or throwing out or displacing something old.*

A parlor organ being delivered
Photograph by Andrew Dahl, c. 1875
Vicinity of Madison, Wisconsin
State Historical Society of Wisconsin,
Madison

They also knew from experience that purchasing a major object could be a significant and momentous occasion in itself, a time of heightened positive emotions and feelings of well-being, importance, and power. They knew, although we cannot say to what extent they expressed it, that a major purchase would transform them in their own eyes and in the eyes of others. They would become worth more on the social and pecuniary scales and would acquire greater status. By so doing, they would receive more respect and deference from others. These, in turn, would make them feel better about themselves. In short, buying a parlor organ could make them something they had not been before. With this object, they might construct new or expanded selves.[13]

In addition to these very real and important feelings about the transformational potential of the act of purchase, people had other specific functions they expected parlor organs to perform and certain statements about their positions in society, their attitudes and values they hoped to make through purchase of the object. These were not necessarily stated, for people are often silent about and even unaware of their own motivations.[14] One way to gain access to those concealed or unarticulated motivations is to examine pictorial sources from the period, particularly advertising.[15] Designed to sell products, advertising images of the nineteenth century generally appealed to and endorsed the values of mainstream America. Profit lay in giving the society what it wanted, not in trying to reform it. Advertising exploited the shared fictions of Victorian America.

Advertising is sometimes described as a sinister plot to generate artificial needs in people and then to sell those people products that meet those needs. A more cynical view is that advertising generates bogus needs in order to sell unending waves of consumer goods that inevitably fail to meet those needs. In both scenarios, advertising is presumed somehow to alter negatively the basic conditions of human life, to falsify some underlying, more authentic, more noble essence of humankind. This point of view gives advertisers—and people in general—more credit than they deserve, for advertising is hardly capable of altering the basic needs of a society. What distinguishes capitalist society is not the invention of new needs but a rapid succession of alternative and competing solutions proposed to meet persisting needs. Advertising creates desires, but it does not create needs; needs already exist. What some advertisers have done with great success is to identify and exploit those needs. The most successful advertising also responds to people's values and ideals, hopes and dreams, fantasies and delusions, and even their weaknesses and insecurities. It is the packaging of this complex bundle of factors that makes advertising fascinating to historians, anthropologists, sociologists, psychologists, and others interested in the dramas of continuity and change in human culture and the human psyche.

The advertising images designed to promote the sale of parlor reed organs provide valuable clues about Victorian society in general and about how Victorians thought parlor organs might fit into their lives in particular. From the little vignettes lithographed on trade cards, we gain considerable information about the hopes, dreams, and insecurities the Victorians thought the parlor organ might address. As it turns out, advertising provides access to this inner reality better than many other classes of documents.[16]

An examination of advertising imagery reveals four clusters of needs Victorian Americans expected a parlor organ to meet: They expected it to help them engage in and extend conventional social roles; achieve social and cultural continuity over time; ensure social bonding over space, whether it be of a couple, a family, or some larger group; and enhance their lives through the self-actualization and interaction with others it would make possible. These expectations overlap; it might be more accurate to describe them as different ways to sustain social order.

CONVENTIONALIZED ROLES

Like playing the piano in the home, playing the parlor organ was an attribute of the genteel Victorian lady. It fit within that broader category of the cultivation of refined sensibilities considered appropriate to the female role (4.10). In Hamlin Garland's boyhood home, for example, only his sister knew how to play the melo-

4.10 *Stereotypical female gentility. Women were the keepers of culture and of manners. Women were also delicate, fragile, vulnerable, sweet, and innocent. The sentimentalized image on this book cover captures the dominant culture's ideology of womanhood. The avoidance of a directly frontal pose, the downward tilt of the head, and the absence of eye contact are all ways in which female modesty, passivity, and subjugation were represented and reproduced. The rustic* frame around the image "naturalizes" the cultural content.

Book cover
Black and gold embossed on dark blue cloth, applied chromolithograph in the center
Decorum: A Practical Treatise on Etiquette and Dress
New York: Union Publishing House, 1880
Photograph by Craig Williams

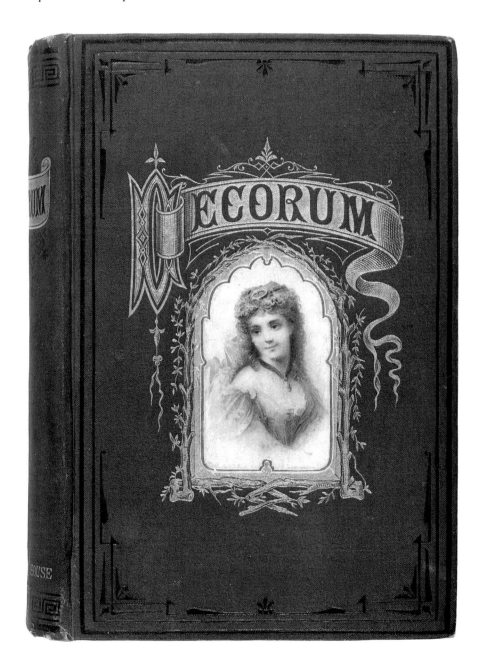

4.11 *Queen of the domestic sphere. Playing a keyboard instrument within the home was an appropriate attribute of the genteel lady. Women were acculturated to use the power of music to socialize and educate men and children. The illustration on the cover of this book of music follows cultural convention in showing a woman at the keyboard of an early parlor organ. The presence of the nine other figures is important. They show that she is not playing for her own amusement or enjoyment but, appropriate to her role, is engaging in activity for the benefit of others. Here is female unselfishness (or selflessness) reified. Here, her culturally constructed satisfaction comes from providing the occasion for a decorous, multigenerational experience.*

Book cover
Printed paper on pasteboard
William H. Clarke, Home Recreations for the Parlor Organ: A Collection of New Songs and Instrumental Pieces
Boston: S.D. & H.W. Smith, 1867
Photograph by Craig Williams

deon, a forerunner of the parlor organ.[17] Garland's family situation was typical. In most nineteenth-century pictorial materials showing someone playing an organ within a domestic environment, that person is female (4.11). In the outer world of the stage or the church, roles are reversed, and males are typically shown at the keyboard. Context is clearly the determining factor in this gender casting. This sexually stereotyped behavior is repeated through scores of normative images that support the now-familiar argument that the nineteenth century witnessed the heightened division of male and female realms. Today, references to a masculine world of commerce and industry outside the home and a feminine world of domesticity and childrearing within—a male world of energy and action, a female world of sentimentality and reflection—seem not merely trite but offensive, oppressive, objectionable. In the 1870s and 1880s, this division was viewed positively by many who shared the dominant culture. Advertising images and photographs of parlor organs in homes consistently link them to the culturally constructed feminine sphere. The parlor organ was presented as an occasion to display feminine accomplishment. Not only was playing the organ an elegant skill in itself but the ability to play made possible the successful performance of a whole string of socially valued tasks.

To maintain that the ability to play a parlor organ was merely an aspect of being an ornamental lady or a manifestation of what Veblen called conspicuous leisure is to oversimplify and trivialize the matter.[18] As Ann Douglas argued, "the lady's function in a capitalist society was to appropriate and preserve both the values and commodities which her competitive husband, father, and son had little time to honor or enjoy; she was to provide an antidote and a purpose to their labor."[19] The roles of consumer and saint (4.12) were combined in the genteel nineteenth-century woman. Among her "saintly" functions was the performance of what might loosely be identified as clerical or priestly duties within the home. If the parlor organ represented, as I have argued, the intrusion of the church into the household, it was woman who presided over those churchly activities within the home that were centered on the parlor organ.[20]

It is a commonplace that people use goods to play roles and that, in turn, they use those roles to define themselves. In this way, playing a parlor organ helped a woman fulfill herself as a genteel lady and moral mother. It allowed her to demonstrate the moral and spiritual superiority conventionally attributed to women. Indeed, it helped her construct her own self-identification. With the self-consciousness typical of the age, she could watch herself—sometimes literally, in the mirror in the upper section of the parlor organ case—and hear herself, just as literally, being a genteel lady, enacting the role written for her by the larger society. By playing the parlor organ, she brought beauty into the home. She sensitized her family and friends to accepted episodes of the world's music. By playing the organ, she could set the

4.12 *Intimations of sainthood trivialize and distort a story of systematic victimization. She, trapped at home by the doctrine of separate spheres and a double social standard, has been waiting for him to return. She waits anxiously because conventional gendering of behavior and opportunity have made her dependent on him. If he does not return, she may find herself destitute, with small children to care for and no marketable skills. The tragedy of her circumstance is muted and obscured by the clever, and manipulative, reversal of roles. She, in fact socially powerless and dependent, plays the role of mother. He, holder of much greater legal, cultural, and physical power and subject to fewer social restrictions, takes on the role of the naughty child. Thus the very real imbalance of power and the pressing pragmatic reasons for her concern are undercut and brushed aside. Behind the two figures looms their double bed, symbol of their conjugal union—and of her subjugation—and sardonic commentary on the pious injustices of Victorian culture. To Victorian audiences, this image demonstrated the moral superiority of women, a superiority women displayed at the keyboard as well as waiting alone by the fireside in the wee hours of the morning.*

The Old, Old Story Was Told Again at
3 O'Clock in the Morning
*Chromolithograph, unknown printer,
probably eastern United States, 1870–1880
Photograph by Ted Beblowski*

THE OLD, OLD STORY WAS TOLD AGAIN AT 3 O'CLOCK IN THE MORNING.

tone of the household, establish its mood, its character. In short, the parlor organ enabled her better to embrace the role of the bourgeois Christian lady.

Gospel hymns and parlor organs were popular at about the same time.[21] At first glance, these cultural forms may not seem closely related. Hymns are for churches, after all, and parlor organs for homes. But sales of sheet music, the contents of books of organ music, personal recollections, and other forms of evidence give plenty of reason to believe that these hymns were sung in the home to the music of the parlor organ. Thus the links between the larger world and the smaller world, the church and the home become clear. The microcosmic activities within the home take on macrocosmic meanings. The parlor organ was assuredly a tool for extending female influence over the family. Female power within the home, however, was related to broader currents of social, cultural, and religious power outside the home. The parlor organ was the link that joined together those two spheres of power.

By assuming major responsibility for home life, women also helped preserve and promote socially functional values and behaviors. The parlor organ was an element within an elaborate normative system that unified the home and the outside world (4.13). For many, the possession of a parlor organ was a nonverbal statement of affiliation with that system. Victorian life was, however, built on contradictions—and apparent contradictions. If woman might be both consumer and saint, as Douglas claims, the parlor organ could be both a product of materialism and a producer of spirituality. The intense materialism and fervent revivalism of the last century, presumably antithetical, were both accommodated in the parlor organ and in Victorian culture. In acquiring the fashionably detailed object, woman's desires as a consumer were satisfied. Yet, once purchased, the object became a useful tool for fulfilling her saintly role, which she also desired. Thus apparent opposites were reconciled, desires made congruent, demonstrating not only objects' capacities to perform widely varied and seemingly opposing functions but also the falseness of the conventional dichotomy between materialism and spirituality, a falseness the Catholic church had recognized centuries before and which American Protestants found increasingly acceptable in the nineteenth century.

4.13 *Connections. Ironies. Contradictions. According to prevalent ideology, women were both powerful and weak. Male-dominated society sanctioned female power within the domestic realm but resisted it in public. Women's power in the public realm was understood to operate indirectly and through others. As the subtitle here put it, "The housewife makes the home and the home makes the nation." The imagery within the central sphere was carefully chosen to underline this principle. Plants at the* window *suggest nurture, caring, and the natural order. Food on the table addresses family maintenance and nurture. The shelf of books endorses literacy and learning, while the cradle specifically invokes maternity and the cycle of human life. It also alludes to the familiar deceit that the hand that rocks the cradle rules the world.*

Pictorial banner
The Housewife, *December 1888*
The Winterthur Library

CONTINUITY OVER TIME

The parlor organ was a nonverbal statement of belief in the importance of perpetuating values, behaviors, and social affiliations over time. If the object's elaborately stylish case proclaimed the value of change, some of its uses endorsed continuity. Advertising and other images are rich in references to continuity. One Mason & Hamlin trade card, for example, skillfully synthesizes words and images into a cohesive ideological package (4.14). At the bottom of the image appear the words "Church, Chapel & Parlor Organs." On one level, these words indicate the range of goods manufactured by the firm. On another, the linking and ordering of the words suggest both a logical association of the three places and a hierarchy, descending from church through chapel to parlor. Strung together in this way, these words confirm the ecclesiastical associations of the artifact and establish a parallel between the formal, institutionalized worship within a church, presided over by a male, and the less formal socialization within the home, presided over by a woman.

4.14 *Selling family, selling religion, selling materialism, selling organs. This trade-card image is small but powerfully manipulative. Fashionably dressed people, all seeming intelligent, thoughtful, and well-socialized, gather around a new Mason & Hamlin organ. Performing a stereotypical role, a woman plays the organ and facilitates cross-generational bonding. The central location of the organ suggests that it is inseparable from this web of activities, values, and beliefs.*

Chromolithographed trade card
Mason & Hamlin Organ Co., Boston,
c. 1890
The Winterthur Library: Joseph Downs Collection of Manuscripts and Printed Ephemera, No. 71 × 247.13, Album No. 35

As the young woman in the Mason & Hamlin advertisement performs her sexually stereotyped role of playing the organ, other members of the family gather near her. The act of playing the organ provides an occasion for three generations of her family to assemble. The meditative and reflective expressions on their faces suggest that their souls and spirits are uplifted by sharing the melody and its sentiments. Outside the window, the tapering spire of a church points heavenward against the sunset sky, casting a sacred benediction over the assembled family group. This diminutive vignette is thus framed top and bottom by ecclesiastical references: the words "church" and "chapel" at the bottom, the church spire at the top.

This image also efficiently exploits the popular appeal of three clusters of associations, each designated by a single powerful word: mother, home, and heaven (4.15).[22] In this picture, as presumably in the larger American society, mother performs a gender-typed role within her home, within her sphere of influence, instilling Christian virtues and values in the family and preparing them for their eventual home in heaven. In this view of the family, no male of working age is present; he is presumably working to support the leisurely and spiritually uplifting activities of those within the image.

Specific references to continuity, to connectedness, to relatedness over time, across generations, appear in the organ advertisement through the juxtaposition of people of widely different ages: the small child, the middle-aged mother, the grandparents. Yet the advertisement shown in Figure 4.14 also contains within it a more succinct Victorian cliché for continuity: the image of the very young and the very old side by side. This formulation is common in the nineteenth century and occurs on the canvases of high-culture artists (4.16) as well as in inexpensive prints for a mass audience. In an 1866 painting by Junius R. Sloan, a young girl practices her knitting under the watchful eyes of an old woman (4.17). Knitting is a form of needlework long understood as an appropriate activity for women, indeed, as a central component of women's role. By placing the scene in an undatable vernacular interior, Sloan suggests that the activity is traditional, venerable. The old woman represents the past and past ways; the young girl's presence is an assurance that

4.15 *Ideology made visible. This pictorial book cover is rich in meaningful symbols. The title is enclosed within a sphere that includes a nonverbal presentation of the same theme. At the left is a portion of a fireplace, literally referring to hearth and, more emblematically, to Home. Beside the fireplace sits a smiling Mother holding a child, while another child approaches. Above this terrestrial scene flies an angel, an emissary from Heaven. Outside this sphere or disk are other images that reinforce this conservative ideology. The house is not only a single-family, free-standing structure but is located in the country, with no other buildings in sight. The chickens suggest farming and self-sufficiency, the wellsweep old-time ways and values, and the child with hoop, the joys of innocent childhood. The prominent branch entering from the left, supporting a bird feeding its nesting young, again stresses the "naturalness" of this imagery and the values it promotes.*

Book cover
Black and gold embossed on ochre cloth
Golden Thoughts on Mother, Home, and Heaven
Philadelphia: Garretson & Co., 1878–1882

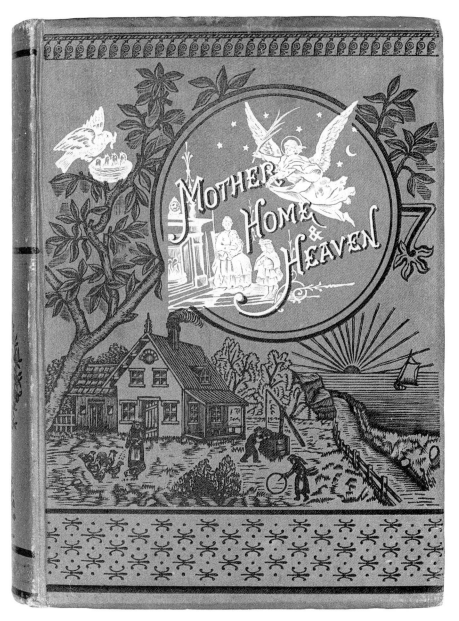

4.16 *A Victorian cliché in the making. This unfinished drawing exploits a popular pictorial device for indicating cultural continuity: the very old and the very young side by side.*
Unfinished drawing of an old woman and a child
Eastman Johnson, c. 1866
Ink, charcoal, and chalk on paper
Georgia Museum of Art, The University of Georgia
University purchase GMOA 77.3622
Photograph by Helga Photo Studio

4.17 *Passing on old ways to the new generation. This image centers on the long-standing association of women with textiles and needlework. Here, not only are skills transmitted but definitions of womanhood and appropriate female behavior as well. The scene takes place in an enclosed domestic space, with little or no evidence of an outside world. Hearth, knitting, and Bible are all prominent. This is also an image of nostalgia. Only the child is contemporary with the date of the picture. The old woman and all the visible material culture were formed in the first two decades of the nineteenth century. Painted in Victorian America, this image is free of Victorian things. And in the not-too-distant future, the little girl will be the only living link with this earlier time. Thus the image responds to a sense of impending cultural loss.*
The Knitting Lesson
Junius R. Sloan, 1866
Oil on canvas, mounted on masonite
Art Museum, Valparaiso University, Indiana

4.18 *"For everything there is a season . . . a time to be born and a time to die." The conjoined image of the very young and the very old is a confrontation with the passage of time, with mortality, with the inevitability of death. The child in this image, innocent and unaware, sleeps peacefully. The old man stares before him, meditating on what was and, perhaps, what was not and now cannot be.*

The Past and the Future
Frontispiece from T. L. Haines and L. W. Yaggy, The Royal Path of Life
New York: Standard Publishing House, 1881

4.19 *Eastman Johnson's famous variation on the theme of the ages of humankind. Here the motif of the very young and the very old is placed in the fuller context of the cycle of human life. The picture is dominated by the figure of work, the central theme of human existence. To one side a male and female, intent on each other, allude to sexual union and the reproduction of the species. He has returned from hunting and has laid before her, as offering and invitation, two gamebirds he shot. At the other side of the picture sit the marginal figures, the old man almost at the end of usefulness and the young child who has not yet entered the age of usefulness.*

Corn Husking
Eastman Johnson, 1860
Oil on canvas
Everson Museum of Art, gift of Andrew D. White, Syracuse, New York
Photograph by Courtney Frisse

the lore and learning of the past will be carried on to future generations. It is an assurance that, in the future, at least some things will be the same. The image is a nonverbal tale of temporal continuity, of ongoing connectedness.

The frontispiece of *The Royal Path of Life* deals with the same theme (4.18). In this image, an old man holds a sleeping child in his arms. While the child slumbers, the man stares vacantly into the space before him, presumably meditating on the passage of time, his own mortality, and the unending cycles of human life. The title beneath the engraving, *The Past and the Future*, states what was obvious to nineteenth-century viewers.

The designer of the Mason & Hamlin advertising card knew that contemporary viewers would understand the allusion to past and future and therefore continuity implicit in the close placement of the child and its grandparent (4.19).[23] Victorian Americans did not find the idea that a parlor organ might perpetuate values from one generation to another ridiculous or offensive. Quite the contrary, they sought mechanisms to retard change and fragmentation; the parlor organ seemed a likely candidate. Whether it had any appreciable impact on the course of human lives is difficult to know. What we do know is that Victorians were vulnerable to sales pitches built on the promise of continuity. To them, it seemed a reasonable expectation. A hope, at least.

BONDING OVER SPACE

If the parlor organ was perceived as a means to temporal continuity, it seems to have been even more important as a device for spatial or geographic continuity, or what might be termed *social bonding*. The goal of social bonding is to create or maintain amiable relations among people or groups of people, ranging from the intimate level of a couple to the more extended realm of an entire society or even several societies.[24]

At the level of the family, the parlor organ was advertised as a means to enhance and fortify the bonds of a marital pair or a nuclear family, to enhance relatedness and encourage intimacy. In an advertisement for the Packard Orchestral Organ (4.20), the wife is shown at the instrument, while her husband stands at her side; the organ and its music bring them together in a moment of intimacy. On the floor in the foreground, a small child plays with blocks. In this context, the child not only testifies to the drawing power of the organ but also sanctifies the relationship of the two adults and identifies the setting as domestic. Depictions of a man and woman in close proximity in an elegant environment were not always images of marital life; they could as easily be bordello scenes. The child functions as a signal that the situation is domestic and the close encounter of members of the opposite sex is socially nonthreatening. The child dispels potentially lascivious connotations.[25] Put in more positive terms, the presence of the child, healthy and well dressed like its parents, not only implies that the parlor organ belongs in the home of cultivated, well-mannered, attractive, and happily married people but is even a way of attaining those ends.

Photographs suggest that parlor organs meant a lot to consumers, for they depict the instrument prominently and repeatedly. In a photograph by Charles Van Schaick, for example, a parlor organ serves as a backdrop for a double portrait of an elderly couple in their Wisconsin home (4.21). The sitters and the photographer apparently agreed that the parlor organ provided a suitable and appropriate setting for the portrait. In fact, the organ is the largest and most prominent artifact in the photograph, the dominant element within the constellation of artifacts drawn together for this commemorative image. In this Wisconsin interior, the organ acts as a magnet, drawing to it not only the two sitters but also their extended families; three generations in portraits rest on the organ or hang on walls nearby. These images of relatives are augmented by attributes of learning and civilization, including books, music, an album, floral wallpaper with a frieze, a textile scarf on the table, doilies on the chair and lounge, a frilly glass vase on the organ, and, in the corner, a gold-framed print or photograph of some natural wonder. The parlor organ dominates this

4.20 *Music enlivens home life and brings the little family together.*
This trade card argues that a parlor organ is an appropriate component of genteel domesticity and that it promotes cohesion of the nuclear family. The elaborate table at the lower left, the large vase of flowers, and the profusion of textiles—upholstered footstool, rugs, curtains—all signal civilization and polite comfort. This world of conventional meanings is built on conventional roles; the genteel lady plays the organ.
Chromolithographed trade card for the Packard Orchestral Organ
Fort Wayne Organ Co., Fort Wayne, Indiana, c. 1885
The Winterthur Library: Joseph Downs Collection of Manuscripts and Printed Ephemera, No. 71 × 247.13, Album No. 35

4.21 *The upper section of this parlor organ held not only music but also books, a frilly glass vase, and photographs. The organ and the things on it were, in turn, flanked by framed portraits hung high on the wall. Together, all these objects formed not only a composition but also a shrine to home and family. The aggressive symmetry of the arrangement extends the equally aggressive symmetry of the organ case. Interlocking layers of meaning are sug-* gested by the photograph of the house centered on the organ, itself centered within a composition within a (the same?) house. To understand the difference money could make, compare this image with the interior of "Netherleigh" (see 4.7).
Mr. and Mrs. Simon in their parlor
Photograph by Charles Van Schaick, vicinity of Taylor, Wisconsin, c. 1900
State Historical Society of Wisconsin, Madison

accumulation of nonverbal communicators, becoming the focal point of a domestic shrine to learning, civilization, and familial continuity over both time and space.[26] In an uncanny way, distant and departed relatives and experiences are reunited at the parlor organ, and it becomes an element of stability in the face of aging and separation.

Division of space and time may, on occasion, be artificial or inappropriate, for space always implies time. Remembering another space always means remembering another, necessarily earlier time. Parlor organs, then, also become vehicles to carry memories. As such, they are doubly powerful. First, the object itself may bring to mind people who once played it or sang to its music. Second, the music played on it may generate memories unrelated to the musical instrument.[27] For music is one of the most emotionally stirring and affecting of cultural forms. From the rousing strains of national anthems to the haunting melodies of songs of love and remembrance, it has the power to move and transport people.[28] Music seems particularly important to people as they pass through the major stages that lead to adulthood. It is a rare person who does not attach special meaning to the music of his or her formative years. The memory-evoking qualities of music were heightened for Victorian Americans by the fact that a large proportion of popular lyrics dealt with days and experiences gone by. Memory and nostalgia were stock elements of Victorian popular music. The parlor organ and its music took people back over space and time to other days, other people, other times of union and bonding, real, fancied, or unattained.[29]

The parlor organ expressed affiliation beyond the limits of family and friends. In much the same way that it nonverbally suggested contact with other people for the elderly couple in their west Wisconsin home, the parlor organ became a popular and familiar symbol of civilization and community for Americans on the frontier. The rich associations of the parlor organ, as well as its synthesis of functions, made it valued evidence of contact and affiliation with the larger world. Both written and nonverbal evidence for this association are abundant. In Lady Mann's music school on the Idaho frontier (4.22), for example, the organ figures prominently as a device for bonding, affiliation, and learning. If it helps teach the children music, it also

4.22 *Music on the frontier. The parlor organ is the largest object in this cheaply furnished interior, where children learn music and appropriate social behavior. A girl plays the organ, a boy the violin. And here they are introduced to art and culture as it could be captured and conveyed with little money at great distance from an urban center. The room is self-consciously and deliberately adorned with pictures, small sculptures, photographs, flowers, and a clock. In the relative barrenness of this interior, each object seems to take on heightened symbolic and didactic significance.*
Cynthia Pease Mann with Snowden Reed, Emily Wood, Frank Wood, and an unidentified boy
Boise, Idaho, c. 1900
Idaho State Historical Society, Boise, 2024-1

educates them to social roles; boys are present in the photograph, but a girl is shown playing the organ. If the music the children learn is for the benefit of their local community, it serves both to bond them to that community by providing occasions for interaction and to affiliate them, still relatively isolated in sparsely settled Idaho, to the rest of Western civilization, both present and past.

Few images of the parlor organ's powers of linkage are more arresting than Solomon Butcher's photograph of the Hilton family at the edge of the Nebraska prairie (4.23). In this well-known image, family members flank this icon of civilization. Close behind them, a rude fence stands as a jagged and tentative barrier between culture and nature. At one level, the image seems silly, ridiculous, absurd. At another, sublime. Here again, we confront the hyperbole of the Victorian world. Fact is stranger than fiction. Powerful human and cultural dramas are performed before our eyes—and here the key player is an artifact, a parlor organ. Few images offer more convincing testimony that people are willing to believe that they are, to a large extent, what they own, that their selves, their identities are constructed from material culture.

4.23 *The parlor organ links them to the world they left behind. Members of the Hilton family squint into the sun as they pose for photographer Solomon Butcher, who may have mounted his camera on top of his wagon to obtain this view. In this stark environment, the parlor organ seems dramatically out of place, a bizarre and alien presence in a land still largely unshaped by human will.*

Photograph of Mr. and Mrs. David Hilton and children
North of Weissert, rural Custer County, Nebraska, c. 1880
Solomon D. Butcher Collection
Nebraska State Historical Society, Lincoln

SELF-ACTUALIZATION AND INTERACTION

Enhancing life by attaining a skill or sharing experience is implicit in the three situations we have discussed. In the case of the organist, achieving and demonstrating mastery or just competence to oneself or others can be immensely rewarding, allowing one to feel a sense of accomplishment and satisfaction. Success may even bring prominence and flattering attention. For those who sing along or only listen, there come the indescribable but very real delights of music, of being moved bodily and emotionally by the sounds and of forming, if only for a short time, that powerful emotional bond that unites those who make music together or share it. Singing together is a ritual of bonding well understood within many religions and social organizations. Like eating or drinking together, it generates communion through shared activity and fosters strong feelings of affiliation, belonging, even union, feelings that cannot be easily verbalized. As an agent for music, the parlor organ participated in one of humanity's most efficacious modes of generating feelings of positive identification with others, a mode perhaps exceeded only by—and perhaps therefore sometimes considered an appropriate prelude to—making love.[30]

In discussing the parlor organ's social function, the needs it met or was presumed to meet, my emphasis has been on the performance of established roles and the maintenance of bonds already formed. Yet the object's utility also reached a step further back to the initiation of roles and bonding. Put differently, we can say that the parlor organ was a tool for change as well as continuity. In a trade card distributed by the Estey Organ Company (4.24), for example, the arrangement of the visual information suggests formation rather than maintenance of bonds. The explicitly religious, familial, or marital associations of the previous images are absent in this interaction of elegantly dressed young people. While a pair of children gaze out the window at Estey's thriving industrial plant in Brattleboro, Vermont, and a chaperon sits in a lavishly upholstered chair at the left of the illustration, neither is the real subject of the picture. The larger area of the advertisement emphasizes the interaction of handsome, expensively attired young people. The delights and

4.24 *Estey offers a taste of the fashionable life. Parlor organ manufacturers did not always use piety and religion to sell organs. This card used secular materialism. While the seated chaperon at the left and the small children at the window were included to assure decorum and proper behavior, the image stressed a lavish lifestyle, affluence and grandeur, handsome men and beautiful women, all splendidly attired, all well mannered, all accessible.*

Chromolithographed trade card
Estey Organ Co., Brattleboro, Vermont,
c. 1885
The Winterthur Library: Joseph Downs
Collection of Manuscripts and Printed
Ephemera, No. 71 × 247.11, Album No. 34

excitements of the fashionable life are the real theme of this advertisement; with the Estey organ, the world of high culture, of the Victorian equivalent to the "beautiful people," might be attained. The setting radiates richness through the luxurious rugs, window hangings, wallpapers, furniture, ceramics, sculptured bust, plants, and other trappings of the life of affluence and abundance.

The organ shown in this advertisement is one of the most expensive produced by the firm for domestic use, Estey's Grand Salon Organ, style 900. This model approached the piano in price and perhaps in secular associations for the setting illustrated in the advertisement is fashionable and worldly, only slightly modified by the domesticating and sanctioning devices of children and chaperon.[31] Thus the parlor organ may also have meant upward mobility through social interaction to some people. Although in certain contexts the instrument may have served to promote continuity, in others it initiated mobility and the breaking or at least straining of old bonds. These variations, even contradictions, in function are not lodged in qualities within the objects. The same object could be used for completely different purposes by different people. Objects are receptacles for people's projected needs and desires.

MEANING THROUGH INTERACTION

Because objects are receptacles, because they have little if any inherent meaning but only the meanings people make of them, there can be no real certainty in discovering the meanings of such objects as parlor organs or in nailing down exactly what they communicated nonverbally to people in late Victorian America. While I have outlined some of the social functions of the parlor organ in Victorian America, some of the needs it was presumed to meet, and offered a few guidelines for interpretation, I want to conclude by stressing the uncertainties that remain. For it is one thing to analyze the sales pitch of an advertisement and another to determine which, if any, of the many and sometimes conflicting possibilities were meaningful to any given individual or group of individuals. Put another way, there may be considerable difference between the public meanings of objects as expressed in advertising imagery and the personal or private meanings that the objects had for their owners and users. What, for example, can historians say about Charles Van Schaick's photograph of two girls at a parlor organ (4.25)? We know the image records a modest interior in the vicinity of Black River Falls, Wisconsin, in the early years of the twentieth century. But with which of the previously discussed images can it fairly be juxtaposed? Certainly it resembles all the advertisements in showing a woman acting out a sexually determined role. Yet the humble surroundings, the inexpensive rocking chairs, the plant in the paper-wrapped tin can in the window, and the crazed window shade strongly contrast with the elegant or at least prim settings of the prescriptive images. The discrepancy between those advertisements and this photograph reminds us not only how far dreams and hopes may depart from reality but how difficult it is for historians to move beyond generalized statements of meaning for some aspect of the past. The best we may be able to do is offer a range of plausible meanings in the hope that at least one may prove applicable to a given instance.

The interactionists have shown how people make meanings when they interact with objects.[32] People may receive and share generalized meanings current in society, yet they may also generate a realm of very private meanings that, if never recorded or shared, slip away with few traces or clues. This distinction runs parallel to that between what Berger and Luckmann call "objective facticity" and "subjective reality."[33] About objective facticity, there is little question or debate. This Van Schaick photograph records the demonstrable fact of two young women at a parlor organ in a room of describable artifacts. But the subjective reality of the moment, of the interaction of these two people, is locked inside their minds and inaccessible to us. To historians' frustration, while the available evidence can be combed for clues, the conclusions can never be more than tentative.

In this chapter, I have tried to widen the range of possible interpretations that might be offered for a prosaic artifact like the Victorian parlor organ. In doing so, I have also tried to demonstrate the value of advertising images as historical tools. Despite their limitations and obvious hyperbole, these combinations of words and pictures are useful reminders of some of the many subtle ways people use objects in their social lives. And, as noted earlier, it is remarkable how familiar some of those uses are. Today's advertising still appeals to many of the same values and needs, but it offers different products to sustain or fulfill them. In comparing Victorian needs and the goods created to meet them with modern needs and our own material culture, we are again struck by the force of both continuity and change. For the pitches in the advertisements all seem so familiar, so obvious, yet the goods seem so alien, so strange (4.26). But here we miss half the point. Parlor organs and all the other

4.25 *The dream object in the real world. What does it mean? How does it mean? Two young women share this modest setting with a Newman Bros. parlor organ and a few rocking chairs. The "objective facticity" of the moment has been captured by the camera and can be described in considerable detail. But the subjective reality experienced by these two women is irretrievable. Here we confront the limits of history. All people have, to varying degrees, outer lives and inner lives. Outer lives are objective facts and, like most facts, have limited meaning by themselves. Inner lives are subjective realities, difficult if not impossible to access. But within these subjective realities lie the keys to interpreting and making meaning of the outer life. The critical point is that neither parlor organs nor any other objects have fixed meanings. People make meanings—both knowable and unknowable—with, through, and about things.*

Two young women at a Newman Bros. parlor organ
Photograph by Charles Van Schaick, vicinity of Black River Falls, Wisconsin, c. 1910
State Historical Society of Wisconsin, Madison

4.26 *The end of a culture. Cultures are not organic or natural. They do not flower and then die. They are artifacts, products of artifice. They are constructed by people and, after time, they are demolished or abandoned by those people or, more likely, those who follow them. Sometimes, the end of a culture is catastrophic. More often, it is gradual and prolonged, and so historians have difficulty determining exactly when one culture eclipsed another. The culture that dominated Victorian America has been in large part abandoned, but pieces of it are still cherished. They lurk within living minds and still shape public and private life. This parlor organ was destroyed, but its likeness lives on into the present. So too Victorian culture.*

Aftermath of Flood, Mount Vernon, Indiana
Photograph by Russell Lee, 1937
Division of Prints and Photographs
Library of Congress

components of Victorian culture are surely strange, but so are the components of our culture. All cultures are strange because they are, like parlor organs, artifacts. They are arbitrary, artificial, tentative. Reflections on parlor organs thus bring us face to face with persisting realities of culture and life. Beneath the constructed, rationalized world of objective facticity, behind the undeniable, hard, tangible reality of things, always lurk the same dark shadows of subjective reality, the same unsolved mysteries, the same unanswerable questions. Only the surface, the superficial, can be known. The history of culture is the record of successive attempts to dispel those dark shadows, to explain those mysteries, to answer those unanswerable questions. But the darkness, the mysteries, the great questions still remain. And if we come no closer to overcoming or resolving them by studying parlor organs, hallstands, sideboards, and mottoes, we at least come closer to understanding some of the strategies mounted by one society to do so. We understand better some of the elaborate fictions one society created to keep at bay the terrifying realization that little of any real importance is known—or is knowable.

5 : Posture and Power

I n 1842 the French silhouette cutter Auguste Edouart created a composite silhouette of an extended American family of seven (5.1).[1] The picture was more elaborate than Edouart's typical products, which showed one or two figures against a stock lithographed background. Instead of his usual formulaic setting, Edouart painted in watercolor a highly detailed neoclassical interior, complete with carpet or floor cloth, square sofa, center table, pier glass with pier table below, astragal lamp, a collection of seashells, and lavish swags of expensive curtains at the windows. The background alone is a useful document of fashionable furnishing in New York in 1842.

The large number of figures, while not unknown in silhouettes, is uncommon; it gives the picture significance to historians of this medium and, more broadly, to those who study group portraiture. A group portrait is more than a collection of individual likenesses. As in all portraits, the challenge is to represent sitters in ways that meet their expectations and conform to cultural norms. Group portraiture, however, poses the additional challenge to likeness makers of arranging the figures in a plausible diagram of relationship and interaction. Edouart seems to have succeeded well on both counts.

If this silhouette provided only an accurate profile, literally and figuratively, of a family in its fashionable 1842 setting, it would have value as a historical document. But there is more going on here, and this image has further value. This silhouette also records cultural conventions, particularly those associated with age, gender, and power. And here the limitations of the silhouette medium literally help us see how these cultural conventions were represented in Victorian America.[2] Compared to painters or photographers, cutters of silhouettes have a narrow range of expressive devices at their disposal. Placement and outline are the two most obvious. Placement reveals relationships; outline reveals physical features and clothing—and it reveals posture. To some extent, posture is determined by physiology and by such psychic factors as self-esteem, but it is also, perhaps even more, shaped by culture. My emphasis here is on posture, particularly sitting posture, as an artifact. Posture

5.1 *A profile of power. This silhouette reveals not only the physical features of a family but also their power relationships. The adult male sprawled across the middle of the image dominates a group of subservient women and children. His posture is expansive, relaxed, and authoritative. Theirs is more introverted, controlled, and submissive.*

Silhouette of a New York City family
Black paper on a watercolor background
Cut by Auguste Edouart, dated 1842
The Winterthur Museum

is a way of presenting the self conditioned and shaped by culture. In short, posture is material culture.

Edouart's silhouette offers alluring entry into the study of posture as material culture. Look again at the image. Edouart depicted seven figures: one adult male, four females of varying ages, and two children of unidentifiable sex. The composition is dominated by the male figure, in part because it is in the center and in part because it occupies the largest area. Other figures in the picture either stand or sit confined within their chairs. The male sits on one Grecian chair and leans back with his elbow resting on another.

The male is located at the power point of the picture. He is flanked by two standing women, one apparently middle-aged, the other younger. Moving from the middle to the sides of the picture, we encounter the two children and finally the two older women, identifiable by their bonnets and facial features. What might have seemed at first an informal family interaction turns out to be a diagram of social power, with both a center and margins.

Some figures stand; some sit. There is meaning here. When a mixed group of standers and sitters occurs, seating belongs to those of highest status and to those due deference or special privilege (5.2).[3] The male in the Edouart silhouette sits because of his high status, the old women because of their frailty, vulnerability, and venerability. While the two standing women occupy relatively high status within this group because they are at the peak of their physical powers, for a variety of cultural and ideological reasons they still stand, literally, in something of a servant relationship to the others.

In this image, those who sit are not peers. If sitting has meaning, so do where someone sits and the way someone sits. Edouart's attention to center and margins has already been noted. Equally important communication is located in the ways sitters arrange their bodies and engage the space around them. It becomes clear at once that clothing plays a critical role here. Because of differences in clothing, male and female bodies not only look different but are enabled or empowered to greater or lesser degrees.[4] Outline is created both by clothing and by posture, working in collusion, conspiring to the same ends. People are gendered both by their clothing and by their posture.

The older women at either side of the picture hold their arms and legs relatively close to their bodies. Their silhouettes are smooth, flowing, confined, even introverted. The silhouette of the male, in contrast, cuts a jagged pattern across the picture. One hand forward, one elbow back, feet kicking out into space, the male's contour is irregular, unconfined, dynamic, extroverted. The seated women project passivity and restraint. The male projects assurance, confidence, power, control.[5]

Still more can be said about sitting, power, and gender in this image. The two elderly women both sit erect, backs pulled away from their chairs. The male leans back, not just on one chair but on two, in an easy, comfortable, confident, natural-looking posture of dominance. The extent to which and the ways that people engage objects, the extent to which they dominate or are dominated by those objects, also

5.2 *When there are two people but only one chair, the person of higher rank sits. Photographs of young married couples taken in the second half of the nineteenth century often adopt the convention shown here. The more powerful male sits. The female stands, demonstrating the submissiveness and obedience her society expects of her.*

Photograph of a young couple Charles A. Tenney, Winona, Minnesota, dated 1884

provide evidence of their culturally constructed character, their roles, their positions within power structures. Here too is communication.

The Edouart silhouette of 1842 shows that there is meaning in the commonplace activity of sitting. In Victorian America, the posture of sitting was generally facilitated by artifacts of seating. In analyzing the Edouart silhouette, I have commented at length on posture but have said little as yet about chairs. Chairs are the other half of the culturally constructed performance called sitting. They are designed to allow or suppress a variety of postures. Once created, chairs are used by people who conform to or violate the postures enabled by and asserted by these objects. From patterns in this conformity and violation come still further meanings.

The following discussion is about the ways in which people in Victorian America used chairs and postures to construct identities and to reveal them. My emphasis is on three discrete postures and the artifacts that facilitated or sustained them: formal sitting, tilting, and rocking. Each of these was distinctive, recognizable, and meaningful. Although physical comfort, insofar as that can be measured objectively, was an active agent here, careful examination of nineteenth-century imagery suggests that ideology played an even greater role. In Victorian America, sitting was not merely taking a load off your feet. It was a way to reveal character, gender, social class, and power.

FORMAL SITTING

Formal sitting was characterized by a combination of restraint and artfulness.[6] It took place in or was considered appropriate for settings and situations understood as public or ceremonial or both. Formal sitting was equivalent to official, on-stage behavior; it was meant for occasions when presentation of self was staged, controlled, held up for public scrutiny and evaluation.[7]

Formal sitting did not necessarily require formal furniture or even furniture at all. Nobility, dignity, and gentility could be expressed through body language alone and

5.3 *Personal dignity and aspiration to genteel values expressed without benefit of material culture. Victorians placed heavy emphasis on goods for conveying cultural meaning, but they acknowledged that body language by itself could eloquently reveal decency and personal nobility. The black man depicted here was understood to possess those qualities, but in order to render him nonthreatening to whites, he was also portrayed as docile, submissive, and deferential.*

The Chimney Corner
Eastman Johnson, 1863
Oil on cardboard
Munson-Williams-Proctor Institute Museum of Art, Utica, New York
Gift of Edmund G. Munson, Jr.

without artifactual props (5.3). Within genteel homes, however, formal sitting was one of the major performances that took place in the highly self-conscious realm of the highly furnished parlor.[8] There it was artifactually endorsed and enforced by the distinctive constellation of seating forms known as the parlor suite. The formulaic Victorian parlor suite seems to have been developed in the 1850s. The concept was fully codified by the 1860s (5.4) and dominated the 1870s. Like hallstands, side-boards, and many other domestic artifacts, it was rethought in the 1880s and went into decline in the 1890s.

In the 1870s, the conventional middle-class and upper-middle-class parlor suite consisted of seven pieces: a sofa, a gentleman's chair, a lady's chair, and four small chairs (5.5). What made this cluster of furniture a suite was its unified visual character. As the suites illustrated here show, the repetition of key elements of design and materials helped viewers recognize at once that these pieces were related; they were, in a sense, all parts of the same multicomponent artifact.

The parlor suite was one of the most explicitly courtly references within Victorian houses. The concept of an extensive set of matching or coordinated furniture—or even of rooms—had its origins in courtly contexts of the past, best exemplified by the grand furnishing schemes of French monarchs and aristocrats of the seventeenth and eighteenth centuries. While industrialization had dramatically reduced the cost

5.4 *Social structure reified. Suites were created by repeating distinguishable forms and motifs throughout the design of a related group of objects, in this case seating furniture. This repetition made it possible to recognize several different pieces of furniture as parts of the same system, of the same extended artifact. As in human societies, hierarchy was both present and evident. In Victorian parlor suites, high rank correlated with size,* *comfort, and cost. The highest-ranking form was the sofa. The lowest-ranking were small chairs with open backs.*
Parlor suite No. 6
Sales catalog of an unknown manufacturer, possibly Boston, c. 1870
The Winterthur Library: Joseph Downs Collection of Manuscripts and Printed Ephemera, No. 70 × 86

of furniture by the 1870s, the suite still carried with it connotations of the power to command labor and materials. Placed in a room, suites conveyed the message that the room had been furnished at a single moment by people with the means to do so. This new sense of pecuniary and social power was highly attractive to Americans who could remember a time when people of their social class could only construct their interiors piecemeal and over time, from unrelated or loosely related components. For many in Victorian America, suites were expressions of newfound power and status.

The formality of parlor suites was manifest in several ways. First, parlor suites enforced upright posture. In each of the four different forms in the suite, the back of the object was nearly perpendicular to the floor. When sitters conformed to the postures asserted by these objects, they sat bolt upright or nearly so, in a position that confirmed their status as competent human beings and projected both gentility and control.[9]

Second, parlor suites endorsed frontal sitting. The chairs and sofas themselves were very much backdrops, settings, props. They framed, contained, and presented their occupants much as elaborate settings present gemstones. When sitters arranged their bodies in conformity with the design of the objects, particularly the chairs, they necessarily sat in fully frontal positions. Upright, frontal sitting pos-

5.5 *These four forms made up a seven-piece parlor suite in the 1870s. Above, the sofa. Below, in the center, the gent's chair. On the right, the lady's chair. On the left, what was variously described at the time as a small chair, wall chair, or parlor chair; suites normally included four of these.*

Parlor suite No. 112
Sales catalog of Phoenix Furniture Co.
Grand Rapids, Michigan, c. 1878
Grand Rapids Public Library

ture has long been the dominant mode in depictions of seated rulers, whether those rulers be terrestrial or celestial. Examples range from Horatio Greenough's heroic statue of Washington and Jean Auguste Ingres's portrait of Napoleon, back over centuries of images of Christ and the Virgin Mary enthroned, to statues of Zeus and the pharaohs and queens of Old Kingdom Egypt. The regal and divine associations and antecedents of the posture contributed to its meaning in Victorian America.

Third, parlor suites encouraged static sitting. Although sitters might move about, shift their weight, lean one way or the other, the chairs themselves did not change their positions or configurations. The objects were fixed. People could move, but the objects made neither concessions to that movement nor offered encouragement. Stasis in objects implies stability, durability, permanence, security. Stasis in formal sitting posture also implies self-control, the triumph of the mind over the body, of reason over what the Victorians believed were powerful but less admirable forces within people. The issue of self-control became a near obsession for Victorian Americans.[10] The occasion for self-control provided by parlor suites fit into a much larger pattern of culturally shaped occasions for demonstrating controlled behavior and creating order.[11] As we see shortly, both tilting and rocking demonstrate a more relaxed attitude toward this conception of self-control.

The parlor suites illustrated here, and most suites created in Victorian America, were richly, even luxuriously upholstered. In the nineteenth century, upholstery and textiles were broadly equated with civilization. The civilizing process was in part a textiling process.[12] In the West, textiles had long performed honorific functions. Like suites of furniture and, for similar reasons, textiles were downwardly mobile in the nineteenth century, although they continued to retain their close association with status and luxury for most of the century. The yards of fine-quality fabric on these parlor suites of the 1860s and 1870s demonstrated the rise of civilization in dramatic, tangible, purchasable, and personally meaningful form.

Important tools for demonstrating and enforcing genteel behavior, parlor suites were a key means through which Victorians convinced themselves of the progress of civilization and the improved condition of their own household. Possession of a parlor suite was a mark of elevated social and financial rank, of higher standing in the social hierarchy. When we turn from examining the entire suite as a unified artifact to individual pieces within the suite and their relationship to each other, the idea of hierarchy takes on additional meaning. As I noted earlier, conventional parlor suites of the 1870s contained four different seating forms. An additional and critical point is that these forms were hierarchically arranged. The highest-ranking object was the sofa. It afforded the greatest space for sitting and allowed its sitters the greatest leeway in the selection of postures. It was the most expansive and expensive, the least restrictive form. By contrast, the chairs were designed for single occupancy. They were also divided into three distinct, visually separable classes. The top-ranked chair was the largest, usually fitted out with arms and padded armrests. The second-ranked chair was usually slightly shorter and had lower arms without padded armrests. In some designs the arms were little more than brackets. The lowest-ranking chairs were the four small chairs that completed the suite. These chairs had seats farther from the floor and of smaller proportions than those of the other chairs. Backs were also lower and less substantial. Many of these chairs had no arms at all.

Like society at large, these suites were a form of structured inequality. Encountering a parlor furnished with a parlor suite was to be reminded of inequality, of power and hierarchy. Such an encounter encouraged self-consciousness. It generated an awareness of social difference and social deference. Parlor suites reified distinctions. Their nineteenth-century users learned that within the system of formal seating, greatest status allowed the opportunity for greatest comfort. In short, rank had its privileges.

People who encountered parlor suites in the nineteenth century were also reminded that males outranked females. Sofas and small chairs seem not to have been gender specific, but the two large chairs were understood as gendered artifacts in Victorian America. The large chair was sometimes called an easy chair or a large easy chair but just as often a gent's chair or a gentleman's chair. The smaller chair was sometimes a small easy chair but also a sewing chair or a lady's chair. While not emphasized in a heavy-handed way—and even playfully treated in the story of Goldilocks and the three bears—gender hierarchy was nonetheless expressed.[13] The male chair was larger and therefore dominant, providing slightly more comfort, slightly more support than the female chair. The artifactual statement here was clear. Even in the feminized domestic sphere, males ranked higher on the scale of social power.

How were the objects actually used? Did men sit only in gent's chairs and women only in sewing chairs? What happened when only adult women were present? Where did children sit when parents or guests were present? When they were not? The evidence supports a conclusion that intuition also suggests: Sometimes people followed the social diagram expressed in the goods (5.6), and sometimes they did not. Regardless of actual behavior, Victorian parlors were furnished with a tangible statement of social distinction. To enter the parlor was to enter the presence of privilege, hierarchy, and deference. To enter a parlor furnished with a parlor suite was to encounter a transatlantic, bourgeoisified extension of courtly European culture.[14] To enter that room was to experience once again the self-consciousness generated by the hall and its furnishings, by the dining room, and, for that matter, by all the material culture of formal life. To enter that room was to enter an environment where artifice and artificiality were paramount.

TILTING

But a formal style of life grounded in courtly models was not universally accepted or universally encountered, nor did it remain unmodified. Notable resistance and alternatives to the courtly model appeared in popular culture long before the design reform movements of the 1870s. Some of this enduring resistance can be seen in sitting postures and seating furniture. If the formal tradition had long experimented with elegant artifactual frameworks for the middle posture between standing and reclining, Americans of the nineteenth century who were physically, culturally, or politically uncomfortable with this posture, its associations and meanings, devoted considerable energy to exploring postures and furniture for the terrain between upright sitting and reclining.[15] American fascination with the sitting–reclining continuum is at some level a rejection of, or retaliation against, European formal culture. Although issues of class and gender are relevant here, political sentiments also play a part. Attention to alternative postures and forms of seating furniture reveal conscious American resistance at a variety of social levels to the authority of European courtly models and to the European social and political structures sustaining those models. Some Americans conceived of themselves as culturally and politically located between "civilized" Europeans of the Old World and "natural" Indians of the New.[16] In this vision, neither alternative provided an appropriate model. The American way would be a new synthesis. Americans would map out new political and cultural terrain.

Interest in this new terrain was manifest in both posture and artifact. The posture was tilting, usually accomplished by leaning a chair back on its two rear legs. While specific seating forms were eventually generated to accommodate this posture (5.7), it flourished apart from them. My emphasis here is on the posture, not on those objects.

The artifactual manifestation was the rocking chair. The rocking chair enabled sitters to assume something like the posture achieved through tilting. Indeed, it allowed a dynamic continuum of postures from upright to nearly reclining. It also encouraged the continuous movement known as rocking, from which its name is derived. As practiced in the nineteenth century, tilting and rocking were related behaviors, but clearly they were not the same. In tilting, the sitter subjected the chair to a function for which it had not been explicitly designed. In rocking, the sitter conformed to the function expressed by the chair. Not surprisingly, these two behaviors tended to be gender linked. Tilting was normally associated with males, rocking more frequently with females. Together, they can be interpreted as manifestations of American nationalism. Contrasted, they suggest ways that this nationalism

5.6 *Following the formula. This Wisconsin family left the sofa in the house, but they brought the rest of the parlor suite outside and arranged the pieces around the marble-topped center table. Then, posing for Andrew Dahl's camera, they seated themselves according to rank. The senior male sat in the gent's chair on the left, the senior female in the lady's chair on the right. The others occupied the four small chairs. To judge from the group's facial expressions and posture, parlor suites were more often valued for their social and cultural meanings than for the physical comfort they provided.*

Family seated in front of their house
Photograph by Andrew Dahl, vicinity of Madison, Wisconsin, c. 1875
State Historical Society of Wisconsin, Madison

5.7 *The new technology accommodates tilting. At mid-century, most tilters still used chairs that had not been designed for the position. An imaginative inventor saw a need, and this was the result. Thomas Warren's centripedal spring chair drew on recent advances in the production of cast iron for forming the base and much of the upper section of the chair. Motion was made possible by the eight C-shaped steel springs under the seat. When this chair was in use, the base remained flat on the floor, but the upper section tilted freely in any direction the sitter leaned—and swiveled as well. This particular chair was popular for only a few years, but the idea survives today in the form of tilting and swiveling office chairs.*

Centripedal spring chair
Cast iron, steel, wood, and upholstery materials
Thomas E. Warren, American Chair Co., Troy, New York, c. 1850
State Historical Society of Wisconsin, Madison

was shaped by cultural conventions of gender. Taken one step further, they reveal the relationship of gender and power. In short, they show how, in the commonplace activity of sitting, ideology was made visible.

Tilting was not invented by Americans. Europeans were tilting back in their chairs in informal settings at least as early as the seventeenth century. This practice seems to have become commonplace in America by the early nineteenth century. Evidence for tilting is artifactual, pictorial, and verbal.[17] Careful examination of the back legs of ordinary chairs will often reveal disproportionate wear on the rear undersides of the feet. Sometimes wear is also visible on the upper backs of chairs where they rested or scraped against a wall. These clues, while subtle, are also widespread. They argue that tilting was a familiar posture in nineteenth-century America.

The pictorial record provides especially rich insights into the meaning of tilting. An early image is John Lewis Krimmel's *Village Tavern* of 1814 (5.8). Krimmel's painting depicts a public but very ordinary setting in which people of different ages, genders, and social classes mingle and interact. This is a republican, egalitarian image largely free of pretense, of formality, of courtly allusion. Off to one side a boy sits close to the stove, resting his feet on the grate and tilting back in a common Windsor chair. This vignette of tilting enjoys a reciprocal relationship with the rest of the picture. On one hand, the presence of tilting helps to deformalize the scene. It provides one of many clues that we are in the presence of unpretentious people. On the other hand, the larger setting serves to contextualize tilting, confirming that it is a posture, a mode of self-presentation appropriate to an egalitarian, informal environment.[18]

Informality, nonformality, even antiformality are persisting themes in depictions of tilting. J. G. Clonney's *Mexican News* of 1847 (5.9) shows two men of different ages seated on a porch. The older man is dressed in formal, sedate, even conservative attire. He sits firmly on an eighteenth-century high-backed chair. His hand holds a mochaware mug of traditional form. He is the product of earlier socialization, an embodiment of earlier values.

5.8 *Early image of tilting as a characteristic American male posture, complete with ambivalent meanings. The
young man on the left, tilting back on
a bamboo-turned Windsor chair, turns
from his newspaper to observe the family
drama being acted out at the table,
where a distressed wife and barefoot*
*child confront a drinking male. The
tension and conflict depicted here re-
verberated throughout the century as
males and females struggled to come
to terms with gender roles and expectations, with gender-connected limitations
and opportunities.*

Village Tavern
John Lewis Krimmel, 1813–1814
Oil on canvas
*Toledo Museum of Art, gift of Florence Scott
Libbey*

5.9 *Two generations, two cultures. The passive, elderly man on the right signifies earlier, more conservative ways. His clothing is staid and formal. He drinks from a low-technology, hand-decorated mochaware mug. He sits firmly in a crook-back chair probably made in the eighteenth century. His active and brash younger companion wears more assertive and informal dress. He pours his drink from a hexagonal pitcher in a current shape fashionably transfer deco-* *rated with a view of romantic scenery. He tilts back in a cane-seat fancy chair new or only a few years old. He belongs to the aggressive republicanism of the 1840s; the old man is part of the deferential society of the past.*

Mexican News
James Goodwyn Clonney, 1847
Oil on canvas
Munson-Williams-Proctor Institute Museum of Art, Utica, New York

Beside him sits a younger man, who seems brash and assertive. His clothing is more current. The transfer-decorated jug and glass tumbler beside him are new or nearly so. And his posture is different as well. As he reads his newspaper and offers commentary, probably unsolicited, to his companion, he tilts his newer-style chair back on its rear legs. Here, in this nondomestic setting, males of different generations communicate verbally and nonverbally.

What are we to make of the age difference so carefully depicted by Clonney? Are we to conclude that in the 1840s old men assumed one posture while young men assumed another? Is age the significant variable? Or are these two men meant to represent different cultures or phases of a culture? Both age and culture may be part of the message here, but culture is probably more significant. In his image of the younger man, Clonney was illustrating an emerging American type, a mythologized ideal. While it is dangerous to attempt to read the character of a painted figure, we have to recognize that painters gave their figures postures and expressions precisely in order to enable viewers to do so. Here those clues suggest boldness, assertiveness, irreverence. The figure seems alert, outspoken, independent. In short, he seems to be the mythic American republican male.[19]

Clonney's painted interaction of two figures and two cultures takes place on a porch, probably of an inn or tavern. Krimmel's scene had been set in a tavern. At first, differences between the two paintings might seem more striking. Krimmel painted an interior, Clonney an exterior. Krimmel painted many figures, Clonney only two. Krimmel included one woman, Clonney included none. But both pictures share a focus on a predominantly male culture. The male emphasis corresponds to the setting: Taverns were largely male domains. The more important lesson here is that tilting was largely a male posture that took place in environments either dominated by males or apart from women and their influence. This conclusion is borne out by subsequent imagery.

Krimmel and Clonney had both linked tilting to social contexts that might be described as popular or even as working class, at least in part. It is true that illustrators and writers sometimes used tilting to suggest that their characters or settings were of lower-class or working-class status. Yet, often the point was to demonstrate masculine behavior in a masculine sphere. When it came to tilting, gender was often more important than class. An illustration from *Harper's Weekly* of 1871 (5.10) shows three well-dressed and obviously affluent males enjoying themselves at Cape May. As they sit on the porch of a hotel, savoring their drinks and seemingly oblivious to the activity around them, one of them tilts his plank-seat chair back at a dramatic and precarious angle. In another illustration, this one from a Joel Chandler Harris novel published at the end of the century (5.11), the owner of the local newspaper, identified as a member of the gentry, tilts his chair back on its two rear legs during a scene of confrontation. In many other scenes, and in literary texts as well, the posture is repeatedly associated with males in a range of contexts that transcends social class.

This male posture of tilting is always literally an act of pulling back, of pulling away. While it is physically possible to tilt a chair forward on its two front legs, this is rarely done. The preferred posture of tilting backward creates distance, emphasizes separateness, controls connectedness. Tilting backward allows one to survey a situation better, to assume the role of spectator, of voyeur. It allows one to assess, to order, and to render more abstract a given situation. All this is congruent with what we know of conventional male patterns of thought and behavior.[20]

Tilting was not, however, a clear or consistent signal in nineteenth-century America. Although I have not attempted to trace it here, the posture has a history, as do the meanings attached to it. Some of these meanings reinforced one another, some were contradictory. A survey of images from the third quarter of the century gives some indication of the mixture of meanings associated with tilting at that time.

In J. G. Brown's painting *The Boat Builder* (5.12), tilting is associated with old-time values, with tradition, with the vernacular. The picture shows an old man tilting his traditional turned chair back against the unpainted door of his boat shed. He is accompanied by a variety of hand tools, a sleeping dog, and a boat. The setting is clearly unpretentious, clearly not formal. We see a utilitarian interior where unglamorous and unglamorized work takes place, a traditional interior where traditional

5.10 *According to stereotypical understanding, males will shed the trappings of civilization and gentility when left to their own devices. These obviously affluent men are fulfilling this cultural expectation as they lounge on a veranda in Cape May. They lean back and relax, savor their drinks, and ignore the bustling activity around them. As is so often the case, tilting and alcohol appear together. And, as usual, the meanings are mixed, contradictory, equivocal.*

Gossip, Cobblers, Romance
Engraved illustration from Harper's Weekly, *August 26, 1871*
Photograph by Craig Williams

5.11 *Tilting and superiority. In this scene, the Major tilts back in his Windsor office chair, teasing Hamp about a notice he threatens to put in the newspaper he publishes. The Major can sit as he pleases. He owns the paper, controls its content, and is white. The setting is Reconstruction Georgia, and Hamp has just been elected to the state legislature. But Hamp is black and defers to the higher-caste status of the Major.*

"Sholy you-all ain't gwine put dat in de paper, is you?"
Illustration by A. B. Frost
Joel Chandler Harris, The Chronicles of Aunt Minervy Ann
New York: Charles Scribner's Sons, 1899
Photograph by Craig Williams

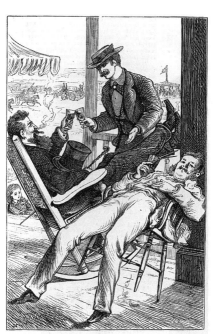

GOSSIP, COBBLERS, ROMANCE.

"Sholy you-all ain't gwine put dat in de paper, is you?"

5.12 *Tilting and tradition. This painting was created from a folkloric point of view, for it is a detailed visual ethnography of traditional boatbuilding. The authenticity of the image is certified by the obviously old and worn interior crafted from traditional materials, by the old hand tools and evidence of their informed use, by the low-technology wooden boat visible on the right and, above all, by the presence of the old*

boatbuilder. Inserted into this traditional context, the tilting posture adds yet another traditional note and, at the same time, is itself legitimized as old-timey.

The Boat Builder
John George Brown, c. 1890
Oil on canvas
The Cleveland Museum of Art, the Hinman B. Hurlbut Collection, CMA 905.72

tools and materials are employed to create traditional objects. In this utilitarian and traditional context, tilting back in a utilitarian and traditional chair seems entirely appropriate. In this vernacular interior, where vernacular products are crafted by vernacular means, vernacular sitting rightly takes place.[21]

The chair in Brown's painting is not entirely visible, but we can see enough to know that it is a simple turned chair. Look back at all the tilting chairs illustrated so far, and a pattern emerges: Men tilt in plain, utilitarian, vernacular chairs. In part this is because these chairs are sturdily constructed, with numerous stretchers to resist the stress of tilting. Genteel parlor chairs normally lack stretchers and will not hold up under this sort of use. The recurrent use of ordinary chairs in this context points to a Victorian cultural equation: Vernacular means, at least in part,

A male temporarily beyond the feminine sphere, beyond genteel norms, beyond polite behavior. The stone wall behind him not only separates the inside of the house from the outside but one sphere from another. The implements of knitting on the windowsill signify the women's sphere within. While the male occupies the transition zone of the porch—a space conjoined to the house, *yet open to nature—he engages in behaviors that associate him with nature even as his formal clothing reveals that he is a participant in the dominant, self-consciously "civilized" culture. This image and many others like it reveal that males were deeply conflicted over the roles and expectations of their culture.*

Independence (Squire Jack Porter)
Frank Blackwell Mayer, 1858
Oil on paperboard
National Museum of American Art,
Smithsonian Institution
Harriett Lane Johnston Collection

masculine. Whatever else the concept may suggest, the no-frills, straightforward, utilitarian concept of design it connotes was widely understood to have a male bias.[22]

Frank B. Mayer's 1858 painting *Independence* (5.13) provides material for a somewhat different yet congruent interpretation of the tilting posture. Here a rugged Andrew Jackson look-alike sits on a rude porch bench, his legs supported by the porch rails and his back by the stone exterior of a country house. Strictly speaking, the figure is not tilting, but approximating the posture as closely as he can on a heavy bench not easily tilted. On the windowsill beside him a ball of yarn with needles sticking from it and a partially finished bit of knitting suggest female presence and female standards of civilization within the structure.

In this painting, Mayer has cleverly reversed the Romantic painting convention

5.14 *On the other side of the window, in the world of women. A younger girl helps an older friend or sister prepare for a social event that will take place in the outside world. The image is in part about coming of age, but it is also about the restricted, constrained world of women and women's conventional association with household interiors.*

The small rocking chair beneath the window feminizes and domesticates an otherwise relatively barren room in a country house.
The Party Dress
Eastman Johnson, 1872
Oil on composition board
Wadsworth Atheneum, Hartford. Bequest of Mrs. Clara Hinton Gould
Photograph by E. Irving Blomstrann

of the open window. As it is usually employed, the open window is seen from inside domestic interiors. These interiors usually contain and constrain female figures (5.14), for whom the open window represents escape, excitement, adventure, and the world beyond with all its lures and dangers.[23] In reversing this convention, Mayer provides an alternative perspective. Now women and their world are out of view. Outside, male values and male identities prevail. The title of the picture, *Independence*, turns out to have more layers of meaning than are at first apparent. The male seated on the porch outside his home, in a space artifactually defined but close to nature, is independent, at least for the moment, of European-derived furnishings, of formal definitions of sitting, of socially reinforced patterns of self-control, and of self-conscious and artful deployment of his body. He is independent of the constrictions and limitations of genteel culture.

The images of tilting discussed so far have been largely positive or, at most, neutral. Tilting was sometimes understood to convey explicitly negative meanings as well. Just as the positive images derive much of their appeal from suggestions of the sitter's control, the negative images are negative precisely because the sitters seem to have lost control or to lack it. Put one way, when tilting revealed strength, it was acceptable; when it revealed weakness, it was not. Put another way, the same posture defined as "natural" in one context could be defined as "savage" in another.

Tilting as unequivocally negative, even savage, behavior appears in Thomas Nast's imaginative graphic re-creation of a Rebel Civil War raid on a border town (5.15). As in the Krimmel painting (5.8) discussed earlier, tilting both contributes to and derives meaning from the larger image. Nast has created a characteristically hyperbolic scene of barbarism and depravity.[24] Cruel and vicious soldiers rape and pillage, torture babies, shoot puppies for sport, terrorize blacks, and engage in other vicious acts. Their cruelty is heightened and fueled by drink, which flows freely. A male figure on a second-story porch surveys this scene of violence and savagery with apparent enjoyment. Holding a glass in one hand, he tilts his chair back on its rear legs and rests his feet against the post in front of him. Here is the familiar posture of tilting, but in this context it has become evil, sinister, even satanic.

5.15 *Tilting and bestial behavior. A Confederate raider tilts back in his chair as he surveys his comrades' descent into wanton violence and destruction. Feet above head suggests the elevation of humanity's baser aspects over the more noble, a regression from adult behavior and adult understandings to total amorality and immersion in sensation. The tilting spectator overlooking this* scene of horror has become completely dehumanized. He has lost all sensitivity to human suffering, all revulsion from human depravity.

A Rebel Guerilla Raid in a Western Town (detail)
Illustration by Thomas Nast
Harper's Weekly, *September 27, 1862*
Photograph by Craig Williams

The Confederate raiders in Nast's illustration have lost self-control and personal nobility. Their bestiality has triumphed over their humanity. This inversion of the normal order is symbolized in the posture of the tilter, whose feet rise above his head. Western formal sitting reified assumptions about the moral value and meaning of being upright and controlled. In formal sitting, the feet, which are utilitarian parts of the body, rest on or near the ground. The head, site of higher faculties, is held erect. In this position, the mind and reason are uppermost. In the case of Nast's sadistic raider, the situation is reversed. Feet above head mean animal over human, emotion over reason, the base over the noble.

This posture was a convenient and effective way to illustrate drunkenness. A usefully explicit example appears on the lithographed cover of an 1874 temperance ditty entitled "Papa, Don't Drink Any More" (5.16). In this bar scene, inebriated Papa wobbles back on his chair, his left leg crooked over the keg of liquor in front of him. As he scowls drunkenly into space, his young daughter begs him not to take another drink. Here, alcohol is indicted as the agent of bestiality. Alcohol induces men to let down their guard so that their baser natures triumph. Alcohol in excess is the enemy of genteel behavior and, by extension, of civilization. Alcohol sabotages the progress of humankind. In its gender stereotyping—drunken, bestial male and saintly, civilizing female—this image plays out a complicated Victorian drama that ultimately demeaned and enslaved both sexes.[25]

To link tilting with drunkenness obviously complicated its interpretation in the nineteenth century, but drunkenness was not its only negative association. Tilting was also sometimes understood to demonstrate lower-class status, to reveal a lack of gentility. One particularly accessible equation of tilting with lower-class status comes, appropriately enough, from a popular etiquette book of the 1880s, *Hill's Manual of Social and Business Forms*.[26] Most etiquette books provided directives for behavior; *Hill's Manual* went one step further to illustrate acceptable and unacceptable behavior. Images of contrasting behaviors were juxtaposed so that readers could participate in comparative analysis. For example, page 156 contained an illustration entitled *Bad Manners at the Table* (5.17). Facing it, on page 157, appeared *Gen-*

5.16 *Drink turns men into animals. Genteel people stand upright and sit upright. But when people drink too much, gentility and propriety evaporate and behavior declines. Here, tilting becomes one of the symptoms of a drink-induced collapse of polite behavior.*

"Papa, Don't Drink Any More"
Lithographed sheet music cover
Boston: G. D. Russell & Co., 1874
Henry Ford Museum and Greenfield Village, Michigan
(Negative No. B65363)

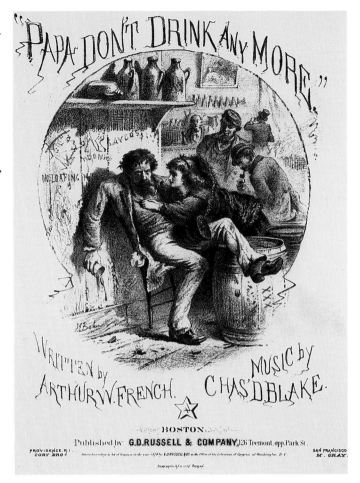

tility in the Dining Room (5.18). Each image was meaningful in itself but became doubly meaningful when compared to the other. The combined message about tilting seemed to be that it could be equated with both masculinity and lower-class status. Implicit in this equation was yet another, more fundamental equation: that masculine and lower-class behavior were much the same. Analysis of these two images shows how this nonverbal reasoning was expressed.

Bad Manners at the Table usually gets a laugh when shown to audiences in the late twentieth century. The manners are so obviously bad, the meal so riotous, the image so lacking in subtlety that it is easy to find this scene humorous. *Gentility in the Dining Room*, in contrast, usually does not provoke much comment, perhaps because it seems so obviously appropriate. It is necessary to examine *Gentility* with some care, however, for it generates a context for making meaning of *Bad Manners*.

Gentility shows twelve well-dressed people at a formal meal. The event takes place in a dining room, as the caption in the book plainly states, apparently within an affluent private house. Host and hostess sit at opposite ends of the table. The diners are all adults, males and females in equal number, seated according to an obvious formula. The dining party is waited on by a servant, visible in the doorway leading in from the kitchen.

5.17 *A middle-class perspective. In the nineteenth century, middle-class people wanted everyone to be middle class or at least to subscribe to middle-class values and behaviors. Values and behaviors that were not middle class were not merely different; they were morally evaluated as "bad." Although this image allegedly demonstrates "bad" manners, it can be more accurately described as recording certain working-class manners. Victorians recognized that there were links between economics and culture, but they often seemed to imply that "bad" manners made people poor or kept them poor. They rarely seemed to take seriously the proposition that poverty might limit and structure culture. In short, as this image demonstrates, they preferred to blame the victims.*

Bad Manners at the Table
Thomas E. Hill, Hill's Manual of Social and Business Forms
Chicago: Hill Standard Book Co., 1882

5.18 *The concept of gentility was a product of top–down cultural diffusion. It was the behavioral equivalent to the courtly mode of furnishing. To behave in a genteel manner meant to emulate the behavior of the aristocracy. To live in a genteel manner meant to emulate the lifestyle of the aristocracy. In short, gentility meant pretending. And if its aristocratic origins gave gentility its social and economic power, the element of pretense and the emphasis on social distinction brought it into conflict with American political ideology. Were this kind of behavior and this kind of lavish living appropriate in republican America? Gentility seems boring or oppressive today because it means living according to scripts, self-consciously attempting to play roles written for other people in other times.*

Gentility in the Dining-Room
Thomas E. Hill, Hill's Manual of Social and Business Forms
Chicago: Hill Standard Book Co., 1882

The dining room is well appointed. A chandelier hangs over the extension dining table. The chairs all match. A carpet covers the floor. Luxurious curtains hang at the windows, and a framed dining room picture graces the back wall. The cloth-covered table is heavy laden with elegant tablewares and presumably equally elegant foods. The evidence of the picture suggests that gentility means behaving formally, being affluent, having a servant, dining in a specialized room furnished with luxurious and appropriate goods, and living in an environment where males and females exist in equal numbers and in some degree of parity.[27]

Now turn to *Bad Manners*. Here, too, twelve people are drawn together, but the gender balance is badly skewed—ten males, a baby of unknown sex, but only one woman. This is not the only difference. *Bad Manners* takes place, not in a dining room, but in the kitchen of a boardinghouse with few if any trappings of gentility. The floor is of bare boards. The wall is cracked and unadorned. The light fixture is damaged. Lunch pails rest on the mantel. Hats and coats hang on pegs in the room where people eat, rather than on a hallstand or in a closet or wardrobe. The table is only a kitchen table, with no tablecloth. The chairs do not match. Men crowd around the table in a variety of attires, none of them formal. One young man still wears his shop apron. The solitary woman waits on all these men and contends with a boisterous child who is at the moment throwing a tantrum and has just kicked a plate into the air.

Around the overcrowded table, the men perform a medley of graceless activities, each numbered for easy identification. Bad manner number one is tilting a chair back on its rear legs while at the table. Ten other inappropriate behaviors are also illustrated. The evidence of this picture suggests that bad manners means not dressing well, being poor, eating chaotic and noisy meals in the kitchen of a boardinghouse, and living in a predominantly male world.

Together, these two images open several lines of interpretation. The one I wish to stress here is the constructed equation of women to gentility, of women to civilization. Setting aside for a moment the ambiguous role of economics in this formulation, we can say that *Bad Manners* suggests that, left to themselves, males will live little better than animals. *Gentility* suggests that when women are present in sufficient numbers, gentility and civilization become possible. Women are the agents of civilization.[28] This construction still operates in the late twentieth century.

One final image of tilting helps to summarize some of its contradictory meanings and at the same time underline the ideological factors shaping the apparently natural act of sitting. Winslow Homer's 1872 oil *The Country Store* (5.19) depicts the interior of a plain, rural general store, probably in northern New England or the Adirondacks. The image has four figures. In the background, only barely visible, the shopkeeper weighs something on a scale. The three seated figures in the foreground are more visible and more important. One sits on the counter. Another sits on a chair and rests a foot on top of the woodstove. The third tilts his chair back on the rear legs.

No dialogue takes place. These are strong, silent, rough-hewn types, the hardy, handsome rural males Sarah Burns discusses so capably.[29] Low-crowned hats worn indoors, large, heavy boots, and rough-textured clothing all indicate the rural working class. Seen from one perspective, these men embody idealized American republican values. Seen from another, they demonstrate the coarseness and crudeness of the back country. Their posture is a key element of meaning in this image, regardless of its interpretation. The posture displayed here was not acceptable within genteel settings shared by both sexes, but here, in this male domain, it is fitting. While middle-class people encountering a similar scene in town might dismiss it as merely working class, placed in a north woods setting it becomes mythologized. Here, this posture is natural, authentic, American, virile, and independent.

Tilting was part of the male world (5.20). This male world was also understood as a backstage world, an informal, allegedly unaffected world. It was not a civilized or civilizing space, not a genteel space, not a space touched in any evident way by women. Again and again, when tilting occurs, it is apart from women. The one conclusion hard to avoid is that civilization, at least as it was manifest within Ameri-

5.19 *Rural working-class males my-thologized. Heavy boots, coarse-textured clothing, hats worn indoors, cheap furniture, an old box stove, and the jumble and clutter of a remote country store, all contrast markedly to the elegance, richness, and finely finished surfaces of a feminized, civilized, fabric-draped genteel parlor or drawing room. In this rough, male environment, country types commune in silence. Tilting was considered a natural component of this allegedly unaffected, unpretentious world.*

The Country Store
Winslow Homer, 1872
Oil on panel
Hirshhorn Museum and Sculpture Garden,
Smithsonian Institution
Gift of Joseph H. Hirshhorn, 1966
(66.2490)

5.20 *A consistent constellation of artifacts. They all go together: a plain, vernacular interior with no textiles to soften or feminize; a low-crowned hat worn indoors; romantic shirt, vest, and cravat; thick trousers; heavy boots; a cheap but durable Windsor chair; and tilting. Together, they constitute a culturally constructed male alternative to culturally constructed female gentility.*

Evening Newspaper
Eastman Johnson, 1863
Oil on paper board
Mead Art Museum, Amherst College, gift of
Herbert W. Plimpton for the Hollis W.
Plimpton, Class of 1915, Memorial
Collection (1977.62)

5.21 *Posture shaped by gender; gender revealed by posture. In this rude frontier setting, the male tilts back on his cheap, plank-seat chair. The female, more formally dressed, sits upright. They share the same physical environment, but they are differentiated and distinguished by their culturally formulated and gender-linked scripts for posture.*

Charles Koehler family in their yard
Photograph by Charles Van Schaick, Black River Falls, Wisconsin, c. 1900
State Historical Society of Wisconsin, Madison

can domestic contexts, was female. Males found a variety of ways to resist, reject, or counteract cultural conventions that were courtly and therefore neither republican nor democratic, and female and therefore effeminate or feminizing. The tilting behavior, so aggressively uncourtly, ungracious, unfeminine (5.21), was a way in which males revealed and affirmed their politics and their gender.

ROCKING CHAIRS

Genteel Victorian women did not tilt chairs back on their rear legs, but they did rock in rocking chairs. Tilting and rocking are related; the major difference lies in the sitter's power relationship to the object. In tilting, males subjected chairs to their wills; they appeared to transcend the cultural signal embodied in the object. In rocking, sitters conformed to the will expressed in the chair; they appeared to accept culture. Tilting was undomesticated, masculine behavior. Rocking domesticated, civilized, feminized that behavior (5.22). The rocking chair made tilting and related postures acceptable within American domestic contexts. Put differently, the rocking chair is the feminized version of the American, republican, antiaristocratic interest in the terrain between sitting and reclining.

The rocking chair is not a product of courtly culture. It comes from humble origins.[30] In America, rocking chairs first appeared around the middle of the eighteenth century. In their early form, they were little more than normal chairs and armchairs with rockers added. Chairs that rocked became more common gradually, and in the early nineteenth century, they became standard components of popular culture (5.23). Unlike the parlor suite, which originated in courtly culture and was disseminated through top–down diffusion, the rocking chair spread upward through society from its lower levels and inward toward the center from its margins, an example of bottom–up and margin–center diffusion. The upward mobility of the rocking chair was limited, however, by the countervailing culture of formality, which was endorsed by centuries of historical precedent and by its long associations with situations of power and high status. The net result was that although they were highly popular throughout the nineteenth century, rocking chairs rarely rose above the median level of formality. Through the 1870s, they were excluded from most parlor suites. Only in the 1880s and 1890s, when the concept was in decline, were rocking chairs made parts of parlor suites and then usually at the mid and lower levels. Even today, the rocking chair does not conform to the prevailing conception of formality. It continues to be, as it has always been, a challenge and an alternative to the European, upper-class mode of formality.[31]

5.22 *The rocking chair sanctions, domesticates, and feminizes the posture of tilting. Here, a lady's rocker forms part of the furnishings of a woman's space. Beside the rocker is a basketwork sewing stand. The corner of the room is furnished with a heavily draped toilet table or personal shrine. Pieces of women's clothing and a quilt lie at the foot of the bed. Taken together, these artifacts suggest the close association of women, textiles, and rocking.*

Interior of Floy's room at "Uplawn"
Photograph by Leonard Dakin, Cherry Valley, New York, c. 1888
New York State Historical Association, Cooperstown

If rocking chairs moved up from the bottom, they also moved in from the margins toward the center of society. Look once again at the Edouart silhouette (5.1). One of the elderly women in that image sits in a rocking chair. She is positioned at the edge of the picture, far removed from the center of power. This image expresses what we know from other sources about the early status of the rocking chair. The form was originally closely related both to cradles and to invalids' chairs. The earliest users of rocking chairs seem to have been children, the aged, and the infirm.[32] Rocking chairs were not originally intended for adults at the height of their powers.

5.23 *The well-rockered household. This densely furnished middle-class interior contains many of the appropriate icons of Victorian bourgeois culture. Over the front door hangs a chromolithographed motto with the text Thou Art My Hope. In the center of the front room stands the conventional center table. Near the junction of the* two rooms, a small bentwood table supports an electroplated ice-water urn. In the near room are an elaborate cast-iron parlor stove and a parlor organ. Together, the two rooms contain at least three rockers: a cane-seated Grecian rocker, an upholstered platform rocker, and, near the front door, a Grecian rocker upholstered in horsehair. The wicker chair partially reflected in the mirror may also be a rocker.

Interior of a middle-class house
Photograph by Andrew Dahl, vicinity of
Madison, Wisconsin, c. 1879
State Historical Society of Wisconsin,
Madison

The association of the rocking chair with marginal people continued well into the nineteenth century, as many forms of evidence indicate. Consider an Andrew Dahl photograph of a family of ten in the vicinity of Madison, Wisconsin, in the 1870s (5.24). Of relatively modest means, these people apparently do not own a parlor suite. In fact, they seem to own only two pieces of upholstered furniture. One is a lounge with brilliantly colored and boldly figured covering. This object was probably new when the photograph was taken; it provides a seat for the top-ranking male in the group. The other piece of upholstered furniture is a Grecian rocker covered in horsehair. Its occupant is an obviously ailing older woman. As was the case with her counterpart in the Edouart silhouette, she too is positioned at the very edge of the picture, at the edge of power. Her age and invalid condition earn her the compensatory right to sit in the most comfortable chair available.

Despite the limiting associations of its early history, the rocking chair was widely, one might even say wildly, popular at certain levels of society, design, and formality in the nineteenth century. By the 1820s, it had moved into the mainstream of American popular culture. The first chair successfully produced as a rocking chair, rather than merely a chair with rockers added, was the famous Boston rocker (5.25). A second major type, which appeared by 1840, was the so-called Grecian rocker (5.26). Both attained great popularity. Both were commonly found in homes around the country.

The second half of the nineteenth century seems to have been the great age of the rocking chair. Upholstered rockers (5.27), while not normally parts of parlor suites, were produced for use in a variety of contexts: parlors, sitting rooms, bedrooms, even theater boxes. The so-called Lincoln rocker is named after the upholstered rocking chair Lincoln was seated in on the night of his assasination in Ford's Theater (5.28).

The configuration, material, and functional workings of the rocking chair were actively contested by inventors and manufacturers attempting to define and dominate the lucrative rocking-chair business. Inventories and photographs show that even ordinary households often had several rocking chairs. Some were the familiar Boston

5.24 *The ambiguous meaning of rocking chairs. In this family portrait, an ailing woman occupies an upholstered Grecian rocking chair. Her weakened physical condition extends the rocking chair's long association with invalids. Her age and seniority within the group also suggest that her presence in the best chair is a mark of status. But this is a generally troubling image. Relationships are not clear. Why is an empty nurse rocker so prominent? Is a woman absent? Dead? Is this a symbolic empty chair?*

Family group in front of their house Photograph by Andrew Dahl, vicinity of Madison, Wisconsin, c. 1875 State Historical Society of Wisconsin, Madison

5.25 *The Boston rocker was the first widely successful realization that the rocking chair could be more than a chair with rockers added. The anonymous inventor of this form fused the scrolling shapes of neoclassicism with the spindle-and-plank construction of Windsor chairs and the decorative properties of fancy furniture to produce what has become an American design classic. The form was introduced sometime in the 1820s and is still produced today.*

Child's Boston rocker
Eastern United States, 1840–1880

5.26 *The Grecian rocker was the second major form of rocking chair to be defined in the nineteenth century. Made from sawed rather than turned elements, finished with clear or colored varnish rather than paint, and seated and backed with cane rather than wood, the Grecian rocker represented a step toward greater formality and greater gentility.*

Grecian rocker with caned seat and back
Detroit Chair Co.
Detroit, Michigan, c. 1870
From the Collection of the Michigan Historical Museum, Lansing

5.27 *Upholstered rocking chairs. The low or nearly nonexistent arms on these chairs indicate that they were intended for female use, probably in the bedrooms of fairly affluent households.*
Photograph of three upholstered rocking chairs
Sales catalog of Phoenix Furniture Co.
Grand Rapids, Michigan, c. 1876
Grand Rapids Public Library

5.28 *Psychohistorians might ponder the meaning of the fact that Lincoln was sitting in a rocking chair when he was assassinated. Further, they might wonder what, if any, connection there might be between this expression of domesticated behavior and Lincoln's famous "House Divided" speech.*

and Grecian forms, both made through the end of the century, but rockers made of bentwood, rattan or wicker, or from branches with the bark still on in the rustic style (5.29) were commonplace.[33] Seats could be of wooden planks, as in Boston rockers; of cane, as in Grecian rockers; of woven rush or splint, as on traditional turned rockers; or upholstered with fabrics ranging widely in price and durability. Gardner & Co. tried to cut into the market with their perforated three-ply seats (5.30). To compete with both cane and fabric upholstery, George Hunzinger patented and produced rockers seated with woven steel strips about the same size as cane encased in colored textile sheathing.[34]

Chairs equipped with the familiar curving wooden rockers were the dominant form throughout the period, but they encountered competition from a new type of rocking chair, which used a variety of mechanisms to elevate the rocking part of the chair above the floor on some sort of platform or base (5.31). Variously called patent rockers, platform rockers, and base rockers, these were highly popular in the 1870s and 1880s. The manufacturers of traditional rockers, subsequently termed floor rockers, in turn responded by producing a line of fancy and sometimes bizarre floor rockers in the 1880s and 1890s. At the end of the century, Gustav Stickley and other manufacturers of Arts and Crafts furniture made massive and sturdy oak rocking chairs staples of their lines.[35]

Inventories and pictorial evidence show rocking chairs used in many settings in homes, at resorts and hotels, and particularly on porches (5.32). Porches seem, in retrospect, to have been appropriate settings for these objects. For just as porches were transitions from one zone to another, from one mode to another, rockers bridged the gap between the artificial and the natural, between the posture of decorous formality and the posture of unaffected naturalness.

This is only a brief outline of the rich and complex history of the rocking chair in nineteenth-century America. My point here, however, is less to present a survey of the form than to suggest some of the meanings these artifacts held for Victorian Americans. Some of that meaning was related to the perceived nationality of the object. The rocking chair was widely understood to be an American form of seating.

5.29 *Rocking made "natural." Rustic furniture often looked as though it had merely happened or as though it had been grown rather than manufactured. Rustic furniture was produced as a culturally sanctioned alternative to the highly artificial, highly artifactualized appearance of the dominant styles, most of which emphasized their distance from nature. Rustic furniture looked natural, but it was yet another assurance that humankind could shape nature to its own needs.*

Rustic bentwood rocking chair
Probably western Pennsylvania, c. 1900
Collection of Gail J. Ames

5.30 *Technology in the service of piety? Piety fronting for technology? Gardner & Co.'s products demonstrate how Victorian manufacturers built cultural balance into their products. The firm countered its innovative technological thesis with a conservative cultural antithesis in order to create an acceptable synthesis. This rocking chair was manufactured with an innovative one-piece seat and back fabricated from three plys of veneer glued together at right angles. This radical departure from the known was rendered familiar by perforating the back with a design that included a pair of Gothic arches,*

imagery readily and usually associated with Christian churches. Thus progressive technology was married to orthodox theology.

Child's rocking chair with one-piece perforated veneer seat and back
Gardner & Co., New York City, 1875–1885

5.31 *The rocking chair gentrified. Platform rockers, like the one shown here, combined the easy back-and-forth movement and variety of postures long associated with the rocking chair and the visual stability and formality of conventional parlor seating. Like most parlor chairs, this one rests on four feet, which remain in place when the chair is occupied. It has no long rockers to wear out rugs, scrape walls, or trip over. And while many conventional rocking chairs tilted back when not in use, the spring mechanisms of platform rockers kept unoccupied chairs genteely upright.*

Upholstered platform rocker
Ebonized hardwood; upholstery not original
Probably Chicago, c. 1885
Galloway House, Fond du Lac, Wisconsin
Fond du Lac County Historical Society

It existed in other places and could be encountered in other parts of the world, but in America it took on nationalistic significance.

Second, as I have indicated, as a genre rocking chairs were considered somewhat more appropriate for women than for men. It is true that certain kinds of rocking chairs were explicitly intended for women. The most familiar were the low, armless types conventionally known as nurse or nursing rockers (5.33). These were standard equipment with bedroom suites in the 1870s (5.34). But there were no specifically identified male equivalents. Large rocking chairs with arms were normally called arm rockers and were not necessarily associated with males either in trade catalogs or in period images. It is difficult to avoid the conclusion that rocking chairs carried female or feminine connotations, at least within the culture constructed by Victorian Americans. These feminine connotations rested in part on the chairs' early links to weakness and marginality (5.35) and in part on the heightened degree to which

5.33 *Specifically for women. Nurse (or nursing) rockers and sewing rockers— the names were interchangeable—were intended for female use in those activities. The typical low seat enabled lap and knees to become usable surfaces, while the absence of any arms allowed the sitter's arms and elbows to move about freely.*

Boston nurse rocker
New England or upper Midwest, 1850–1880

5.34 *All the furniture needed to furnish a bedroom in 1870: a double bedstead with full tester top, a chest of drawers with looking glass, a commode washstand, a towel bar, a teapoy with four small chairs (only one of which appears here), and a nurse rocker. The routine inclusion of nurse rockers with bedroom suites indicates that these objects were integral parts of the reigning concept of appropriate middle-class bedroom furnishing. While the presence of*

these rockers can be explained on solely functional grounds, the omission of any male equivalent, even at the symbolic level, argues that bedrooms were culturally constructed as more female than male.

Painted bedroom suite
From the sales catalog of an unidentified firm
Probably Boston area, c. 1870
The Winterthur Library

the artifacts controlled posture. Hundreds, perhaps even thousands of nineteenth-century images record males and females sitting in rocking chairs (5.36), but women appear somewhat more frequently than men (5.37). Moreover, women's association with rocking chairs has a mythic dimension that men's association lacks. While women appear in many settings and engaged in a variety of activities, the prototypical image, at least in normative culture, is of woman as mother holding a child in her arms and gently rocking (5.38).[36] This is a powerful and pervasive icon of nurture, of comfort, of maternal love and care, of intimacy. Rocking a child in a rocking chair suggests a safe, secure, and soothing experience, a stereotypical feminine experience. Juxtapose with this the conventional image of male tilting (see 5.20) or even an actual image of a male tilting while holding a small child (5.21). Compared to rocking, tilting has something reckless, risky, dangerous about it. Compared to tilting, rocking provides safety and security that seem sensible, responsible. Within

5.35 *Males are strong and females are weak, at least according to conventional Victorian gender dichotomies. Thus, as males age and become weak, they also become womanlike, feminized. There is, therefore, no incongruity in this image of a very old man who has fallen asleep in a Boston rocker.*

Old man asleep in a rocking chair
Edward Lamson Henry, 1872
Pencil and oil on paper
New York State Museum, Albany
Photograph by John Yost

5.36 *A picture of prosperity and contentment. Three people sit on the lawn in front of their stone and brick mansion, each in a rocking chair. The male occupies a relatively plain and austere chair with little ornament or elaboration. The two women sit in intricately wrought wicker or rattan chairs. The imposing house in the background suggests that these were people of considerable affluence, people who owned and could have been photographed amid very formal furniture. And yet, perhaps not to appear* pretentious or overly formal, they chose to have themselves recorded relaxing in rocking chairs.

A family on the lawn in front of their house
Photograph by Andrew Dahl, Trenton, Wisconsin, 1875–1880
State Historical Society of Wisconsin, Madison

5.37 *The old, familiar image. An old house, filled with old furnishings. And in the back room, an old woman, sitting in an old-fashioned rocking chair. By the later years of the nineteenth century, the rocking chair had been mythologized into a symbol of tradition, of olden days and old-time ways, of republican values and virtues, and of domestic comfort and nurture. The image of an old woman in a rocking chair evoked* all these associations, commingled with the cluster of warm emotions and sentiments constructed around the concept of grandmother.

The Old Clock on the Stair
Edward Lamson Henry, 1893 or earlier
Watercolor on paper
New York State Museum, Albany
Photograph by John Yost

5.38 *The rocking chair and motherhood. Held tight in her mother's arms, the young child sleeps peacefully to the gentle rocking motion of the chair. At this moment, the child's sense of security, the mother's warmth, and the movement of the chair are one. This image provides insight into the powerful sensory factors and sensory memories that underlay the appeal and success of the rocking chair in the nineteenth century. For before ideology, there was feeling; before thought, there was sensation. Encountered in the haze of infancy, the rocking chair came to partake of the powerful experiences and associations that constituted and surrounded early childhood.*

Since I Last Listened Your Lullaby Song
Engraved illustration from Elizabeth Akers Allen, Rock Me to Sleep, Mother
Boston: Estes and Lauriat, 1884
Photograph by Craig Williams

"Since I last listened your lullaby song."

the Victorian division of gender roles, the rocking chair and security became associated with women's sphere. The rocking chair assumed and retained deep if subtle links to culturally constructed feminine values and traits.

What of all those men sitting in rocking chairs recorded by nineteenth-century painters and photographers? When males used rocking chairs, regardless of who they were, the inference was that they had become civilized or domesticated (5.39). And just as male tilting sometimes had negative readings, so did male rocking. An illustration entitled *Helping Churn* (5.40) indicates that an able-bodied man who rocked while a woman worked in his presence had serious moral deficiencies, that he was exploitative and lazy.[37]

Far more could be said about rocking chairs and nineteenth-century strategies for using them to convey cultural meaning. My purpose in discussing them, as well as tilting and formal sitting, has been to show how far culture reaches into ordinary behavior. Parlor suites seem artificial. The fact that they are extinct today inclines us to see them as culturally constructed, arbitrary, artificial, transitory. But people still rock and tilt. When they do so today, they just seem to be making themselves comfortable. Perhaps they are, but in the nineteenth century these seemingly natural postures carried heavy cultural baggage.

In the nineteenth century, an activity, a posture as basic as sitting was invaded by culture and ideology because other very basic dimensions of life had become problematic. Manners and gender were two of the most obvious. Today, what the Victorians called manners are still an issue. Definitions of appropriate formality or informality for a given situation are still contested. Cultural pluralism and diversity are much easier to accept in the abstract than in the emphatically real arenas of America's cities and neighborhoods. What were issues of manners for the Victorians we recognize as authentic cultural conflicts. And with the escalation of terminology has come an escalation of consequences.

The destructive effects of the intense gendering of the nineteenth century are also still being felt. We are still learning how far culture reached into psyches to

5.39 *The thoroughly domesticated male. Why is Dr. Blodgett looking at the camera so sternly? Is it because his son is photographing him sitting in a nurse rocker? Dr. Blodgett's action was probably no more meaningful than when a late-twentieth-century man momentarily holds a purse for a woman. Just a little crossing of gendered behavior that commonly takes place among intimates. This same act, however, would* be considered not merely inappropriate but self-destructive in formal public or ceremonial settings. Not the kind of behavior most contemporary males would want recorded in a photograph.

Dr. Thomas S. Blodgett on the porch
Photograph by his son, George L. Blodgett
Cooperstown, New York, c. 1890
New York State Historical Association, Cooperstown

5.40 *Male laziness embodied. The thoroughly victimized Widder Doodle has been reminiscing about her beloved former husband. She remembered how he helped her churn butter. Sometimes she would churn for an entire day, and her back would be sore for a week afterward. But while she churned, Doodle would sit in his cushioned rocking chair and read to her from his newspaper. The paper was strong against women's rights. The editorials argued persuasively that voting would be too much for the weaker sex. Yes, the Widder loved Doodle. She remembered fondly that he could sit and watch her work for hours and hours, telling her how delicate and pretty she looked. And yes, there are still Doodles and Widder Doodles today.*

Helping Churn
Engraved illustration from [Marietta Holley], Josiah Allen's Wife as a P. A. and P. I.: Samantha at the Centennial
Hartford, Conn.: American Publishing Company, 1888

HELPING CHURN.

make constructed gender seem natural. Today, both males and females struggle with gender roles that prevent or hinder their development into fully actualized human beings. And sometimes the pain and anger created by gender typecasting find violent and tragic outlets. Sitting was only a little piece of a larger phenomenon that we now recognize as subtle and pervasive. But it is from such little pieces that effective ideologies are built. It is through such little pieces that effective ideologies shape the world and the meanings people make of it.

Conclusion

What does it mean to be human? In part, it means to make, use, and live with things. And what does it mean to live right and live well? In most societies, it means, in part, to own, experience, and live with things of certain kinds and qualities. In this book, I have examined five classes of little-studied objects, five groups of ordinary things of Victorian daily life, to learn something about Victorian Americans' sensory, emotional, and cognitive experiences. But even more, I have examined these things to understand what Victorian Americans thought it meant to be human, to live right and live well.

A major assumption permeating this study is that, in very important ways, Victorian American life centered on things. Despite a lengthy history of denial and lamentation, Americans have long been a materialistic people. I use "materialistic" in a nonprejudicial way. To me, it means that Americans have invested goods with powerful meanings. Goods matter to them. Owning things, living with things, experiencing things, longing for things years ago became normal and accepted parts of American life. Studying Americans' lives, then, necessarily means studying Americans' things. In this book, I have tried to complement and extend the work of the many scholars who have studied the roles of goods in American life.

While I stop short of maintaining that people are, in any literal or essentialist way, what they own, I have argued throughout that people rely heavily on goods to know and define themselves and others, to structure and give meaning to life, to make and find meaning in the world around them, and to express and advocate systems and patterns of belief. Thus pivotal humanistic issues of identity, meaning, and belief are at the core of this study and appear repeatedly throughout the book.

I noted at the outset that this was something of an experimental work. I have drawn sometimes sweeping conclusions about culture from close examinations of specific objects. I have offered findings—*assertions* may be a more accurate word—about the nature and texture of Victorian life as retrieved from that society's objects for others to weigh and evaluate. I have tried to apply the traditional methodology of art history to goods that are not conventionally considered art. I have tried to bring rigorous analysis to ordinary things.

In this spirit, I have used largely an Aristotelian or inductive method in framing the essays. In each chapter, I have given a prominent place to a detailed investigation of one or more objects. I have tried to learn as much as possible from the goods themselves and from their location within various settings, sequences, and contexts. I have initiated inquiry with a few objects, then moved outward toward larger cultural issues.

Verbal evidence does not play a prominent part in this book. As a student of material culture, I have come to recognize that relatively few people are comfortable with directly confronting objects. Furthermore, many share prejudices that elevate verbal evidence over nonverbal evidence, what people say or write over what they build or buy. For that reason, some prominent books about material culture approach things through the words written about them. I have tried to counter those prejudices and have consciously rejected that method. I have assumed that words and things are both cultural products, equally limited, flawed, contrived to reveal or conceal, persuade, convince, or deceive. Neither is more "truthful" than the other. Neither is more "authentic." My goal has been to explore the peculiar powers of things. Therefore, this book, I think appropriately, favors things, both because they are its main evidence and in order to compensate for others' favoring of words.

Taken together, the five studies presented here illuminate several areas of cultural and psychic continuity. For one thing, they demonstrate compellingly the mutability, artificiality, and uncertainty of culture. Objects and behaviors only a century or less behind us not only seem strange today but, in the case of sideboards, even a little distasteful. These studies show that the constant change of the late twentieth century has deep roots. For another, they suggest that cultural change might be conceived of as a series of successive and often contradictory doctrines and dogmas swirling around a core of fixed, persisting, even universal, questions and problems, issues and needs. They also make it clear that people of Victorian America, like those of the present, were tormented by inner conflicts, anxieties, and ambivalences. This is a valuable lesson about continuities in American psychic life.

Other strands of continuity run through these chapters and tie Victorian America to the present. It is still true, for instance, that change produces stress and that people are conflicted over the gains and losses brought about by major transformations. There is still acute tension within our society between tradition and innovation, between orthodoxy and the unorthodox, between convention and the unconventional. And different cultural components continue to be joined in unexpected—or perhaps all too expected—ways. The wedding of technological modernism and cultural premodernism that appeared in such dramatic form in embroidered mottoes of the last century is just as evident today in, for example, political agendas in Washington. Technology may truly progress, but culture, like art, seems only to change. And so it should not be surprising that hostility to intellectual freedom and inquiry has not noticeably declined, and reductionism in the face of complex issues is as common in contemporary political circles as it is among religious fundamentalists.

There are still centers of power and margins, as anyone even vaguely familiar with American society plainly knows. And there is still pressure to conform, with rewards for those who do and costs for those who do not. Wealth still legitimizes. Violence is still an accepted part of American life, deeply institutionalized within social and power structures, celebrated in myth and public ritual, and glorified in sports, the entertainment industry, and international politics.

Some people are still truly victimized by culture. Others allow themselves to be. And society still tends to blame victims, without regard to circumstances. There are still differences between "objective facticity" and subjective reality, between people's outer lives and their inner lives, between public actions and private thoughts. And the meanings of things are still not fixed; people make meanings from things. And as people and their conditions change, meanings change.

The meanings of most of the objects discussed in this book have changed since the time when those objects were new. Much of their cultural intensity is gone. Today, they are viewed primarily as antiques and collectibles. But when they were new, they played important parts in some of the larger cultural dramas of their time. One of the most important of these dramas revolved around the rise and fall of gentility. In one definition, gentility means belonging to the gentry, being a member of the upper class. Gentility became the dominant paradigm for middle-class behavior in the nineteenth century and therein lies a contradiction, a paradox; by definition, middle class can never be upper class. The middle class can only pretend, only emulate.

Few objects better demonstrate the aspiring orientation of Victorian gentility than the hallstand. The hallstand embodied and enshrined Victorians' fixation on appearance, formality, theatricality, ceremonialization, and self-control. It captured in tangible, enduring form the studied imitation and self-consciousness at the core of Victorian gentility. To live as those of higher rank lived, to behave as those of higher rank behaved, these impulses lay at the heart of Victorian gentility.

All culture is artificial. But Victorian Americans' culture was more artificial than most. Theirs was consciously and deliberately a culture of artificiality, of imitation, of pretending and pretension. And it was in opposition to these qualities that the modern cult of authenticity was formulated. Modernist notions of authenticity cannot be fully understood without reference to Victorian culture, without appreciating how much movement toward authenticity was also movement away from imitation, away from the Victorian formulation of gentility.

Even in its own time, gentility generated resistance and alternatives. If parlor suites encoded conventional understandings of gentility, rocking chairs compromised many of gentility's basic tenets, and tilting rejected them altogether. Victorian society also acknowledged the fragility, the tentativeness of genteel behavior. The uninhibiting power of alcohol, for example, could subvert a carefully constructed and otherwise controlled presentation of self all too easily. The descent from genteel behavior to animalistic behavior could be swift and destructive.

Gentility was a widely shared set of aspirations—or illusions—sustained by particular forms of material culture. The material culture counterpart and complement to genteel behavior was, predictably enough, patterned after courtly furnishings, after the furnishings of the upper classes. The second major drama deals with the ascendance and then decline of these courtly furnishings, with the rise and fall of the courtly paradigm. Like genteel behavior, courtly furnishings spread through the middle class, generating a sensation of progress, of rising levels of civilization, and of elevated taste.

This courtly paradigm not only acknowledged hierarchy but depended on it. It was understood and valued as diffusion from the top down. The courtly paradigm was an international phenomenon grounded in cosmopolitan values. The model was European in a general sense and French in particular, not only in America but throughout the Europeanized world. In the 1850s and 1860s, Americans bought parlor suites in forms that replicated or at least emulated currently fashionable French furniture. That French furniture, in turn, emulated French aristocratic furniture of the sixteenth, seventeenth, and eighteenth centuries.

The decline of the courtly model parallels the decline of gentility. While neither has disappeared, both survive in significantly modified and diminished form. In the later nineteenth century, international cosmopolitanism of the courtly mode was contested by the nationalism of the Colonial Revival and by the preindustrial nostalgia of the Arts and Crafts movement. Reintroduced historic vernaculars challenged the hegemony of the courtly mode. While some of the very wealthy continued to set themselves up in palatial settings, the middle class increasingly turned to other patterns of references and associations. Today, courtly styles are among the many furnishing options available. But in Victorian America, particularly during the third quarter of the century, French courtly styles and aspirations to lead courtly lives were dominant.

The third drama centers on the rise and fall of specialized furniture forms. It is not self-evident that furniture forms must be differentiated or specialized. The core functions of furniture are finite and few. Put succinctly, people use furniture to support, contain, or both. All forms fit into one of these three categories. But in the nineteenth century, considerable ingenuity was devoted to devising new and specialized forms to support and contain. Hallstands are again among the best examples. These artifacts combined a variety of mundane, unglamorous support and container functions within a ceremonializing frame, creating in the process discrete and distinctive furniture forms. These specialized furniture forms were often accompanied by specialized forms of seating called hall chairs and specialized holders or containers called card receivers. In a similar way, parlor suites refined the gross concept of sitting according to gender and power hierarchies.

Specialization produced objects that could with propriety serve only one purpose or a closely related set of purposes. These objects were appropriate only in designated spaces, which they in turn helped to define and distinguish. Hallstands could be placed only in halls, sideboards only in dining rooms, parlor suites only in parlors. This formulation of artifact use and location was sustained by a set of assumptions about the high value of specialization. Specialization was endorsed by apparent truths discovered in the study of both the natural world and humankind. Specialization was as much an attribute of highly developed organisms as it was of highly developed societies. To many Victorians, the concepts of specialization and refinement were inseparable. Living well meant living in a highly specialized world. Victorian homes were created as elaborate specialized landscapes, laid out according to widely shared rules and principles. Each specialized space was furnished with specialized artifacts that provided appropriate settings and props for the specialized rituals and ceremonies of everyday life.

The fourth drama highlights changing expressions of power within the domestic realm. On one level, this means the display of financial power, of wealth. A century ago, Veblen coined the term "conspicuous consumption" and offered a trenchant analysis of the phenomenon. The uninhibited display of wealth, of pecuniary power, reached its zenith in the late nineteenth century and the early years of the twentieth. Wealth is still visible in Americans' homes, but bombastically splendid furnishings in palatial settings, all closely modeled on the settings of Europe's wealthiest monarchs, are comparatively rare today and a phenomenon we now think of as typically Victorian.

What is equally Victorian is the explicit expression of power relationships within objects or groups of objects. The parlor suite, with its overt articulation of hierarchy, is perhaps the most obvious example. More dramatic, perhaps, was the commentary on power and domination conveyed by elite culture sideboards at the middle of the century. The rise and fall of these objects is tied in part to the fortunes of the courtly paradigm and in part to shifting patterns of gendered responsibility and authority within the home.

Looking back, these bizarrely assertive furniture forms seem to appear at the very moment of a dramatic shift from male to female control of the domestic sphere. It may be too melodramatic to call these extraordinary creations the last hurrah of male domination of the home, but within an American context at least, the correlation is striking and provocative.

The gender shift marked by these exceptional objects brings us to the fifth drama woven into these five chapters, the gendering of culture. Victorians cannot be accused of inventing the gendered world. It antedates them by millennia. But the Victorians intensified gender distinctions and sometimes gave them new form. Through the doctrine of separate spheres, houses became terrain overseen by women. Within this sphere, women exerted their authority through such means as parlor organs and embroidered mottoes. But objects were gendered too. Chairs in parlor suites were differentiated by sex. Rocking chairs had feminine connotations, and even posture could be masculine or feminine. But more than these inventions and adaptations of prior cultural patterns, what most distinguished Victorian culture was the intensity of its gendering, the distance between the masculine and feminine poles.

Together these five dramas constitute a constellation of interrelated values that gave Victorian culture much of what we now regard as its distinctive character. These values did not merely coexist but were tightly interrelated. At their center rested the concept of gentility. Surrounding and reifying gentility was the courtly model, for courtly styles and forms of furnishings were gentility's material culture equivalents. The third strand, specialization, was legitimized in part by rationalism but also in part by the courtly furnishings of the eighteenth century, when aristocratic material culture became increasingly refined and delicate; the specialization of Victorian American middle-class furniture still pales beside the exquisite subtlety of differentiation of French eighteenth-century upper-class goods.

Specialization sustained both overt expressions of power and extreme gendering. Specialization was but another form of classification, a major Victorian compulsion. The nineteenth century was comparatively comfortable with classifying people according to power and rank. Expressions of power were appropriate manifestations of a differentiated world. Gender is one of the most fundamental classifications of all. Intensive gendering, like dramatic expressions of wealth, advanced classification and differentiation.

But values are invisible. It is through behaviors and through things that they become visible. Things, in turn, frame and structure behavior. Behaviors may or may not be recorded, but things often endure. In this series of glimpses into Victorian culture, I have tried to examine a sampling of things that have endured. I have tried to draw from them some of the cultural values and meanings they were meant to contain. I have tried to demonstrate the richness of material culture as historical evidence, as a way to understand those parts of a past culture, those aspects of experiences gone by, that were rarely if ever put into words yet were unarguably real and powerful.

As a materialist and student of material culture, I have become convinced that human life, and American life in particular, is in large part about things and cannot be understood apart from those things. This book is an attempt to understand Victorian Americans by exploring just a few of the things that were once parts of their lives. The book has a more modest and more basic goal as well. I wrote this book in large part to share the excitement of exploring things. I have tried to convey, without exactly saying so, that looking at and thinking about things is a stimulating and creative activity in itself. Discovery of great truths is always a possibility but is hardly necessary to justify the adventure. The point of material culture study is not just the conclusions but the thinking as well. Material culture study is more than a utilitarian enterprise. It yields deep personal joys and satisfactions.

It is incontrovertible that goods are for using. Many will agree that goods are for visual enjoyment. I believe that goods are also for thinking, for contemplating, reflecting, meditating. A major intention behind this book was to provide examples of thinking about goods. The opportunity to look closely at things, to ponder things, to see things in new ways, to identify patterns, to make connections, to ask questions, to have insights, and to see the world in new ways—these are the very real benefits of object study.

People sometimes ask, why study objects? This entire book is one extended answer, but I have a second, more succinct response. Study objects because objects open minds.

Notes

INTRODUCTION

1. The term *visible proofs* is from Simon J. Bronner, "Visible Proofs: Material Culture Study in American Folkloristics," in *Material Culture: A Research Guide*, ed. Thomas J. Schlereth (Lawrence: University Press of Kansas, 1985), 127–153.

2. The meaning of "Victorian" has been capably discussed elsewhere. I share the interpretations found in Daniel Walker Howe, "Victorian Culture in America," in *Victorian America*, ed. D. W. Howe (Philadelphia: University of Pennsylvania Press, 1976), 3–26; Louise L. Stevenson, *The Victorian Homefront: American Thought and Culture, 1860–1880* (Boston: Twayne, 1991); and Rodney D. Olsen, *Dancing in Chains: The Youth of William Dean Howells* (New York: New York University Press, 1991). On the twentieth-century deconstruction of Victorian culture, see Stanley Coben, *Rebellion against Victorianism: The Impetus for Cultural Change in 1920's America* (New York: Oxford University Press, 1991).

CHAPTER ONE

This chapter originally appeared, in much different form, as "Meaning in Artifacts: Hall Furnishings in Victorian America," *Journal of Interdisciplinary History* 9, no. 1 (Summer 1978): 19–46.

1. On the so-called primacy effect, see David I. Kertzer, *Ritual, Politics, and Power* (New Haven: Yale University Press, 1988), 83; and Richard Nisbett and Lee Ross, *Human Inference: Strategies and Shortcomings of Social Judgment* (Englewood Cliffs, N.J.: Prentice-Hall, 1980). On impression management, see James T. Tedeschi, ed., *Impression Management Theory and Social Psychological Research* (New York: Academic Press, 1981). See also Dale Carnegie, *How to Win Friends and Influence People* (New York: Simon & Schuster, 1964). First impressions are also directly related to cognitive development. A typical nineteenth-century statement of this understanding is found in Jean Paul Richter, "Thoughts," *The Diadem* (Philadelphia: Carey & Hart, 1846): "In advanced age the grandest moral examples pass by us, and our life-course is no more altered by them than the earth is by a flitting comet; but in childhood the first object that excites the sentiment of love or of injustice flings broad and deep its light or shadow over the coming years" (p. 71).

2. For various perspectives on this issue, see Alan Trachtenberg, *The Incorporation of America* (New York: Hill and Wang, 1982); T. J. Jackson Lears, *No Place of Grace: Anti-Modernism and the Transformation of American Culture* (New York: Pantheon, 1981); Mark Twain and Charles Dudley Warner, *The Gilded Age: A Tale of To-Day* (Hartford: American Publishing Co., 1874); and the observations of various foreign visitors to this country during the nineteenth century.

3. In the most general terms, American middle-class housing can be said to shift from few multifunctional rooms in the seventeenth century to many specialized rooms in the nineteenth century. For extensive commentary on specialization in nineteenth-century material

culture, see Siegfried Giedion, *Mechanization Takes Command* (New York: Norton, 1969).

4. The literature on reality as constructed socially through culture is enormous. The seminal text is Peter L. Berger and Thomas Luckmann, *The Social Construction of Reality* (New York: Doubleday, 1966). Two titles particularly relevant here are Grant McCracken, *Culture and Consumption* (Bloomington: Indiana University Press, 1988); and Kertzer, *Ritual, Politics, and Power*.

5. For an overview of domestic building and an annotated listing of key titles, see David Schuyler, "Domestic Architecture," in *Decorative Arts and Household Furnishings in America*, ed. Kenneth L. Ames and Gerald W. R. Ward (Winterthur: Winterthur Museum, 1989), 61–75.

6. On eighteenth-century house plans, see George B. Tatum, *Philadelphia Georgian* (Middletown: Wesleyan University Press, 1976); and Bernard L. Herman, *Architecture and Rural Life in Central Delaware* (Knoxville: University of Tennessee Press, 1987).

7. Vincent J. Scully, Jr., *The Shingle Style and the Stick Style* (New Haven: Yale University Press, 1971). Thousands of house plans appear in the numerous nineteenth-century architectural manuals published for the lay public. For an extensive listing of these, see Henry-Russell Hitchcock, *American Architectural Books* (New York: Da Capo Press, 1976). Models for "living halls" are illustrated in Joseph Nash, *The Mansions of England in the Olden Time* (New York: Bounty Books, 1970; originally published 1839–1849).

8. For discussion of competing models for middle-class domesticity, see Wendy Kaplan, *"The Art That Is Life": The Arts and Crafts Movement in America* (Boston: Little, Brown, for the Museum of Fine Arts, 1987); and Rosalind H. Williams, *Dream Worlds: Mass Consumption in Late Nineteenth Century France* (Berkeley: University of California Press, 1982).

9. In some more costly homes, the hall was separated from the outside by a vestibule. On one level, the vestibule served further to insulate the interior of the house from the outside by keeping out wind and weather. On another, it heightened the sense of drama associated with entering or leaving the house by adding another stage to the process.

10. A seminal discussion of front and back zones appears in Erving Goffman, *The Presentation of Self in Everyday Life* (Garden City, N.Y.: Doubleday, 1959). Benjamin Disraeli, *Sybil; or The Two Nations* (London: H. Colburn, 1845). Explicit acceptance of stratification is found in Andrew Jackson Downing, *The Architecture of Country Houses* (New York: D. Appleton, 1850). Downing argues that a cottage is appropriate for a family with no more than two servants, but three or more servants entitle one to a villa. Much of Downing's approach can be traced to John Claudius Loudon, *Encyclopædia of Cottage, Farm, and Villa Architecture and Furniture* (London: Longman, Rees, Orme, Brown, Green, & Longman, 1833). Recent research on Downing is summarized in George B. Tatum and Elisabeth MacDougall, eds., *Prophet with Honor: The Career of Andrew Jackson Downing* (Washington D.C.: Dumbarton Oaks, 1989). John Ruskin, *The Seven Lamps of Architecture* (New York: Wiley, 1866).

11. The hallstand is atypical in that, unlike most genteel middle-class furnishings of the nineteenth century, it has no obvious courtly antecedents. Hallstands are an international phenomenon, found throughout the Western and Westernized world in the last century. Comments on the history of the form can be found in Christopher Gilbert, *Loudon Furniture Designs* (East Ardsley, England: S. R. Publishers, 1970), 56–57; Thomas Webster and Mrs. Parkes, *An Encyclopædia of Domestic Economy* (New York: Harper & Brothers, 1845), 287–288; Rudolph Ackermann, ed., *The Repository of Arts, Literature, Commerce, Manufacture, Fashions, and Politics* (London: R. Ackermann, 1809–1828); Charles F. Montgomery, *American Furniture: The Federal Period* (New York: Viking, 1966), 435;

Henry Havard, *Dictionnaire de l'Ameublement et de la Décoration* (Paris: Maison Quantin, 1887–1890), 4:512–514, 516–517. Despite its prominence and extensive production, the hallstand has not held much appeal for twentieth-century enthusiasts of elegant furniture: "As a piece of furniture, it was seldom designed; it merely occurred." John Gloag, *A Short Dictionary of Furniture* (New York: Holt, Rinehart and Winston, 1965), 282. To contextualize Gloag's condescending comment, see Kenneth L. Ames, "The Stuff of Everyday Life," in Schlereth, *Material Culture: A Research Guide*, 79–112. On the 1870s as the visual high point of Victorian style (and the high point of Victorian culture?), see Carroll L. V. Meeks, *The Railroad Station* (New Haven: Yale University Press, 1964), 1–25. The story of the decline of the hallstand is capably told in Leslie A. Greene, "The Late Victorian Hallstand: A Social History," *Nineteenth Century* 6, no. 4 (Winter 1980): 51–53.

12. For more on Grand Rapids furniture of the 1870s, see Kenneth L. Ames, "Grand Rapids Furniture at the Time of the Centennial," in *Winterthur Portfolio* 10, ed. Ian M. G. Quimby (Charlottesville: University Press of Virginia, 1975), 23–50.

13. For documentation and analysis of an expensive example, see Elizabeth Agee Cogswell, "The Henry Lippitt House of Providence, Rhode Island," *Winterthur Portfolio* 17, no. 4 (Winter 1982): 203–242.

14. On umbrellas, see William Sangster, *Umbrellas and Their History* (London: Cassell, Petter, and Galpin, c. 1870); Louis Octave Uzanne, *Les Ornements de la Femme* (Paris: Librairies-imprimeries reunies, 1892); A. Varron, "The Umbrella," *Ciba Review* 42 (1942): 1510–1548; T. S. Crawford, *A History of the Umbrella* (Newton Abbot, England: David and Charles, 1970). Canes were also placed on hallstands. For a classic analysis of this object in nineteenth-century society, see Thorstein Veblen, *The Theory of the Leisure Class* (New York: Macmillan, 1912), 265. The connotations of the umbrella and the cane or walking stick differed significantly. While both were widely used by males, as images amply record, the umbrella was often associated with the parson, the cane with the dandy or rake.

15. James Laver, *Modesty in Dress* (Boston: Houghton Mifflin, 1969), 121–123. Today Laver's point seems debatable. Top hats are gone and American society is still male dominated. It might be more accurate to say that such explicit signs of male domination subside at times when expression of male domination must be muted. For more on the dynamic relationship of male and female attire, see Grant McCracken, "The Voice of Gender in the World of Goods: Beau Brummell and the Cunning of Present Gender Symbolism," a paper delivered at the Winterthur conference on material culture and gender, November 1989.

16. For closets in eighteenth-century houses, see Tatum, *Philadelphia Georgian*; and Herman, *Architecture and Rural Life in Central Delaware*.

17. On grooming rituals, see McCracken, *Culture and Consumption*, 86–87. On appearances in nineteenth-century America, see Karen Halttunen, *Confidence Men and Painted Women* (New Haven: Yale University Press, 1983). On glass and mirrors, see *Glass: History, Manufacture and Its Universal Application* (Pittsburgh: Pittsburgh Plate Glass Co., 1923); and Serge Roche, Germain Courage, and Pierre Devinoy, *Mirrors* (New York: Rizzoli, 1985). Trade catalogs document the full range of mirrors and mirror-bearing goods available in the nineteenth century. A helpful guide to one major collection is E. Richard McKinstry, *Trade Catalogues at Winterthur: A Guide to the Literature of Merchandising* (New York: Garland, 1984). The modern use of the mirror in the fine arts occurs in the work of Michelangelo Pistoletto, among others. See Edward Lucie-Smith, *Late Modern, The Visual Arts Since 1945* (New York: Praeger, 1969).

18. Giedion, *Mechanization Takes Command*, 329–332.

19. People with less space or

money could purchase the components of the hallstand as separate artifacts. Metal umbrella stands and wooden, wall-mounted hat and coat racks, usually with small mirrors, were the most common.

20. Ray Faulkner and Edwin Ziegfield, *Art Today* (New York: Holt, Rinehart and Winston, 1969); Henry Glassie, *Folk Housing in Middle Virginia* (Knoxville: University of Tennessee Press, 1975), 170–175; Glassie, "Folk Art," in *Folklore and Folklife, an Introduction*, ed. Richard M. Dorson (Chicago: University of Chicago Press, 1972), 272–279. It is not symmetry, however, that distinguishes Victorian artifacts and design from those that precede or follow them but profusion, elaboration, complexity. The latter traits are simultaneously self-conscious expressions of affluence, knowledge, and a high level of civilization. When symmetry is added, the whole becomes a demonstration of order and of control of self, materials, techniques, machinery, natural substances and laws, and the culture of other people, past and present. In short, in the Victorian world, complex symmetry demonstrated mastery in the broadest sense.

21. For comments on issues of style and symbol, see Dell Upton, "The Power of Things: Recent Studies in American Vernacular Architecture," in Schlereth, *Material Culture: A Research Guide*, 57–78; Karl Lehmann, "The Dome of Heaven," in *Modern Perspectives in Western Art History*, ed. W. Eugene Kleinbauer (New York: Holt, Rinehart and Winston, 1971), 227–270; Earl Baldwin Smith, *The Dome, a Study in the History of Ideas* (Princeton: Princeton University Press, 1950); John Summerson, *Heavenly Mansions* (New York: Norton, 1963), 1–28. Most of the hallstands illustrated here are examples of what was known as the néo-grec style in the 1870s (although explicit naming of styles of household goods in mainstream culture was no more prevalent than it is today). For comments on the néo-grec, see Kenneth L. Ames, "What Is the Néo-Grec?" *Nineteenth Century* 2, no. 2 (Summer 1976): 12–21; and Ames, "Sitting in (Néo-Grec) Style," *Nineteenth Century* 2, nos. 3–4 (Fall 1976): 50–58.

22. Todd S. Goodholme, ed., *A Domestic Cyclopedia of Practical Information* (New York: H. Holt & Co., 1877), 223.

23. Clarence Cook, *The House Beautiful* (New York: Scribner, Armstrong & Co., 1878), 31. A similar sentiment appears in Goodholme, *Domestic Cyclopedia*: "Probably the worst possible step is to buy the stereotyped hat and umbrella rack. No matter how elaborate, they are always the same thing over again, and generally very ugly" (p. 223). Both texts were part of what has been called the household art movement; see Martha Crabill McClaugherty, "Household Art: Creating the Artistic Home, 1868–1893," *Win-*terthur Portfolio 18, no. 1 (Spring 1983): 1–26.

24. If anything, the reformers were more self-conscious. For design reform in this country in the 1870s, see Doreen Bolger Burke et al., *In Pursuit of Beauty: Americans and the Aesthetic Movement* (New York: Rizzoli with the Metropolitan Museum of Art, 1986).

25. Self-consciousness in the nineteenth century takes many forms. It can be seen in the establishment of what would become state historical societies in the Midwest with the first wave of Yankee immigration: Wisconsin in 1846 and Minnesota in 1849. It can also be seen in the widespread popularity of diaries. See Gayle R. Davis, "Women's Frontier Diaries: Writing for Good Reason," *Women's Studies* 14 (1987): 5–14; Elizabeth Hampsten, *Read This Only to Yourself, the Private Writings of Midwestern Women* (Bloomington: Indiana University Press, 1982); Thomas Mallon, *A Book of One's Own: People and Their Diaries* (New York: Ticknor, 1984); and Lillian Schlissel, *Women's Diaries of the Westward Journey* (New York: Schocken, 1982).

26. As at the Lippitt house in Providence. See Cogswell, "Henry Lippitt House."

27. Plank-seat chairs were inexpensive but durable forms of seating, normally used by the poor or in utilitarian contexts where upholstery was not necessary or appropriate. Unlike hallstands,

hall chairs can be readily traced to antecedents in eighteenth-century Britain and Europe. They were, for example, found in great Palladian houses of eighteenth-century England, occasionally adorned with a family crest. Hall chairs are additional instances of the devaluation of aristocratic symbols. The quotation is from Cook, *House Beautiful*, 33. Psychological manipulation in a particularly bald form can be seen at the Lippitt House, where the hall chairs are so overscaled that they dwarf normal-sized people who try to sit on them. See Cogswell, "Henry Lippitt House."

28. Esther B. Aresty, *The Best Behavior* (New York: Simon & Schuster, 1970); Norbert Elias, *The Civilizing Process* (New York: Urizen Books, 1978); Arthur M. Schlesinger, *Learning How to Behave* (New York: Macmillan, 1946).

29. Continuities and changes in the prescriptive literature of calling and cards can be traced through the following volumes: *Etiquette for Gentlemen* (Philadelphia: Lindsay & Blakiston, 1845); George Winfred Hervey, *The Principles of Courtesy* (New York: Harper & Brothers, 1852); Emily Thornwell, *The Lady's Guide to Perfect Gentility* (New York: Derby & Jackson, 1856); Henry Lunettes (Margaret Cockburn Conkling), *The American Gentleman's Guide to Politeness and Fashion* (New York: Derby & Jackson, 1857); Henry P.

Willis, *Etiquette and the Usages of Society* (New York: Dick & Fitzgerald, 1860); *The Bazar Book of Decorum* (New York: Harper & Brothers, 1871); Florence Hartley, *The Ladies' Book of Etiquette* (Boston: J. S. Locke & Co., 1876); *Decorum* (New York: Union Publishing House, 1880); and George D. Carroll, *Diamonds from Brilliant Minds* (New York: Dempsey & Carroll, 1881). Many of these books acknowledged that the social practices they prescribed were based on English or French practice. Veblen, *Theory of the Leisure Class*, 41–60. Abba Goold Woolson, *Woman in American Society* (Boston: Roberts Brothers, 1873). Carol Gilligan, *In a Different Voice: Psychological Theory and Women's Development* (Cambridge: Harvard University Press, 1982).

30. It is also clear that the authors of etiquette books plagiarized and paraphrased earlier books extensively. The links and correspondences between literary behavior and social behavior are therefore not obvious.

31. Carroll, *Diamonds from Brilliant Minds*, 5:3. Etiquette books articulated four classes of calling: congratulation, condolence, friendship, and ceremony. My discussion focusses on ceremonial calling and the card practices associated with that ritual. The prescribed use of cards in conjunction with so many aspects of social life can be interpreted as social bookkeeping, a kind of

"paper trail" for social debts and obligations.

32. These afternoon calls were sometimes termed *morning calls*, an expression that suggests that work time and social time might have been conceived differently— or that there may have been an attempt to heighten the distinctions between the work world of males and the social world of females. While males participated in calling rituals, the emphasis on female maintenance of a household's social linkages suggests a very self-conscious division of labor.

33. "Never call without cards," an imperative from Hartley, *Ladies' Book of Etiquette*, 81, bears a remarkably close resemblance to an advertising slogan used by American Express. Continuity may account, in part, for the widespread acceptance of charge cards. The quotation is from Carroll, *Diamonds from Brilliant Minds*, 5:7. The use of "Miss" prescribed by etiquette books varies over time.

34. "A visit and an umbrella should always be returned" (*Etiquette for Gentlemen*, 86). The card system provided mechanisms for indicating absences. See any of the etiquette books listed in note 29.

35. The courtly origins or models for ceremonial calling are revealed by the heavy dependence on servants, although the practice also occurred where there were no servants to mediate and formalize the ritual. In significant

ways, the calling ritual was about status, hierarchy, and stratification. Some modern observers find calling (only leaving a card) with no intention to visit difficult to understand. One explanation is that such calling was an attenuated form of social bonding, that it was an efficient and effective way of "keeping in touch." Cards offered artifactual answers to the hypothetical question: "Who thought of us (me) today?" Even in etiquette books tolerance of the practice varied. *Decorum* noted, "It is becoming more usual for visits of ceremony to be performed by cards; it will be a happy day when that is universal" (p. 75).

The *Bazar Book of Decorum* provided a somewhat cynical endorsement: "Every dame nowadays has what is called a visiting list. This is composed of a number of persons of her own sex who spend money, dress, and make calls very much as she herself does. No other sympathy than is indicated by these is required by mutual visitors of the fashionable sort. They need not be friends; it is not, in fact, necessary that they should be acquaintances, and we actually know of two dames who not long ago met in the street and looked into each other's face as perfect strangers, though they had been on visiting terms for the last ten years or more. There is so little substance in this kind of social relationship that its obligations can be as well performed by a mere symbol as the person it

represents, and thus a bit of cardboard, with nothing but a name upon it, frequently serves every purpose" (p. 235).

Another answer is that the practice does not have to "make sense" in any rational way. Culture is not rational. See Kertzer, *Ritual, Politics, and Power*, and Peter Gay, *Freud for Historians* (New York: Oxford University Press, 1985).

36. These behaviors were defended as polite fictions which eased the pain or discomfort of potential rejection.

37. See Chapter 3 for a fuller discussion of Home, Sweet Home and related sentiments.

CHAPTER TWO

Some of the material presented here was originally planned as a contribution to a *Festschrift* for Robert C. Smith. The volume was never published. I am pleased, therefore, to dedicate this chapter to his memory. I am not sure that Smith would have agreed with my argument, but I know he would have appreciated and enjoyed the images. And he would have been able to say far more about their historic design sources than I. This chapter incorporates ideas suggested to me by Susan Garfinkel.

1. On the cultural dimensions of foodways, see Sidney W. Mintz, *Sweetness and Power: The Place of Sugar in Modern History* (New York: Penguin, 1985), 3–18; and

Peter Farb and George Armelagos, *Consuming Passions: The Anthropology of Eating* (New York: Washington Square Press, 1980).

2. André Leroi-Gourhan, *The Dawn of European Art: An Introduction to Paleolithic Cave Painting* (Cambridge: Cambridge University Press, 1982); John E. Pfeiffer, *The Creative Explosion: An Inquiry into the Origins of Art and Religion* (New York: Harper & Row, 1982); Ann Sieveking, *The Cave Artists* (London: Thames and Hudson, 1979).

3. The term *affecting presence* is from Robert Plant Armstrong, *The Affecting Presence: An Essay in Humanistic Anthropology* (Urbana: University of Illinois Press, 1971).

4. The concept of *prime objects* is formulated in George Kubler, *The Shape of Time* (New Haven: Yale University Press, 1962), 39–45.

5. For an overview of some of this firm's most prominent products, see Kenneth L. Ames, "The Furniture of Fourdinois," *Antiques* 110 no. 2 (August 1976): 335–343. For more on this object, see Ames, "The Battle of the Sideboards," in *Winterthur Portfolio* 9, ed. Ian M. G. Quimby (Charlottesville: University Press of Virginia, 1974), 1–27. A period photograph of the Fourdinois sideboard is reprinted in Elizabeth Aslin, *Nineteenth Century English Furniture* (New York: Thomas Yoseloff, 1962), pl. 39.

6. On sideboards, buffets, and cognate forms, see appropriate

entries in Gloag, *Short Dictionary of Furniture*; Havard, *Dictionnaire de l'ameublement*; Percy Macquoid and Ralph Edwards, *The Dictionary of English Furniture* (London: Country Life, 1954). Changes in dining room furnishings are discussed in Mark Girouard, *Life in the English Country House* (New Haven: Yale University Press, 1978); Eric Mercer, *Furniture, 700–1700* (New York: Meredith Press, 1969); Peter Thornton, *Authentic Decor: The Domestic Interior, 1620–1920* (New York: Viking Penguin, 1984).

7. Put in somewhat different terms, the primary function of the object was to facilitate ceremony and ritual. Seen from this perspective, no other utilitarian function was necessary. An emphasis on ceremonial and ritual function is characteristic of the courtly mode of furnishing in the nineteenth century. Like many other forms of material culture, these immense sideboards also served to "locate" their owners on class, status, and other social, economic, and political grids. See Kenneth L. Ames and Michael J. Ettema, "Unseating Style," *Art and Antiques*, March 1984, 72–79.

8. On innovation as reconfiguration of the familiar, see H. G. Barnett, *Innovation: The Basis of Cultural Change* (New York: McGraw-Hill, 1953).

9. On still-life painting, see Ingvar Bergstrom, *Dutch Still-Life Painting in the Seventeenth Century* (New York: Thomas Yoseloff, 1959); Michel Faré, *Le Grande Siècle de la Nature Morte en France* (Fribourg: Office du Livre, 1974); William H. Gerdts and Russell Burke, *American Still-Life Painting* (New York: Praeger, 1971). On Parisian hotels, see Michel Gallet, *Stately Mansions: Eighteenth Century Paris Architecture* (New York: Praeger, 1972), 86–87. On Rococo ornament, see Peter Jessen, *Das Rokoko im Ornamentstich* (Berlin: Verlag für Kunstwissenschaft, c. 1920).

10. For cross-cultural perspectives, see Helena Hayward, ed., *World Furniture: An Illustrated History* (New York: McGraw-Hill, 1965); and Noel Riley, ed., *World Furniture* (New York: Mayflower Books, 1980).

11. On the Philadelphia Centennial, see George Titus Ferris, *Gems of the Centennial* (New York: D. Appleton & Co., 1877); Frank Henry Norton, *Illustrated Historical Register of the Centennial Exhibition* (New York: American News Co., 1879); and Walter Smith, "Industrial Art," in *The Masterpieces of the Centennial International Exhibition 1876* (Philadelphia: Gebbie & Barrie, 1876).

12. Aslin, *Nineteenth Century English Furniture*; R. W. Symonds and B. B. Whineray, *Victorian Furniture* (London: Country Life, 1962).

13. B. Silliman and C. R. Goodrich, eds., *The World of Science, Art and Industry Illustrated* (New York: G. P. Putnam & Co., 1854), 168–169. Commentary later in the text (p. 185) reveals ambivalence about the suitability of such explicitly courtly goods for republican America. For Herter, see relevant sections in Berry B. Tracy et al., *Nineteenth-Century America: Furniture and Other Decorative Arts* (New York: Metropolitan Museum of Art, 1970); and Marilynn Johnson, "Art Furniture: Wedding the Beautiful to the Useful," in Burke et al., *In Pursuit of Beauty*, 142–175.

14. Silliman and Goodrich, *World of Science, Art and Industry*, 162. For basic data on Roux, see Dianne D. Hauserman (Pilgrim), "Alexander Roux and His 'Plain and Artistic Furniture,'" *Antiques* 93, no. 2 (February 1968): 210–217.

15. Sideboards, particularly the most expensive examples, seem less functional in a utilitarian sense than hallstands, which were often in an adjacent space only a few feet away. Differences in degree of utility may be linked to differences in degree of ceremony. The more important the ceremonial roles of an object, the less significant its ability to serve utilitarian ends. Halls and dining rooms represent graduated levels of ritual and ceremony within homes. The most important rituals usually intersect with foodways.

16. On universalizing, see Melanie Wallendorf and Eric J. Arnould, "'We Gather Together': The Consumption Rituals of

Thanksgiving Day," *Journal of Consumer Research* 18, no. 1 (June 1991); and Ann Douglas, *The Feminization of American Culture* (New York: Knopf, 1977).

17. On Delacroix, see René Huyghe, *Delacroix* (New York: Harry N. Abrams, 1963); and Frank Anderson Trapp, *The Attainment of Delacroix* (Baltimore: Johns Hopkins University Press, 1970). For the hunts and animal scenes, see Lee Johnson, *The Paintings of Eugène Delacroix* (Oxford: Oxford University Press, 1981–1989), 3:9–32, 4:7–32.

18. *Sculptures by Antoine Louis Barye* (New York: Metropolitan Museum of Art, 1940); Stuart Pivar, *The Barye Bronzes: A Catalogue Raisonné* (Woodbridge, England: Antique Collectors' Club, 1978). Barye also produced numerous sculptures of stags.

19. James A. Manson, *Sir Edwin Landseer, R. A.* (London: Walter Scott Publishing Co., 1902); Frederic G. Stephens, *Sir Edwin Landseer* (London: Sampson Low, Marston & Co., 1880); Estelle M. Hurll, *Landseer* (Boston: Houghton Mifflin, 1901); *Engravings from Landseer* (Boston: James R. Osgood & Co., 1876).

20. For other examples, see Philip Hook and Mark Polimore, *Popular 19th Century Painting* (Woodbridge, England: Antique Collectors' Club, 1986).

21. On imperialism and foodways, see Mintz, *Sweetness and Power*, xvi–xxx.

22. Genesis 1. 26.

23. Human figures appear on European sideboards more frequently than on those produced in the United States. These figures are usually garbed in fifteenth- or sixteenth-century attire. See, for example, sideboards in the photographically illustrated catalog of the Parisian firm of Mazaroz et Ribaillier of about 1856, now in the Bibliothèque Nationale, Paris. On allegory, see Rudolf Wittkower, *Allegory and the Migration of Symbols* (Boulder, Colo.: Westview Press, 1972).

24. On attitudes toward the natural world, see René Dubos, *The Wooing of Earth* (New York: Scribner, 1980); and Donald Worster, "Transformations of the Earth: Toward an Agroecological Perspective in History," *Journal of American History* 76, no. 4 (March 1990): 1087–1106. Lawrence I. Berkove, "The 'Poor Players' of *Huckleberry Finn*," *Papers of the Michigan Academy of Science, Arts, and Letters* 53 (1968): 294–295.

25. John D'Emilio and Estelle B. Freedman, *Intimate Matters: A History of Sexuality in America* (New York: Harper & Row, 1988); Shere Hite, *The Hite Report on Male Sexuality* (New York: Ballantine Books, 1981); Michael S. Kimmel, ed., *Changing Men: New Directions in Research on Men and Masculinity* (Newbury Park, Calif.: Sage, 1987).

26. William Scrope, *Days of Deer-Stalking in the Forest of Atholl* (London: John Murray, 1847); Erich Hobusch, *Fair Game: A History of Hunting, Shooting and Animal Conservation* (New York: Arco Publishing, 1980); Ron Baker, *The American Hunting Myth* (New York: Vantage Press, 1985); Ruth Irwin Weidner, "Images of the Hunt in Nineteenth-Century America and Their Sources in British and European Art," Ph.D. dissertation, University of Delaware, 1988.

27. Claude Lévi-Strauss, *The Raw and the Cooked* (New York: Harper & Row, 1969). On civilizing foodways, see Yi-Fu Tuan, *Segmented Worlds and Self* (Minneapolis: University of Minnesota Press, 1982).

28. Susan Williams, *Savory Suppers and Fashionable Feasts: Dining in Victorian America* (New York: Pantheon, 1985); Kathryn Grover, ed., *Dining in America, 1850–1900* (Amherst: University of Massachusetts Press, 1987).

29. Kertzer, *Ritual, Politics, and Power*; Victor Turner, *The Ritual Process* (Chicago: Aldine, 1969).

30. This formulation may suggest a greater involvement of reason than was actually the case. One of the key features of rituals is that they express what cannot be expressed verbally. Thus, explanation is approximate at best. The situation is further complicated by the fact that rituals are not necessarily reasoned or reasonable. They are about emotions, not thoughts. Bonding, solidarity is

achieved by people doing something together in a shared setting, not by thinking the same thoughts together. Kertzer, *Ritual, Politics, and Power*, 57–76.

31. Cogswell, "Henry Lippitt House."

32. On window shades and window treatments, see Samuel J. Dornsife, "Design Sources for Nineteenth-Century Window Hangings," in *Winterthur Portfolio 10*, ed. Ian M. G. Quimby (Charlottesville: University Press of Virginia, 1975), 90, 92. For information on "Décor Chasse et Pêche," see E. A. Entwisle, *French Scenic Wallpapers 1800–1860* (Leigh-on-Sea, England: F. Lewis, 1972), 45; Catherine Lynn, *Wallpaper in America* (New York: Norton, 1980), 325; and *Trois Siècles de Papiers Peints* (Paris: Musée des Arts Décoratifs, 1967), cat. no. 164. The paper also figures prominently in the wallpaper auction catalog of Sotheby Parke Bernet Monaco for February 14, 1983, 10–11. At the Crystal Palace in 1851, another Paris wallpaper firm, Delicourt, exhibited a pattern called "La Grande Chasse." Like the Fourdinois sideboard, it won a top award. This complex and extensive design consisted of a wooded landscape ornamented with six scenes of dogs attacking prey. The centerpiece of the paper was a stag hunt, closely resembling the "Death of the Stag" dominating the Bulkley & Herter sideboard of 1853. It would seem that the Bulkley & Herter compo-

sition synthesized key elements of the Fourdinois sideboard and the Delicourt wallpaper. See Entwisle, *French Scenic Wallpapers*, 45, figs. 46–48. On dining room pictures, see, for example, Katharine Morrison McClinton, *The Chromolithographs of Louis Prang* (New York: C. N. Potter, 1973), 180–183.

33. For Roesen, see Gerdts and Burke, *American Still-Life Painting*, 61–67; and William H. Gerdts, *Painters of the Humble Truth* (Columbia: University of Missouri Press, 1981).

34. On Thanksgiving, see Wallendorf and Arnould, "We Gather Together"; Diana Karter Appelbaum, *Thanksgiving: An American Holiday, An American History* (New York: Facts on File, 1984); Hennig Cohen and Tristram Potter Coffin, *The Folklore of American Holidays* (Detroit: Gale Research, 1987), 331–351; Ralph and Adelin Linton, *We Gather Together: The Story of Thanksgiving* (New York: Henry Schuman, 1949); Jane M. Hatch, ed., *The American Book of Days* (New York: H.W. Wilson, 1978), 1053–1057; and Robert Haven Schauffler, *Thanksgiving: Its Origin, Celebration and Significance as Related in Prose and Verse* (New York: Moffat, Yard & Co., 1908). On civil religion more generally, see Robert Bellah, "Civil Religion in America," *Daedalus* 96 (1967): 1–21. On Thanksgiving postcards, see George and Dorothy Miller, *Picture Postcards in the*

United States, 1893–1918 (New York: Potter, 1976), 233–236. The authors describe one set of six cards showing "an eagle attacking and killing a turkey," presumably a symbolic enactment of the subordination of nature to nationalism.

35. On Thanksgiving and abundance, see Wallendorf and Arnould, "We Gather Together." Colleen McDannell, *The Christian Home in Victorian America, 1840–1900* (Bloomington: Indiana University Press, 1986), 151.

36. The mid-century iconography of dining enabled international bonding of the upper classes but was potentially disruptive within the nation. Thanksgiving traded international or cosmopolitan bonding for vertical solidarity through all social classes. Nationalism superseded cosmopolitanism. Appelbaum, *Thanksgiving*, 113, 153; Linton and Linton, *We Gather Together*, 90–96.

37. Gilligan, *In a Different Voice*, 40–62.

38. On the Colonial Revival, see Alan Axelrod, ed., *The Colonial Revival in America* (New York: Norton, 1985). On Thanksgiving as an Americanizing ritual, see Lawrence H. Fuchs, "Thinking about Immigration and Ethnicity in the U.S.," paper delivered at a conference on U.S. and French immigration policies sponsored by the American Academy of Arts and Sciences, Chantilly, October 12, 1989, 32–33.

39. Eric Hobsbawm and

Terrence Ranger, eds., *The Invention of Tradition* (Cambridge: Cambridge University Press, 1983).

40. I do not mean to suggest that Thanksgiving is without antecedents, only that its current form was constructed in Victorian America. That construction, however, credits the Pilgrims with inventing the holiday. As Wallendorf and Arnould put it: "Contemporary Americans tend to believe that the holiday was cleverly invented by the Pilgrims in 1621, without any historical precedent in their native lands of Holland and England. This nationalistic myth persists despite the historical roots of Thanksgiving Day in ancient holidays such as the Hebrew celebration of Purim, the Feast of the Tabernacles; Greek festivals honoring Demeter, the goddess of harvests and grain; the Roman festival of Cerealia held in honor of Ceres, the goddess of grain; the mid-autumn festival in China; and Native American tribes' harvest festivals, such as the Vikita ceremony of the Tohono O'Odham" (p. 26).

There is extensive literature on religious celebrations of thanksgiving and on thanksgiving proclamations and addresses. See, for example [Franklin Benjamin Hough], *Proclamations for Thanksgiving, Issued by the Continental Congress, Pres't Washington, by the National and State Governments* (Albany: Munsell & Rowland, 1858). The New York State Library has an extensive collection of thanksgiving addresses and proclamations dating from the seventeenth to the nineteenth century.

41. Ames, "Battle of the Sideboards."

42. Harriet Prescott Spofford, *Art Decoration Applied to Furniture* (New York: Harper & Brothers, 1878), 195.

43. Rhoda and Agnes Garrett, *Suggestions for House Decoration* (London: Macmillan and Co., 1877), 49.

44. Gilligan, *In a Different Voice*. Women played prominent roles in teaching children about nature and in the conservation movement. See Carolyn Merchant, "Gender and Environmental History," *Journal of American History* 76:4 (March 1990), 1118–1119. A late Victorian female perspective on Landseer's painting, "The Hunted Stag" (2.23) comes from Hurll, *Landseer*, 72: "While we admire the art which can produce such a picture, the subject, like that of war, is too painful for enjoyment." While it may be tempting to attribute this change in evaluation to shifting gender relations or roles, those shifts, like these objects, must be examined within an international context.

45. Kirk Jeffrey, "The Family as Utopian Retreat from the City," *Soundings* 55 (1972): 21–41; McClaugherty, "Household Art"; Grant McCracken, " 'Homeyness': A Cultural Account of One Constellation of Consumer Goods and Meanings," in *Interpretive Consumer Research*, ed. Elizabeth C. Hirschman (Provo, Utah: Association for Consumer Research, 1989), 168–183.

46. Norman H. Clark, *Deliver Us from Evil: An Interpretation of American Prohibition* (New York: Norton, 1976); Paul Boyer, *Urban Masses and Moral Order in America* (Cambridge: Harvard University Press, 1978).

47. D'Emilio and Freedman, *Intimate Matters*, 156–164, 222–223.

CHAPTER THREE

The rough contours of this chapter were initially sketched out in a 1979 presentation called "Needlework Mottoes: Icons of Popular Culture," given at the symposium, "Victorian Album: Aspects of American Life, 1865–1900," held in Washington, D.C. and cosponsored by the Victorian Society in America and the National Archives.

1. Assumptions that they will be placed over doors are expressed in Henry T. Williams and Mrs. C. S. Jones, *Beautiful Homes* (New York: H. T. Williams, 1878), 21–23, where they are called "door texts." The authors note: "These cheery and beautiful door embellishments have become so common and deservedly popular that a tasteful apartment is scarcely considered finished without one or more of them." They

add: "We believe the most popular kind of door texts are those worked on the beautiful stamped perforated card-board, of which there are such an innumerable variety, embroidered with silk, chenille, gold and silver thread, cord or bullion, beads, or even zephyrs."

2. Herbert Marshall McLuhan, *Understanding Media* (New York: McGraw-Hill, 1964).

3. A period account of developments in the production of paper is found in Charles Thomas Davis, *The Manufacture of Paper* (Philadelphia: Henry Carey Baird & Co., 1886).

4. Margaret Vincent, *The Ladies' Work Table: Domestic Needlework in Nineteenth-Century America* (Allentown, Pa.: Allentown Art Museum, 1988), 37–39, 57–59.

5. See, for example, *The Lady's Work-Box Companion* (New York: Burgess, Stringer, 1844). The quotation is from *The Ladies' Guide in Needlework* (Philadelphia: Gihon, 1852), 86.

6. Florence Hartley, *The Ladies' Hand Book of Fancy and Ornamental Work* (Philadelphia: Evans, 1859), 100; Mrs. C. S. Jones and Henry T. Williams, *Household Elegancies: Suggestions in Household Art and Tasteful Home Decorations* (New York: H. T. Williams, 1875), 249.

7. The remaining 10 percent are smaller, presumably standard sheets cut in halves, thirds, quarters, and so on.

8. For motto frames, see the following trade catalogs: Hirshberg Bros. & Hollander (Baltimore, 1878), 11; C.F. Rice (Chicago, 1879), 66–67; W. R. Reid (Cleveland, 1880), 14–15; Bowen & Lee (Chicago, 1881), 38; George N. Lee & Co. (Chicago, 1884), 34, 46: Hirshberg Bros. & Hollander (Baltimore, 1884), 81–82; Kohn & Co. (Philadelphia, 1887), 29–31; C. F. Rice (Chicago, 1888), 62.

9. Varieties of perforated cardboard are listed in Hirshberg Bros. & Hollander (1878), 33; W. R. Reid (1880), 49; Bowen & Lee (1881), 73; and G.N. Lee & Co. (1884), 170.

10. Beverly Gordon, "Victorian Fancywork in the American Home: Fantasy and Accommodation," in *Making the American Home*, ed. Marilyn Ferris Motz and Pat Browne (Bowling Green, Ohio: Bowling Green State University Popular Press, 1988), 48–68; Arlene Zeger Wiczyk, ed., *A Treasury of Needlework Projects from Godey's Lady's Book* (New York: Arco, 1972), 181, 226.

11. Giedion, *Mechanization Takes Command*; David A. Hanks et al., *Innovative Furniture in America* (New York: Horizon, 1981).

12. Quoted in Winthrop S. Boggs, *Ten Decades Ago: 1840–1850* (Federalsburg, Md.: American Philatelic Society, 1949), 72. On stamps and perforating, see also Asa Briggs, *Victorian Things* (Chicago: University of Chicago Press, 1988), 327–368.

13. Marvin D. Schwartz, Edward J. Stanek, and Douglas K. True, *The Furniture of John Henry Belter and the Rococo Revival* (New York: Dutton, 1981). A bridge between furniture and paper can be found in the development of the papier-mâché industry, which literally used a paper product for the production of furniture. See Shirley Spaulding DeVoe, *English Papier Mache of the Georgian and Victorian Periods* (London: Barrie & Jenkins, 1971). On paper replacing cotton cloth during the Civil War, see Davis, *Manufacture of Paper*, 61. The history of material culture is in large part the history of materials competing to dominate functions. See Robert Friedel, *A Material World* (Washington, D. C.: Smithsonian Institution, 1988).

14. Kenneth L. Ames, "Gardner and Company of New York," *Antiques* 100:2 (August 1971): 174–183.

15. Trade catalog of W. R. Reid (Cleveland, 1880), 49.

16. Gardner's trade catalog for 1884 illustrates a Sunday school settee with "Our Sabbath Home" perforated in the back (p. 27). Small chairs and rocking chairs marked "Pet" and "Baby" still survive.

17. On mottoes, see Charles Box, *Elegies and Epitaphs* (Gloucester, England: H. Osbourne, 1892); Sophia Frances Anne Canfeild, *House Mottoes and Inscriptions* (London: Elliot Stock, 1908); Warrington Hogg, *The Book of*

Old Sundials & Their Mottoes (Edinburgh: T.N. Foulis, 1922); Laurence Urdang et al., *Mottoes* (Detroit: Gale Research Co., 1986); James Wood, *Dictionary of Quotations* (London: Frederick Warne and Co., 1893).

18. The list of examples is extensive. A few title-page mottoes chosen at random give an idea of the genre: "Thou, God, seest me," John Angell James, *The Young Man from Home* (New York: American Tract Society, c. 1858); "Her ways are ways of pleasantness, and all her paths are peace," Daniel Wise, *Pleasant Pathways; or, Persuasives to Early Piety* (New York: Carlton & Porter, 1859); "Proverbs are the daughters of daily experience," J. G. Holland, *Gold-Foil, Hammered from Popular Proverbs* (New York: Charles Scribner's Sons, 1859); "Politeness, is to do and say the kindest things in the kindest way," Mrs. Manners, *At Home and Abroad; or, How to Behave* (New York: D. Appleton & Co., 1865); "The hand of the diligent maketh rich," Emily Huntington Miller, *The Royal Road to Fortune* (Chicago: Alfred L. Sewell & Co., 1869); "The proper study of mankind is man," *How to Read Character: A New Illustrated Hand-Book of Phrenology and Physiology* (New York: Samuel R. Wells, 1873); "A little child shall lead them," J. Henderson M'Carty, *Inside the Gates* (Cincinnati: Hitchcock and Walden, 1876); "They also serve,

who only stand and wait," *Folded Hands* (New York: American Tract Society, 1878); "Blessed are they that mourn for they shall be comforted," G. W. Quinby, *Heaven Our Home* (Augusta, Maine: Gospel Banner, 1882); "Lengthen thy chords and strengthen thy stakes," Andrew Manship, *History of Gospel Tents and Experience* (Philadelphia [author], 1884).

19. Publisher C. P. Farrell advertised in 1880 that he sold "the best and latest American and English Liberal Works." Authors he listed included Robert Ingersoll, Voltaire, Thomas Paine, John Stuart Mill, Humboldt, Darwin, Huxley, and Spencer. The notice appeared on the back pages of Robert G. Ingersoll, *The Ghosts and Other Lectures* (Washington, D. C.: C.P. Farrell, 1880). McDannell, *Christian Home in Victorian America*, discusses differences between Protestant and Catholic concepts and behaviors.

20. On condensation (or universalizing), see Douglas, *Feminization of American Culture*.

21. Howard Mumford Jones, *The Age of Energy: Varieties of American Experience, 1865–1915* (New York: Viking, 1973), 104–112.

22. Meeks, *The Railroad Station*, 1–25. Probably the most notable architectural expression of this tendency was in the work of Philadelphia architect Frank Furness. See James F. O'Gorman, *The Architecture of Frank Furness* (Philadelphia: Philadelphia

Museum of Art, 1973).

23. This term is used in Peter J. Hugill, "Technology Diffusion in the World Automobile Industry, 1885–1985," in *The Transfer and Transformation of Ideas and Material Culture*, ed. Hugill and D. Bruce Dickson (College Station: Texas A & M Press, 1988), 110–142.

24. On Frances Flora Palmer (1812–1876), see Charlotte Streifer Rubinstein, *American Women Artists* (New York: Avon Books, 1982), 68–70.

25. See, for example, Downing, *Architecture of Country Houses*, 317–321.

26. John F. Moe, "Concepts of Shelter: The Folk Poetics of Space, Change, and Continuity," *Journal of Popular Culture* 11, no. 1 (Summer 1977): 219–253.

27. John F.W. Ware, *Home Life: What It Is and What It Needs* (Boston: Wm. V. Spencer, 1866), 170–171.

28. See, for example, several of the images in Phoebe Stanton, *The Gothic Revival & American Church Architecture* (Baltimore: Johns Hopkins University Press, 1968).

29. Catharine E. Beecher and Harriet Beecher Stowe, *The American Woman's Home* (New York: J.B. Ford & Co., 1869), 22.

30. Colleen McDannell and Bernhard Lang, *Heaven: A History* (New Haven: Yale University Press, 1988). For period constructions of the relationship of home and heaven, see *The Homeward Path* (Boston: Crosby, Nichols,

and Co., 1856); *Heaven Our Home* (Boston: Roberts Brothers, 1864); M'Carty, *Inside the Gates* (1876); E. Prentiss, *Stepping Heavenward* (London: James Nisbett & Co., 1879); Quinby, *Heaven Our Home* (1882); Elizabeth Stuart Phelps, *Beyond the Gates* (Boston: Houghton Mifflin, 1884); and *Golden Thoughts on Mother, Home, and Heaven* (Philadelphia: Garretson & Co., 1878).

31. This imagery is international. A particularly compelling example in the Paris cemetery of Père Lachaise is illustrated in Kenneth T. Jackson and Camilo Jose Vergara, *Silent Cities: The Evolution of the American Cemetery* (New York: Princeton Architectural Press, 1989), 17.

32. Sandra Sizer, *Gospel Hymns and Social Religion* (Philadelphia: Temple University Press, 1979). For changes in the architecture of Congregationalism, see Kathleen Curran, "The 'Rundbogenstil' and the Romanesque Revival in Germany and Their Effloressence in America," Ph.D. dissertation, University of Delaware, 1986.

33. For the literature on samplers and related forms of needlework, see Susan Burrows Swan, "Needlework," in Ames and Ward, *Decorative Arts and Household Furnishings*, 247–255.

34. Sizer, *Gospel Hymns*, 33.

35. Douglas, *Feminization of American Culture*. Lawrence Taylor, "An Anthropological View of Mourning Ritual in the Nineteenth Century," in *A Time to Mourn: Ex-*pressions of Grief in Nineteenth Century America*, ed. Martha V. Pike and Janice Gray Armstrong (Stony Brook, N.Y.: Museums at Stony Brook, 1980), 39–48. James F. White, *The Cambridge Movement* (Cambridge: Cambridge University Press, 1962).

36. Gay, *Freud for Historians*, 75–77.

37. Ingersoll, *Ghosts*, iv.

CHAPTER FOUR

An early version of this chapter was delivered at the annual meeting of the Popular Culture Association, Cincinnati, April 21, 1978, and published as "Material Culture as Non Verbal Communication: A Historical Case Study," *Journal of American Culture* 3, no. 4 (Winter 1980): 619–641.

1. For music, musicians, and high status, see Don J. Hibbard with Carol Kaleialoha, *The Role of Rock* (Englewood Cliffs, N.J.: Prentice-Hall, 1983); and Charles Kaiser, *1968 in America: Music, Politics, Chaos, Counterculture and the Shaping of a Generation* (New York: Weidenfeld & Nicolson, 1988).

2. Robert F. Gellerman, *The American Reed Organ* (Vestal, N.Y.: Vestal Press, 1973); Robert B. Whiting, *Estey Reed Organs on Parade* (Vestal, N.Y.: Vestal Press, 1981).

3. In some pianos of the nineteenth century, the relationship to the harp was explicit. Henry Kroeger of New York City and Kuhn and Ridgaway of Baltimore both produced so-called harp-pianos in the 1850s. See Laurence Libin, *American Musical Instruments* (New York: Metropolitan Museum of Art, 1985), 188–189. The common upright, widely available by the end of the century, was furnished with ranges of strings set perpendicular to the floor.

4. Alfred Dolge, *Pianos and Their Makers* (New York: Dover, 1972).

5. Music for parlor organs can be found in William H. Clarke, *The American Organ or Organist's Parlor Companion* (Boston: G.D. Russell, 1865); William H. Clarke, *Home Recreations: A Collection of New Songs . . . for the Parlor-Organ, Melodeon, or Pianoforte* (Boston: S.D. and H.W. Smith, 1867); H. S. Perkins and Wm. W. Bentley, *The River of Life, for Our Sunday Schools* (Boston: Oliver Ditson & Co., 1873); and C. A. White and Chas. D. Blake, *White's School for the Reed Organ* (Boston: White, Smith & Co., 1875). The popularity of the reed organ can be measured in part from the number of publications generated to provide instruction or music. The end-papers of Perkins and Bentley, *River of Life* (1873) list the following: *Clarke's New Method for Reed Organs*; *Getze's School for Parlor Organ*; *Emerson's Method for Reed Organs*; *Clarke's Improved School for Parlor Organ*; *Kinkel's New Method for Reed Organ*; *Root's*

School for Cabinet Organ; *Clarke's Dollar Instructor for Reed Organs*; *Clarke's Reed Organ Companion*; *Bellak's Method for Organ*; *Melodeon without a Master*; *Mack's Analytical Method for Cabinet Organ*; *Winner's New School for Cabinet Organ*; *Winner's Perfect Guide for Cabinet Organ*; *Winner's Cabinet Organ Tutor*; *Winner's Easy System for Melodeon*; *Amateur's Organ Instructor*; *Leslie's Cabinet Organ*; *Cabinet Organ Treasury*; *Young Organist's Album*; and *Organ at Home*.

6. In the cabinetmaking and furniture trades, the term *piano finish* referred to the highest-quality clear finish available.

7. On verticality and its relationship to picturesque eclecticism, see Meeks, *Railroad Station*, 1–25.

8. For examples of the ways the wealthy expanded functions into many rooms and suites of rooms, see Edward Strahan, *Mr. Vanderbilt's House and Collection* (Boston: George Barrie, 1883–1884); and *Artistic Houses* (New York: Benjamin Blom, 1971; originally published 1883).

9. Comparative retail prices of parlor organs and pianos for the 1870s and 1880s, based on figures provided in trade catalogs:

Organs:	Pianos:
Estey & Co., 1874, $160 to $400	Decker Bros., 1873, $400 to $1,500
Packard, 1884, $200 to $400	J. & C. Fischer, 1878, $350 to $1,200
Mason & Hamlin, 1886, $100 to $400	J. & C. Fischer, 1883, $450 to $1,200
New England, 1880, $150 to $300	Weber, 1880, $650 to $1,600

Prices listed are for domestic models only. Church or lecture hall organs were more expensive. Fischer's $350 piano was an upright; square pianos started at about $500. The highest figures are for grand pianos.

10. Pianos might also be described as belonging to the courtly tradition; parlor organs were more domestic, more privatized. The greater attention to small-scale design elements and the closer involvement with changing styles and fashions make these objects more intimate, more "homey," as that term was understood by advocates of the household art movement in the last third of the nineteenth century. See McClaugherty, "Household Art"; and McCracken, "'Homeyness.'"

11. But worldly design itself sometimes had ecclesiastical associations. This was particularly true of the so-called Modern Gothic style developed in Britain in the 1860s and popular in the United States in the 1880s. Organs in this style were explicitly churchly. For organs in other styles, the visible links to religiosity were fewer or less obvious.

12. This artifactual measuring and "clumping" of time is most frequently associated with large, even inhabitable objects: "When we lived in the yellow house . . ." or "When we had the '57 Chevy. . . ." Through this mental linkage, time is reified, tied to and proven by the concrete.

13. On the artifactual construc-

tion of self, see McCracken, *Culture and Consumption*; and Ames and Ettema, "Unseating Style."

14. Gay, *Freud for Historians*; Kertzer, *Ritual, Politics, and Power*.

15. On advertising, see David M. Potter, *People of Plenty* (Chicago: University of Chicago Press, 1954), 166–188; Samm Sinclair Baker, *The Permissible Lie* (Cleveland: World Publishing, 1968); Raymond A. Bauer and Stephen A. Greyser et al., *Advertising in America: The Consumer View* (Boston: Division of Research, Graduate School of Business Administration, Harvard University, 1968); Yale Brozen, *Advertising and Society* (New York: New York University Press, 1974); Jerry Della Femina, *From Those Wonderful Folks Who Gave You Pearl Harbor* (New York: Simon and Schuster, 1970); Stuart Ewen, *Captains of Consciousness* (New York: McGraw-Hill, 1976); Stephen Fox, *The Mirror Makers* (New York: Morrow, 1984); Philip Gold, *Advertising, Politics, and American Culture* (New York: Paragon House, 1987); Wilson Bryan Key, *The Age of Manipulation* (New York: Holt, 1989); William Leiss, Stephen Kline, and Sut Jhally, *Social Communication in Advertising* (Toronto: Methuen, 1986); Ivan L. Preston, *The Great American Blow-Up* (Madison: University of Wisconsin Press, 1975); Susan Strasser, *Satisfaction Guaranteed* (New York: Pantheon, 1989); and Jennifer Wicke,

Advertising Fictions (New York: Columbia University Press, 1988).

16. Robert Jay, *The Trade Card in Nineteenth-Century America* (Columbia: University of Missouri Press, 1987).

17. Hamlin Garland, *A Son of the Middle Border* (New York: Macmillan, 1917).

18. Woolson, *Woman in American Society*; Veblen, *Theory of the Leisure Class*; Gilligan, *In a Different Voice*.

19. Douglas, *Feminization of American Culture*, 60.

20. McDannell, *Christian Home*, discusses the gender division of domestic priestly roles.

21. Sizer, *Gospel Hymns and Social Religion*. Some of the late nineteenth century's most popular songs are assembled in the *National Magazine's Heart Songs* (Cleveland: World Syndicate Publishing Co., 1909). See also the titles listed in note 5.

22. This trilogy was captured in *Mother, Home, and Heaven* (1878), which contained an introduction by the prominent Presbyterian clergyman Theodore L. Cuyler (1822–1909). On Cuyler, see *Dictionary of American Biography* (New York: Charles Scribner's Sons, 1930), 5:18–19.

23. This formula also appears in images associated with multi-generational bonding at Thanksgiving. See, for example, C. G. Bush, "Thanksgiving Sketches— Frolic with the Children," *Harper's Weekly*, November 27, 1858.

24. On bonding, see Albert E. Scheflen, *Body Language and Social Order* (Englewood Cliffs, N.J.: Prentice-Hall, 1972).

25. The child as sanctioning agent also appears on the illustrated covers of sentimental Civil War music.

26. Examples of shrine making appear in George Talbot, *At Home: Domestic Life in the Post-Centennial Era* (Madison: State Historical Society of Wisconsin, 1977).

27. As in the common expression "They're playing our song," or in the familiar linking of a loved one or intimate with a certain tune.

28. Kaiser, *1968 in America*.

29. A few examples, chosen largely at random: "Auld Lang Syne," "Sweet Genevieve," "The Vacant Chair," "A Thousand Leagues Away," "The Girl I Left Behind Me," "I've Left the Snow-Clad Hills," "Oft in the Stilly Night," "Dream Faces," "Long Ago," "Darling Nelly Gray," "The Old Folks at Home," "Killarney," "The Last Rose of Summer," "My Old Kentucky Home," "Carry Me Back to Old Virginny."

30. Sexuality is explicitly linked to rock 'n roll (Hibbard and Kaleialoha, *Role of Rock*, 8–11) but also to the familiar "soft music" conventionally associated with intimacy and seduction. In many situations, dancing provides the link between music and intimacy. Music's bonding may as frequently be nonsexual, however, for it is often a form of shared flow experience. See Mihaly Csikszentmihalyi and Isabella Selega Csikszentmihalyi, eds., *Optimal Experience: Psychological Studies of Flow in Consciousness* (Cambridge: Cambridge University Press, 1988).

31. Whiting, *Estey Reed Organs on Parade*, 39. This model was introduced about 1880; the company claimed that it was the "finest reed organ yet manufactured." In 1886 it retailed for between $650 and $800, depending on accessories selected. In 1881 Estey claimed to have manufactured its 100,000th organ; all of the company's instruments were numbered consecutively. Eventually, the firm produced over half a million reed organs.

32. Lars Lerup, *Building the Unfinished: Architecture and Human Action* (Beverly Hills: Sage, 1977).

33. Berger and Luckmann, *Social Construction of Reality*.

CHAPTER FIVE

Parts of this chapter were first presented in a paper called "Sitting and Social Class: The Case of the Rocking Chair," delivered at the American Studies Association meeting in Boston, October 1977. My thoughts on tilting were developed during discussions with Michael Owen Jones and Gretchen Townsend.

1. On Edouart, see Andrew Oliver, *Auguste Edouart's Silhouettes of Eminent Americans, 1839–1844* (Charlottesville: University

Press of Virginia for the National Portrait Gallery, 1977).

2. For silhouettes, see Desmond Coke, *The Art of Silhouette* (London: Martin Secker, 1913); and R. L. Megroz, *Profile Art through the Ages* (New York: Philosophical Library, 1949).

3. Mercer, *Furniture 700–1700*, 76–77; Penelope Eames, "Furniture in England, France and the Netherlands from the Twelfth to the Fifteenth Century," *Furniture History* 13 (1977).

4. Claudia Brush Kidwell and Valerie Steele, eds., *Men and Women: Dressing the Part* (Washington D.C.: Smithsonian Institution Press, 1989).

5. Scheflen, *Body Language and Social Order*.

6. Schlesinger, *Learning How to Behave*.

7. Goffman, *Presentation of Self in Everyday Life*.

8. Katherine C. Grier, *Culture & Comfort: People, Parlors, and Upholstery, 1850–1930* (Amherst: University of Massachusetts Press, 1988), esp. chap. 7, "Parlor Suites and Lounges."

9. Karin Calvert, "Children in the House: A Social History of the Material Culture of Early Childhood, 1630 to 1900," ms., 16–56.

10. D'Emilio and Freedman, *Intimate Matters*.

11. Robert H. Wiebe, *The Search for Order, 1877–1920* (New York: Hill and Wang, 1966); *Wooton Patent Desks: A Place for Everything and Everything in Its Place* (Indianapolis: Indiana State Museum, and Oakland: The Oakland Museum, 1983).

12. Grier, *Culture & Comfort*.

13. The story of the three bears was published in England in 1837 by the poet Robert Southey (1774–1843). See Jean-Charles Seigneuret, ed., *Dictionary of Literary Themes and Motifs* (Westport, Conn.: Greenwood Press, 1980), 1:160.

14. Grier, *Culture & Comfort*.

15. See Joshua C. Taylor, *America as Art* (Washington D.C.: National Collection of Fine Arts, 1976), particularly the chapter titled "The American Cousin," 39–94.

16. Bruce E. Johansen, "Native American Societies and the Evolution of Democracy in America, 1600–1800," *Ethnohistory* 37, no. 3 (Summer 1990): 287–288.

17. See, for example, the portrait of Willem van Heythuisen in the Musée Royal des Beaux-Arts in Brussels, attributed to Frans Hals. Literary references to tilting appear in the work of Hamlin Garland, Thomas Chandler Haliburton, Joel Chandler Harris, Benjamin Silliman, Booth Tarkington, and others.

18. On Krimmel, see Milo M. Naeve, *John Lewis Krimmel: An Artist in Federal America* (Newark: University of Delaware Press, 1987), 73–74. Naeve suggests that *Village Tavern* may have been intended as a temperance image, an interpretation supported by the activities of the central family group.

19. Sarah Burns, *Pastoral Inventions: Rural Life in Nineteenth-Century American Art and Culture* (Philadelphia: Temple University Press, 1989).

20. Gilligan, *In a Different Voice*.

21. On nineteenth-century folkloric interest in the American preindustrial past, see Simon J. Bronner, *Folklife Studies from the Gilded Age* (Ann Arbor: UMI Research Press, 1987), 1–49.

22. Michael Aaron Rockland, "The Masculine Bias of the Vernacular," a paper delivered at the Winterthur conference on material culture and gender, November 1989.

23. Lorenz Eitner, "The Open Window and the Storm-Tossed Boat," *Art Bulletin* 37 (December 1955): 281–290.

24. On Nast as cartoonist, see J. Chal Vinson, *Thomas Nast: Political Cartoonist* (Athens: University of Georgia Press, 1967); and Morton Keller, *The Art and Politics of Thomas Nast* (New York: Oxford University Press, 1968).

25. A classic and highly effective example of this typing appears in Timothy Shay Arthur, *Ten Nights in a Bar-room and What I Saw There* (Philadelphia: J. W. Bradley, 1854).

26. Thos. E. Hill, *Hill's Manual of Social and Business Forms* (Chicago: Hill Standard Book Co., 1882).

27. On genteel dining, see John F. Kasson, "Rituals of Din-

ing: Table Manners in Victorian America," in Grover, *Dining in America*, 114–141.

28. Harvey Green, *The Light of the Home* (New York: Pantheon, 1983), 29–58.

29. Burns, *Pastoral Inventions*.

30. The most extensive study of this object is Ellen and Bert Denker, *The Rocking Chair Book* (New York: Mayflower Books, 1979).

31. Consult any major art historical survey of modern furniture and you will find very few rocking chairs. The bentwood rockers of Austrian manufacturer Michael Thonet are among the very few rockers that have been acceptable to the art establishment.

32. Denker and Denker, *Rocking Chair Book*, 13–29.

33. On rustic forms, see Craig Gilborn, *Adirondack Furniture and the Rustic Tradition* (New York: Harry N. Abrams, 1987).

34. On Gardner & Co., see Ames, "Gardner and Company of New York." On Hunzinger, see Richard W. Flint, "George Hunzinger, Patent Furniture Maker," *Art and Antiques* 3, no. 1 (January–February 1980): 116–123.

35. Denker and Denker, *Rocking Chair Book*.

36. Elizabeth Akers Allen, *Rock Me to Sleep, Mother* (Boston: Estes and Lauriat, 1884).

37. [Marietta Holley], *Josiah Allen's Wife as a P.A. and P.I.: Samantha at the Centennial* (Hartford, Conn.: American Publishing Co., 1888), 54–72.

Index

Finn, Huckleberry, 73
"For God So Loved The World . . ."
(motto text), 141, 147
"Forget Me Not" (motto text), 97, 147
Formal sitting, 189–195; definition of,
189; without material culture, 189–
190
Fourdinois sideboard, 46–49, 50, 51,
53, 55, 58, 65, 71, 79, 81, 82; description, 46–48, 49; functions,
49; innovations of, 49–51; as prime
object, 49; replications of, 51–66
France, design authority of, 46, 47, 51,
52, 57, 67, 83, 237
"Friendship Love and Truth" (motto text),
113, 147

Gardner & Co., 109, 111–113, 223
Garland, Hamlin, 161, 163
Garrett, Rhoda and Agnes, 92–93
Gender: and conflict, 4; and stereotypes,
8, 73–74, 88, 186, 187, 215, 228,
230, 231, 232. *See also* Men; Stereo-
types, female; Stereotypes, male;
Women
Gentility, 8, 42, 162; aspirations to, in
hallstands, 236; and calling, 35–43;
decline of, 237; definition of, 195,
211, 212, 236; resistance to, 236; and
rocking chairs, 236
Gentility in the Dining Room, 210–213
Giedion, Siegfried, 25
"Give Us This Day Our Daily Bread"
(motto text), 146, 147
Glass. *See* Mirrors
"God Bless Our Home" (motto text), 97,
99, 100–101, 116, 117, 120, 121,
127–137, 147
"God Is Love" (motto text), 141, 148
Gospel hymns, 117, 137, 166

Hale, Sarah Josepha, 88
Hall chairs, 21, 32–34; antecedents of,
246–247 n11; architectural qualities
of, 33; British, 18; design of, 32–34;
as evidence of specialization, 238;
experimental, 21; functions, 32–34;
similarities to hallstands, 33; use of, in
defining halls, 34
Hall seating, 32–34
Halls, 4, 7–43, 67, 195; activities
within, 11; architectural features of,
11, 16; back, 13; and control, 13;
dimensions of, 11, 14; eighteenth-
and nineteenth-century compared, 9;
English reform, 9–10; front, 4, 8–43;
functions of, 11, 13; furnishings of,

7–43; Georgian, 9–17; as passages, 8,
9–17; types of, 10–17
Hallstands, 17–32, 38, 67, 184; architectural qualities, 18, 19, 20, 21, 28;
and autovoyeurism, 32; British, 18;
cast-iron, 26, 27, 29; ceremonializing
daily life, 8; compared to sideboards,
249 n15; design of, 17–25, 26–28;
functions of, 18, 24, 30, 31; history of,
17, 30; humorous commentary on, 32;
as international phenomenon, 244–
245 n11; meanings of, 26–32; men's
use of, 30, 31; mirrors on, 17, 18, 19,
20, 21, 24, 25, 27, 28, 29, 31, 32;
neoclassical, 19; ornamentation of,
28; placement of, 28–29; prices of,
21; provisions for hats on, 17, 18, 19,
20, 21, 23, 24, 29, 32, 43; provisions
for umbrellas on, 17, 18, 19, 20, 21,
22–23, 29; relation of cost to design,
21; ritual uses of, 30; Romanticism
and, 30, 32; size of, 26; specialization
of, 237–238; symmetry of, 26, 28; as
theatrical backdrops, 30; as tools for
social differentiation, 26, 212
Hats, men's: and male domination, 23,
245 n15; provision for, on hallstands,
17, 18, 19, 20, 21, 23, 24, 29, 32, 43
"He Leadeth Me" (motto text), 144, 148
"Heaven Is My Home" (motto text), 135,
138, 144, 148
Henry, Edward Lamson, 228, 229
Herter, Gustave and Christian, 53
Hierarchy, 77, 95; as expressed in furniture, 237; in halls, 13; in house forms,
14–15; in parlor suites, 191, 194, 195
History, limits of, 2, 183
Holidays, 85
"Home Sweet Home" (motto text), 43,
97, 120, 148
Homer, Winslow, 213, 214
Homes: as expressions of character, 7;
idealized Christian, 134, 136–137,
138; as settings for social strategies, 7
Homeyness, 95
Houses: backs of, 13; continuities in spatial arrangement in, 9; courtly models
for, 10, 14; facades of, 13; Georgian
types, 9–17; images of, on mottoes,
128–134, 136–137; specialization
within, 9, 13
Hunting. *See* Dining iconography; Sideboards
Hunzinger, George, 223
Hyperbole, 121, 125, 127, 177, 182,
206. *See also* Lettering

Impression management, 7, 29, 41

Independence, 205–206
Ingersoll, Robert, 146

Jeffrey, Kirk, 95
"Jesus Loves Me" (motto text), 97, 115,
137, 142–143, 144, 148
Johnson, Eastman, 42, 171, 172, 190,
206, 207, 214
Jones, Howard Mumford, 121

Krimmel, John Lewis, 198, 199, 201,
207

"Labor Has Sure Reward" (motto text),
144, 148
LaCroix, Paul, 79, 81
Landseer, Edwin, 68, 70, 73, 77
Laver, James, 23
Lettering, 117–128. *See also* Mottoes
Leutze, Emanuel, 81, 82
Lincoln, Abraham, 23, 88, 116, 118,
219, 222
Lippitt, Henry, House, 77
"Lord Is My Shepherd, The" (motto text),
120, 149
"Lord Is Risen, The" (motto text), 104,
149
"Lord Will Provide, The" (motto text),
144, 149
Luckmann, Thomas, 182

McDannell, Colleen, 87
McLuhan, Marshall, 97
Marble, uses in furniture, 17, 25, 58,
125, 197
Marx, Karl, 73, 77
Mason & Hamlin, 156, 167–169, 173
Material culture: benefits of studying,
240–241; and construction of self,
177; and culture, 1, 2, 5; functions
of, 233; and gentility, 236; as historical evidence, 240; and ideology and
values, 198, 240; importance of, 9,
233; methods of studying, 3; relationship to words, 3, 234; sacralization of,
119; as way of knowing, 2, 3
Materialism, 3, 166, 233
Mayer, Frank Blackwell, 205–206
Meanings of things, 1, 2, 181–184; generated through interaction, 182; public
and private, 181–184; variability of,
183
Medievalisms in mottoes, 121–123, 129,
130–131, 134
Meeks, Carroll, 123, 125
Men: bestial behavior of, 213; dominance of, 186–189; as hunters, 72–75,
172; and technology, 98–114, 145,